The Law Commission
Consultation Paper No 189

THE ILLEGALITY DEFENCE

A Consultative Report

THE LAW COMMISSION – HOW WE CONSULT

About the Law Commission: The Law Commission was set up by section 1 of the Law Commissions Act 1965 for the purpose of promoting the reform of the law.

The Law Commissioners are: The Rt Hon Lord Justice Etherton (*Chairman)*, Professor Elizabeth Cooke, Mr David Hertzell, Professor Jeremy Horder and Kenneth Parker QC.

The Chief Executive is William Arnold.

Topic: We ask whether a claimant who has been involved in illegal conduct should be entitled to enforce a claim in contract, unjust enrichment, trusts and tort. We welcome views on our provisional recommendations. A summary is attached and an impact assessment is included in Part 1.

Geographical scope: England and Wales.

Previous consultation: This follows consultation papers on Illegality in Contracts and Trusts (1999) and the Illegality Defence in Tort (2001).

Duration of the consultation: from 23 January 2009 to **20 April 2009**.

How to respond

Please send your responses either –

By email to: commercialandcommon@lawcommission.gsi.gov.uk   or

By post to: Helen Hall, Law Commission, Steel House, 11 Tothill Street, London SW1H 9LJ
             Tel: 020-3334-0288 / Fax: 020-3334-0201

If you send your comments by post, it would be helpful if, where possible, you also sent them to us electronically (in any commonly used format).

After the consultation: In the light of the responses, we will decide our final recommendations and present them to Parliament. We hope to publish our final report in autumn 2009.

Freedom of information: We will treat all responses as public documents in accordance with the Freedom of Information Act. We may attribute comments and include a list of all respondents' names in any final report we publish. If you wish to submit a confidential response, you should contact us before sending the response.

PLEASE NOTE – We will disregard automatic confidentiality statements generated by an IT system.

Code of Practice: We are a signatory to the Government's Code of Practice on Consultation and follow the criteria set out on the next page.

Availability: You can view/download the paper free of charge from our website at:
http://www.lawcom.gov.uk/docs/cp189.pdf.

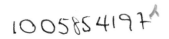

CODE OF PRACTICE ON CONSULTATION

○ **THE SEVEN CONSULTATION CRITERIA**

Criterion 1: When to consult

Formal consultation should take place at a stage when there is scope to influence the policy outcome.

Criterion 2: Duration of consultation exercise

Consultations should normally last for at least 12 weeks with consideration given to longer timescales where feasible and sensible.

Criterion 3: Clarity and scope of impact

Consultation documents should be clear about the consultation process, what is being proposed, the scope to influence and the expected costs and benefits of the proposals.

Criterion 4: Accessibility of consultation exercises

Consultation exercises should be designed to be accessible to, and clearly targeted at, those people the exercise is intended to reach.

Criterion 5: The burden of consultation

Keeping the burden of consultation to a minimum is essential if consultations are to be effective and if consultees' buy-in to the process is to be obtained.

Criterion 6: Responsiveness of consultation exercises

Consultation responses should be analysed carefully and clear feedback should be provided to participants following the consultation.

Criterion 7: Capacity to consult

Officials running consultations should seek guidance in how to run an effective consultation exercise and share what they have learned from the experience.

○ **CONSULTATION CO-ORDINATOR**

The Law Commission's Consultation Co-ordinator is Correna Callender.

○ You are invited to send comments to the Consultation Co-ordinator about the extent to which the criteria have been observed and any ways of improving the consultation process.

○ **Contact:** Correna Callender, Law Commission, Steel House, 11 Tothill Street, London SW1H 9LJ – Email: correna.callender@lawcommission.gsi.gov.uk

Full details of the Government's Code of Practice on Consultation are available on the BERR website at http://www.berr.gov.uk/files/file47158.pdf.

THE LAW COMMISSION

THE ILLEGALITY DEFENCE

CONTENTS

THE ILLEGALITY DEFENCE

SUMMARY

THE PROBLEM

1.1 Where claimants are involved in some form of illegal conduct, how far should this prevent them from enforcing their normal legal rights? This issue arises in many areas of law. In this Consultative Report, we look at the effect of claimants' illegal conduct on claims:

- for contractual enforcement – for example where an employee, seeking to enforce an employment contract, is paid cash-in-hand;

- for the reversal of unjust enrichment – for example where a buyer seeks the return of the money already paid for goods which it turns out may not be sold legally;

- for the recognition of legal title to property – for example where the claimant asserts that property has been transferred to him or her under a contract which breaches statutory hire purchase regulations;

- to enforce equitable interests – for example where the claimant asserts that he or she is the beneficial owner of property held under a trust arrangement originally created to evade tax;

- in tort – for example where the claimant claims compensation for a personal injury sustained while committing a criminal offence.

1.2 In answering this question, it is particularly difficult to set out hard and fast rules. This is because the illegality defence may be raised in such a wide variety of contexts. For example:

- In some cases, the illegal conduct may be relatively trivial. In others, the claimant's conduct may be seriously reprehensible.

- The connection of the illegality to the claim varies. It may be inextricably linked, for example where the claimant seeks to enforce an interest in a trust set up to "hide" the true ownership of assets for fraudulent purposes. Or the illegality may be merely incidental to the claim, as where a road haulier seeks to enforce payment when the delivery driver has exceeded the speed limit.

- The comparative guilt of the parties varies. Sometimes the illegality defence may benefit an innocent defendant who is unaware of the claimant's illegal conduct. Sometimes it provides an unmerited windfall to a defendant who is equally or more implicated in the illegal conduct than the claimant. In some cases, the effect of denying the claimant's claim may be to benefit a "guilty" defendant at the expense of the claimant's innocent creditors.

- Sometimes the consequences of denying the claim may appear just – while in others they may seem disproportionate (as where a minor crime deprives the claimant of an interest in his or her home).

1.3 The courts have attempted to lay down a series of rules to apply in these many different circumstances. The result is a body of law which is technical, uncertain and sometimes arbitrary. It often lacks transparency. Occasionally it produces results which may appear unduly harsh.

PREVIOUS CONSULTATION

1.4 In our two consultation papers on this issue,[1] we provisionally proposed legislative reform. We thought that the courts should be given a statutory discretion to decide whether the claimant's involvement in some form of illegality should act as a defence to a claim. In exercising this discretion the courts should take into account a list of factors such as the seriousness of the illegality involved and the proportionality of denying relief.

1.5 The responses we received to our consultations and the further work we carried out have led us to conclude that we should not recommend legislation for most areas of law. This is partly because it would be difficult to define the ambit of a statutory discretion in a way that did not cause further problems. We also think that in most cases legislation is unnecessary. The courts could reach the desired result through development of the case law.

OUR CURRENT VIEW

Judicial development: illegality and contract, unjust enrichment and tort

1.6 We consider that in contract, unjust enrichment and tort claims it is open to the courts to develop the law in ways that would render it considerably clearer, more certain and less arbitrary.

1.7 In this Consultative Report, we include a detailed discussion of the case law in these areas. We show how in most cases, the courts weigh policy arguments to provide a fair result. However, their task is made more difficult by the perceived need to abide by detailed and ostensibly rigid rules.

1.8 We argue that judges should base their decisions directly on the policies that underlie the illegality defence and explain their reasoning accordingly. The so called "rules" are in fact no more than guidance that show how these policies operate. What matters is how the relevant factors apply in each particular case. The courts should allow the illegality defence to succeed only where it can be justified by a particular public policy rationale.

The policy rationales

1.9 We set out the policy rationales in Part 2. The normal business of the courts is to decide cases according to the law. However, there may be good reasons to deny normal rights to a claimant involved in illegal conduct. We set out five such reasons, which often overlap.

---

[1] Illegal Transactions: The Effect of Illegality on Contracts and Trusts (1999) Consultation Paper No 154; The Illegality Defence in Tort (2001) Consultation Paper No 160.

(1) *Disallowing the claim may further the purpose of the rule which the claimant has infringed.* If, for example, the law makes the sale of hand guns illegal, it furthers the purpose of gun control to prevent a seller from suing for the contract price.

(2) Allied to this, *the law should be internally consistent.* It should not both prohibit the sale of guns and encourage it by protecting the seller's interest.

(3) *The law should prevent a claimant from profiting from his or her own wrong.* As Lord Atkin put it, the courts should not "recognise a benefit accruing to a criminal from his crime".[2]

(4) *The law should deter illegal conduct.* For example, the Court of Appeal has attempted to deter insurance fraud by sending "a clear message" to builders that they will not be entitled to enforce payment if they provide false estimates of work.[3]

(5) An illegality doctrine may be needed *to maintain public confidence in the integrity of the legal system.* As said in 1725, courts are not there to provide an arena in which wrongdoers may fight over their spoils.[4]

1.10 These are all important reasons to deny the claimant's claim. However, they are not always applicable to every case in which there has been unlawful behaviour.

1.11 Sometimes conduct is made illegal partly to protect the weaker party to the transaction. This means that denying redress to the weaker party may undermine the purpose of the rule rather than further it. This point was stressed by the European Court of Justice in *Courage Ltd v Crehan*:[5] preventing the weaker party to an anti-competitive agreement from claiming damages against the stronger party may undermine effective competition law. The Court agreed with the Advocate-General that one should not apply formalistic tests that take no account of the individual circumstances.

1.12 Sometimes claimants are not attempting to seek a profit from the wrongdoing, so the application of the illegality defence cannot be justified on this basis. Instead, the claimant is seeking to return to the position they were in before the crime. Furthermore, a rule that acts as a deterrent to one party may act as an inducement to the other party. For example, denying employment rights to an employee paid cash-in-hand will act as a deterrent to the employee but as an incentive to the employer, who thereby escapes normal employment obligations. And in practice, public confidence in the legal system is unlikely to be undermined simply because it emerges that litigants occasionally break the speed limit.

---

[2] *Beresford v Royal Insurance Company Ltd* [1938] AC 586, 599.

[3] *Taylor v Bhail* [1996] CLC 377.

[4] See *Everet v Williams* (1725) reported at (1893) 9 *Law Quarterly Review* 197.

[5] Case C-453/99; [2001] ECR 1-6297.

Our provisional recommendations

1.13   Our provisional recommendations are listed in Part 8. We do not think it is possible to create a workable system of rules determining when the illegality defence should operate in claims for contractual enforcement, the reversal of unjust enrichment or tort. Instead, the courts should consider each case to see whether the application of the illegality defence can be justified on the basis of the policies that underlie that defence.

1.14   Ultimately a balancing exercise is called for which weighs up the application of the various policies at stake. An illegality defence should only succeed when depriving the claimant of his or her rights is a proportionate response based on the relevant illegality policies. In giving judgment, the court should explain the balancing exercise it has undertaken.

1.15   We do not think that this would lead to a major change in the outcome of cases. The policy rationales are already found within the case law, and courts already apply them so as to do justice. The main change would be in the transparency of the decisions.

1.16   We think a more open approach to the policy issues would make the law easier to explain and to understand. Illegality issues often arise at the last moment. For lay tribunal members and arbitrators who are faced with such issues, the complexities, uncertainties and contradictions of the present law can impede the fair resolution of disputes.

Illegality and trusts

1.17   In one area we do not think that judicial clarification is possible. Where a trust has been set up to hide the true ownership for criminal purposes a House of Lords' decision, *Tinsley v Milligan*,[6] prescribes how the illegality defence should operate. In this case a couple bought a house together but put the legal title to it into the name of one of them only, so that the other could more easily hide her interest and claim social security benefits on the fraudulent basis that she did not own a home. The House of Lords held that a claimant could establish an interest in such circumstances, provided that he or she did not need to "rely" on the illegality to do so. The consequences of this decision have been criticised by academics and judges. However, we do not think that it is open to any lower court to depart from such a clear precedent.

1.18   In this area, we think that statutory reform is needed. We are currently preparing a draft Bill to provide the court with a structured discretion to deprive a beneficial owner of his or her interest in the trust in limited circumstances. We intend to publish it in our final report in Autumn 2009.

---

[6]   [1994] 1 AC 340.

PURPOSE OF THIS CONSULTATIVE REPORT

1.19   We are consulting again both because our scheme is now so different from the one we originally proposed, and because of the length of time since the publication of the original consultation papers. We are particularly interested to hear from judges and practitioners on how far our new approach is workable. Please send responses by Monday 20 April 2009 by email to commercialandcommon@lawcommission.gsi.gov.uk; or by post to Helen Hall, The Law Commission, Steel House, 11 Tothill Street, London SW1H 9LJ (Fax 020 3334 0201).

PART 1
INTRODUCTION

A BRIEF HISTORY OF THE PROJECT

1.1 The Law Commission first agreed to take up this project in 1995 as part of its Sixth Programme of Law Reform, which required us to examine "the law on illegal transactions, including contracts and trusts".[1] Over several years, there had been many comments in the academic literature that the law relating to illegality was unsatisfactory. Then in 1994, in an important House of Lords' decision on illegality and trusts, *Tinsley v Milligan*, Lord Goff specifically suggested that the Law Commission should review the position.[2] In this case, Miss Milligan claimed to be entitled to an interest in the home which she had shared with her partner, Miss Tinsley. Although she did not dispute that Miss Milligan had contributed to the purchase price, Miss Tinsley argued that because Miss Milligan had fraudulently claimed social security benefits on the basis that she did not have any interest in the house, she should not now be allowed to claim one. The minority of the House of Lords agreed that Miss Milligan's unlawful conduct meant that she was unable to enforce the interest which she would otherwise have had in the house. The majority felt able to avoid such a disproportionate result and allowed her claim, but only by adopting a line of reasoning that many commentators and judges have criticised as being artificial and arbitrary.[3] They said that Miss Milligan could succeed because she was able to prove her interest in the house without "relying on" the illegal purpose of the transaction. She simply pointed to the resulting trust that was presumed to arise in her favour because of her contribution to the purchase price. It was against this background that we started our work on the project.

1.2 We published our first consultation paper, Illegal Transactions: The Effect of Illegality on Contracts and Trusts[4] ("CP 154") in 1999. This examined the law relating to the doctrine of illegality as it operates in contract and trusts. In 2001 we published our second consultation paper, The Illegality Defence in Tort[5] ("CP 160"). This examined the law relating to illegality and tort. We received just over fifty responses to CP 154 and just over forty to CP 160; the responses coming from individual academics, solicitors, barristers and judges, and from various institutions and organisations. We found these responses to be enormously helpful in formulating our provisional recommendations and are very grateful to all those who took the time and effort to write them.

---

[1] Sixth Programme of Law Reform (1995) Law Com No 234, Item 4.

[2] [1994] 1 AC 340, 364.

[3] For further discussion of the case and criticism of it, see Part 6.

[4] Law Commission Consultation Paper No 154.

[5] Law Commission Consultation Paper No 160.

1.3 The project has proved to be difficult. Policy issues concerning specific points have taken time to resolve owing to the controversial nature of the subject. Amongst those whom we consulted on the project and within the Law Commission itself, there was a divergent range of views as to when, if ever, the claimant's unlawful behaviour should have an effect on his or her civil claims. In addition, the length of time it has taken us to complete our work has been due, in part, to the fact that at several stages in its history the project has had to give way to matters that required higher priority.

FURTHER CONSULTATION

1.4 In this consultative report, we set out in detail our provisional recommendations concerning the illegality defence in relation to the law of contract, unjust enrichment, property (other than beneficial interests under trusts) and tort. We also outline our provisional recommendations concerning the illegality defence and the law of trusts.

1.5 The provisional recommendations that we put forward concerning the law of contract, unjust enrichment, property (other than beneficial interests under trusts) and tort differ markedly from the proposals that we made in the two consultation papers. In particular, we are no longer recommending that legislative reform is the most appropriate way forward, but rather provisionally recommend that any improvement needed can be best achieved through incremental case law development.

1.6 We have decided to consult again on our recommendations, partly because our scheme is now so different from the one we originally proposed, and partly because of the length of time since the publication of the original consultation papers. We are particularly interested to hear from judges and practitioners on how far our new approach is workable. Throughout the body of the report we have highlighted in bold text all our provisional recommendations. These are also summarised in Part 8. We do not raise any specific questions for consultees, but seek comments on all our provisional recommendations. We would welcome views **by Monday 20 April 2009**, to the contact details on page iii.

1.7 We also outline our provisional recommendations in relation to the illegality defence and the law of trusts. Here, however, we do recommend that legislative reform is necessary in relation to the concealment of beneficial interests. We are currently preparing a draft Bill on this issue.

1.8 After undertaking an analysis of the responses we receive to this consultative report, we plan to publish our final report in Autumn 2009. This will set out our final recommendations in relation to the illegality defence as it applies throughout all areas of the law, and will include the draft Bill.

THE SCOPE OF THIS CONSULTATIVE REPORT

1.9 In this consultative report we consider what effect the involvement of a claimant in some form of illegal conduct may have on his or her legal action against the defendant. In particular we look at when the law allows a defendant to raise such illegal activity as a defence to a claim for breach of contract, for the protection of a legal or equitable property right, in tort or for unjust enrichment. This is an issue which arises in a variety of contexts. In some cases, the claimant's illegal behaviour may be of a fairly trivial nature. There are many modern regulations which make various types of conduct unlawful, often without the need for any criminal intent. In other cases, the claimant's illegality may be far more reprehensible, involving a crime committed with deliberate intent. The connection of the illegality to the claim may also vary. It may be inextricably linked, for example where the claimant seeks to enforce an interest in a trust which he or she has set up in order to "hide" the true ownership of assets for fraudulent purposes. Or the illegality may be merely incidental to the claim, for example where a road haulier seeks to enforce its contractual right for payment when during the course of the delivery the driver has exceeded the speed limit.

1.10 As we shall see in this report, because of the great variety of ways in which illegality can impinge on a civil claim, the law has found it difficult to determine exactly when and how the illegality should prevent claimants from enforcing a right to which they would otherwise have been entitled. It is an area in which the law is technical, uncertain, in some instances arbitrary and lacking in transparency. It occasionally produces results which at least some people think to be unduly harsh.

1.11 For the most part, we have only considered the position where the claimant's conduct or purpose is unlawful. We do not deal with conduct or purpose which, while it might be regarded as immoral or contrary to public policy, is not actually prohibited. In some cases, such behaviour will affect the claimant's civil rights. For example, a transaction which tends to interfere with the administration of justice,[6] or which is prejudicial to the status of marriage,[7] will not be enforced by the courts. However, we do not regard it as part of our project to clarify exhaustively what should constitute conduct that is contrary to public policy. Any attempt at legislative reform of such an area would be extremely difficult and require frequent modification. We believe that the courts remain the best arbiters of which transactions, while not involving unlawful conduct, should be regarded as contrary to public policy, with Parliament intervening only in particular areas as and when appropriate.[8]

---

[6] For discussion of this heading of public policy, see *Giles v Thompson* [1994] 1 AC 142.

[7] For discussion of this heading of public policy, *see Fender v St John-Mildmay* [1938] AC 1.

[8] For example, legislation has been enacted in relation to fees chargeable by solicitors which renders enforceable agreements that were previously held to be contrary to public policy: Courts and Legal Services Act 1990, s 58 as amended by the Access to Justice Act 1999.

SUMMARY OF OUR PROVISIONAL RECOMMENDATIONS

1.12 Unlike the majority of Law Commission reports, we do not for the most part recommend legislation.[9] Our two consultation papers on this issue, CP 154 and CP 160, did provisionally propose statutory reform. In these two consultation papers we proposed that a statutory scheme should be introduced under which the courts would have a discretion to decide whether or not the claimant's involvement in some form of illegality should act as a defence to a claim. In exercising their discretion we suggested that the courts should take into account a number of factors such as the seriousness of the illegality involved and the proportionality of denying relief.

1.13 However, the responses that we received to the consultation papers, and the further work that we have carried out, have led us to conclude that we should not recommend legislation throughout the illegality case law. Our change in thinking is based largely on two important points. First, we found that it would be difficult to devise and draft a broad statutory scheme that would be an improvement on the current law. Secondly, we believe that in relation to most types of claim it is open to the courts to develop the law in ways that would render it considerably clearer, more certain and less arbitrary. Legislation is, therefore, not necessary.

1.14 This is the case in relation to claims to enforce a contract, for the reversal of unjust enrichment, for the protection of a legal property right and in tort. In all these areas we provisionally recommend that substantial improvements, where needed, could be made by way of development through the case law. In particular we recommend that the judiciary should base their decisions directly on the policies that underlie the illegality defence and explain their reasoning accordingly. That is, they should not feel obliged to follow any so-called "rule" applied in previous cases, which might lead to a harsh result on the facts of the particular case before them. Instead, they should focus directly on the facts of the case before them and allow the illegality defence to succeed only where it can be justified by a particular public policy ground. What ground that is should be made clear in the judgment so that it can be seen that the illegality defence applies only where it has some merit.

---

[9] This is not the first time that we have published a Report which recommends judicial development of the law rather than legislative reform. For example, see Damages for Personal Injury – Non-Pecuniary Loss (1999) Law Com No 257; Damages under the Human Rights Act 1988 (2000) Law Com No 266 and The Law of Contract: The Parol Evidence Rule (1986) Law Com No 154.

1.15 However, there is one area where we do not think that such judicial clarification and improvement is possible. This relates to the enforcement of a trust which has been created pursuant to arrangements set up in order to hide the true ownership for criminal purposes. Here, there is a decision of the House of Lords[10] which prescribes the exact way in which the illegality defence should operate. The consequences brought about by this decision have been criticised by academics and the judiciary alike and we believe that this particular area needs reform. However, because this would not be possible by a lower court, and it may be some time before an appropriate case were to reach the House of Lords for reconsideration, we recommend that legislative reform is here needed. We think that the courts should be given a statutory discretion to determine whether the illegality should have any effect in these cases. The legislation should provide some guidance as to how this discretion should be exercised. It should also provide what the consequences of the court's decision should be.

ECONOMIC IMPACT ASSESSMENT

1.16 We have undertaken an assessment process in order to evaluate the impact that our provisional proposals for legislative reform would have on the economy as a whole or on any one individual sector. The legislative reforms would affect those who attempt to conceal assets in order to commit fraud or other unlawful acts and those who deal with such assets. It is not possible to categorise any particular class of persons as falling within this group.

1.17 However we would expect the economic impact of the proposed legislation on the economy as a whole to be small. A search of two electronic databases for cases that would fall within the scope of our proposals revealed only 12 since 2000. This does not, of course, include every relevant decided case at all levels or disputes that have been settled. It is, however, an indication that the number of people likely to be affected is not large.

1.18 One economic benefit that we hope to emerge from our provisional proposals is a reduction in the number of people who use the trust institution to enter into fraudulent arrangements. Under our proposals, people who enter into such arrangements will be at risk of losing their interest in the trust property. Although there is no data to use to test the effect of this reform, it may act as a deterrent. If this proves to be the case, there would be a resultant saving to the State in the form of reduced tax and benefits fraud.

OUTLINE OF THIS CONSULTATIVE REPORT

1.19 The report is divided into eight Parts:

1.20 In Part 2 we explain what we believe are the policies that underlie the illegality rules. That is, we explain why it is that sometimes claimants should be denied their usual legal rights and remedies because they have been involved in some form of illegal conduct that is connected to their claim.

---

[10] *Tinsley v Milligan* [1994] 1 AC 340. For the facts of this case, see para 1.1 above.

1.21 In Parts 3, 4 and 5 we look at the effect of illegality on contractual claims. In Part 3 we look at the position where the claimant is seeking to enforce the contract; in Part 4 we look at what happens where the claimant seeks to withdraw from the contract and recover what he or she has already transferred or be paid for what he or she has already provided; and in Part 5 we examine the position where the contract has already been completed.

1.22 We go on in Part 6 to look at how illegality may affect trusts. Part 7 considers claims in tort. Finally, Part 8 contains a list of our provisional recommendations.

1.23 We have found it helpful for the purposes of exposition to separate out the present law and our provisional recommendations into these various Parts. The relevant case law is so large and the possible variety of illegal involvement so diverse that some division must be made in order to ensure that the report is accessible and comprehensible. However, it must be emphasised that the Parts do overlap. That is, there will be fact situations which fall within two or more Parts. This would be the case, for example, where the parties have entered into a contract to create a trust. Several of the policies that underlie the illegality defence are the same whatever type of claim is being brought, although their application may be different. Because of this we have tried to ensure that our recommendations are consistent throughout the report. Where there are differences in approach, we have explained why we believe this is necessary.

1.24 Appendix A describes the main provisions of the Proceeds of Crime Act 2002 that are relevant to the types of arrangements covered by our report. A list of those who responded to CP 154 and CP 160 is set out at Appendix B.

PART 2
WHY DO WE NEED ANY DOCTRINE OF ILLEGALITY?

INTRODUCTION

2.1 The normal business of the courts is to decide cases according to the law, and in doing so to provide a just resolution to the dispute between the parties. The illegality defence operates to prevent the courts from providing the claimant with the rights or remedies to which he or she would otherwise be entitled. In this Part we examine the basis on which the illegality defence does this and consider whether it can be justified. As we shall see, there is always a difficult balancing exercise to be performed between awarding the claimant his or her usual rights, and seeking to uphold the rationales that underlie the defence.

2.2 One of the initial questions that we considered in CP 154 and CP 160 was whether there was any need to maintain a doctrine of illegality at all. That is, should we simply recommend the abolition of the illegality defence? The reasoning adopted in the case law has made it quite clear that the defence is not aimed at achieving a just result between the parties. The classic statement frequently cited in support of the illegality defence is that of Lord Mansfield in *Holman v Johnson*:

> The objection, that a contract is immoral or illegal as between plaintiff and defendant, sounds at all times very ill in the mouth of the defendant. It is not for his sake, however, that the objection is ever allowed; but it is founded in general principles of policy, which the defendant has the advantage of, contrary to the real justice, as between him and the plaintiff.[1]

2.3 If this is the case, we consider that it is important to examine what *are* the "general principles of policy" on which the illegality doctrine is based. In CP 154 and CP 160 we identified several, of differing importance and application, depending on the type of claim pursued. In CP 160, we asked respondents to tell us which they believed to be the most relevant, and indeed whether they considered that the rationales were sufficient to show that an illegality defence should be maintained. These questions raised a broad range of views. However, with only one exception everyone who responded to the two CPs thought that some doctrine of illegality could be justified and was still needed.

---

[1] (1775) 1 Cowp 341, 343; 98 ER 1120, 1121.

2.4 We look at the policies that we consider underpin the application of the illegality defence in some detail below. We believe that these policies should be at the forefront of any consideration as to how the law should develop in the future. It is important to point out that they are not mutually exclusive, but rather overlap with each other to a greater or lesser degree. It was apparent from the responses that we received that different people held different views on exactly where the boundaries of each lay. However together, it was felt, they operated to justify the illegality defence.

THE POLICY RATIONALES

2.5 Many different rationales have been put forward in the relevant academic literature and case law in order to justify the operation of the illegality doctrine. Here we consider what might be regarded as the six main ones: (1) furthering the purpose of the rule which the claimant's illegal behaviour has infringed; (2) consistency; (3) the need to prevent the claimant profiting from his or her own wrong; (4) deterrence; (5) maintaining the integrity of the legal system; and (6) punishment.

1. Furthering the purpose of the rule which the claimant's illegal behaviour has infringed

2.6 One of the main policies that is said to underlie the illegality defence is that disallowing the claim will further the purpose of the rule which the claimant has infringed. Suppose, for example, it were an offence for the claimant to sell a gun to the defendant. If the defendant failed to pay, then refusing to allow the claimant to sue may further the aim of prohibiting gun sales. This is a rationale which is frequently considered in contract cases where the claimant has breached a statutory provision either in making or performing the contract.[2] An early example is given by *Cope v Rowlands*[3] where the court held that an otherwise valid brokerage contract made by a person who had failed to comply with a statutory requirement to obtain a licence from the City of London was unenforceable. Parke B said:

> The question for us now to determine is, whether the enactment of the statute is ... meant to secure a revenue to the city, and for that purpose to render the person acting as a broker liable to a penalty if he does not pay it? Or whether one of its objects be the protection of the public, and the prevention of improper persons acting as brokers? ... [T]he legislature had in view, as one object, the benefit and security of the public in those important transactions which are negotiated by brokers. The clause, therefore, which imposes a penalty, must be taken ... to imply a prohibition of all unadmitted persons to act as brokers, and consequently to prohibit, by necessary inference, all contracts which such persons make for compensation to themselves for so acting.[4]

---

[2] See paras 3.3 to 3.11 below.

[3] (1836) 2 M & W 149; 150 ER 707.

[4] (1836) 2 M & W 149, 158-159; 150 ER 707, 710-711.

2.7   This question, we consider, is not only relevant in the contract cases dealing with "statutory illegality", but whenever the court is looking at the illegality defence. That is, an important function that underlies the defence is to support the law that the claimant has infringed. In some cases, to allow the civil claim would defeat the object of that law. Many examples could be given from all contexts of the illegality doctrine. In the context of a claim for unjust enrichment, the Court of Appeal's decision in *Awwad v Geraghty*[5] shows that a *quantum meruit* claim for work performed under an unenforceable contract will not be awarded where granting it would undermine the rule that rendered the contract illegal. In this case a solicitor sued for her fees payable under a conditional fee agreement which the court held to be contrary to public policy and therefore unenforceable. The *quantum meruit* claim was similarly denied. Lord Justice Shiemann explained:

> What public policy seeks to prevent is a solicitor continuing to act for a client under a conditional normal fee arrangement. This is what [the claimant] did. That is what she wishes to be paid for. Public policy decrees that she should not be paid.[6]

2.8   In a trusts context, this rationale would also seem to play an important role in the courts' decisions. For example, the court has refused to recognise a trust that had been created in order to evade a statutory prohibition against the use of property belonging to a Member of Parliament in contracts entered into with the Government.[7] Finally, this policy can be seen at work in several of the tort cases. For example, it explains those cases in which the illegality doctrine has prevented the claimant from recovering damages for the fact that he or she has been imprisoned[8] or had to pay a fine or damages to another party.[9] In both cases the award of damages would undermine the penalty imposed by the rule which the claimant infringed.

---

[5]   [2001] QB 570. This case is considered in more detail in para 4.26 below.

[6]   [2001] QB 570, 596.

[7]   *Curtis v Perry* (1802) 6 Ves 739; 31 ERR 1285. This case is discussed in more detail at para 6.28 below.

[8]   *Worrall v British Railways Board* (Unreported) 29 April 1999.

[9]   *Askey v Golden Wine Co Ltd* [1948] 2 All ER 35.

2.9   In all the cases referred to above, to allow the claim would have undermined the purpose of the rule that the claimant had infringed. However, in other cases, the court has reached the opposite conclusion.[10] Indeed in some cases, the court has found that to allow the illegality defence to prevail would actually undermine the purpose of the rule that had been infringed. Such was the decision of the European Court of Justice in *Courage Ltd v Crehan*.[11] The tenant of a pub let by a brewery under terms which included a beer tie agreement sought damages suffered as a result of being a party to the beer tie. He argued that the beer tie was contrary to article 81 (previously article 85) of the European Community Treaty, therefore unenforceable, and that he was entitled to be compensated for losses that he had suffered as a result of being party to the agreement. The brewery defended the claim on the basis of illegality. However, the European Court pointed out that in such a case as this, allowing the claim would actually promote the principle of competition, the purpose behind article 81, rather than frustrate it. The Court said:

> The existence of such a right [to claim damages for loss caused to him by a contract liable to restrict competition] strengthens the working of the Community competition rules and discourages agreements or practices, which are frequently covert, which are liable to restrict or distort competition. From that point of view, actions for damages before the national courts can make a significant contribution to the maintenance of effective competition in the Community.[12]

2.10   We suggested in CP 154 that the question whether denying relief will further the purpose of the rule which renders the contract illegal should be one of the factors that the court should take into account in exercising the statutory discretion that we provisionally proposed. Several of those responding to the paper thought that this should be a prominent factor. Indeed one suggested that it was more in the nature of an overriding principle.

2.11   In CP 160 we asked specifically whether respondents to the paper thought that "furthering the purpose of the rule" was an important justification for the illegality doctrine as it applies in tort cases.[13] A large majority did so, although several thought that this rationale also embraced several other rationales that we go on to discuss, and that it was difficult to separate them. Others thought the policy an "elusive" concept that made it difficult to predict the outcome of cases. Professor Buckley pointed out that when claims do succeed, they tend to do so despite the rule which they contravene, rather than in order to fulfil its purpose.

---

[10] For example, in *Archbolds (Freightage) Ltd v S Spanglett Ltd* [1961] 1 QB 374 the Court of Appeal found that the object of the relevant legislation, the Road and Rail Traffic Act 1933, was to ensure an orderly and comprehensive transport service by the use of licensing arrangements, and not to render contracts for the transport of goods illegal.

[11] Case C-453/99; [2001] ECR I-6314. This case is discussed in more detail at para 3.84 below.

[12] Case C-453/99; [2001] ECR I-6314.

[13] CP 160, para 4.59.

2.12   We accept that this policy will not be easy to apply in all cases. Ascertaining the purpose of any particular invalidating rule is not always straightforward. Then deciding whether allowing the claim in the factual circumstances before the court would undermine that purpose may not be clear-cut. This is not the only rationale that is relevant and its operation may conflict with others. In these cases the courts will have to determine which takes precedence. However, despite these difficulties we do believe that this is an important policy which underlies the illegality defence and justifies its operation in many cases.

2. Consistency

2.13   A similar policy to the one which we have just considered, but perhaps more broadly applicable, is that the law should be seen to be internally consistent. We can see this policy at work already in some of the cases. For example, it is clear that a claim in unjust enrichment will not be allowed where it would have the same effect as a claim for contractual enforcement that the law has refused. To allow such a claim would stultify the law. We look at this policy further when we consider how the illegality defence works in claims for unjust enrichment.[14]

2.14   While the English cases have not relied directly on the principle of consistency to explain the basis of the illegality defence, it has been endorsed by the Canadian Supreme Court for tort cases in *Hall v Hebert*.[15] Here Madam Chief Justice McLachlin said:

> I conclude that there is a need in the law of tort for a principle which permits judges to deny recovery to a plaintiff on the ground that to do so would undermine the integrity of the justice system. The power is a limited one. Its use is justified where allowing the plaintiff's claim would introduce inconsistency into the fabric of the law, either by permitting the plaintiff to profit from an illegal or wrongful act, or to evade a penalty prescribed by criminal law.[16]

---

[14]   See paras 4.5-4.9 below.

[15]   [1993] 2 SCR 159.

[16]   [1993] 2 SCR 159, 179.

2.15   In CP 160 we suggested that the policy of consistency was needed to explain some of the tort cases for which there seems to be no other underlying rationale. We asked consultees whether they agreed. Consistency was seen to have a number of benefits by those who commented on this aspect of CP 160. For many, the rationale absorbed or provided an umbrella for the rationales that we go on to discuss next. Others felt that it added nothing new to the policies that we already clearly have in the English case law. One judge commented that "the attractiveness of the formulation is mainly based on its lack of detailed content".[17] Another respondent pointed out that "it is not really difficult, when judges want to ignore a technical illegality, to embrace all sorts of apparent inconsistencies".[18] While there was therefore a large degree of agreement that the illegality defence helped to maintain internal consistency in the law, this was not seen to be the overriding rationale.

3. The need to prevent the claimant profiting from his or her own wrong

2.16   There is undoubtedly a principle running through English law that a person should not be able to profit from his or her own wrongdoing. Statutory effect is given to this principle by the broad powers for criminal confiscation and civil recovery set out in the Proceeds of Crime Act 2002. We look at these provisions further below in paragraphs 2.32 to 2.33 when we consider whether their existence displaces any need for the illegality defence.

2.17   However, the principle can also be seen at play in the civil case law. For example in *Beresford v Royal Insurance Company Ltd*, Lord Atkin referred to "the absolute rule ... that the Courts will not recognise a benefit accruing to a criminal from his crime".[19] While this rule has an application over a wider area than illegal transactions, it is a maxim to which the courts frequently refer in the type of case that we are considering.

2.18   We believe that this principle has an important role to play in many illegality cases. However, its confines should be noted. The policy can only be invoked where the claimant is indeed a wrongdoer, and not in every case where some element of illegality is involved. Also, it is not clear to what extent it will be relevant in tort claims, where the claimant is often seeking compensation or an indemnity, rather than any element of "profit"; or in unjust enrichment claims, where the claimant is seeking restitution.

---

[17]   The Right Honourable Lord Justice Buxton.

[18]   Professor Patrick Atiyah.

[19]   [1938] AC 586, 599. The personal representatives of a man who had shot himself sought to recover on life insurance policies that the deceased had taken out with the defendants. There was no suggestion that the policies were illegal, but recovery was denied on the basis that to allow it would permit the estate to benefit from the deceased's suicide at a time when suicide was a crime. For other examples of the principle being used, see *In the Estate of Crippen* [1911] P 108; *ex parte* Puttick [1981] QB 767; and *Whiston v Whiston* [1995] Fam 198.

4. Deterrence

2.19 Deterrence is the explanation for the illegality defence that is most frequently cited by the courts. For example, in *Taylor v Bhail*,[20] the Court of Appeal refused a claim for the cost of work carried out by a builder who had falsely inflated his estimate in order to enable his customer to defraud his insurers. Lord Millett, then a Court of Appeal judge, said:

> It is time that a clear message was sent to the commercial community. Let it be clearly understood if a builder or a garage or other supplier agrees to provide a false estimate for work in order to enable its customer to obtain payment from his insurer to which he is not entitled, then it will be unable to recover payment from its customer.[21]

2.20 It has also been forcefully pointed out that in some cases, particularly those involving the breach of a minor technical statutory provision, the potential unenforceability of a contract may provide a far more serious deterrent than the criminal law. This is largely because the risk of discovery and the threat of prosecution for breach of the provision are slight,[22] but also because the amount at stake in any civil claim could far exceed that payable under the fine imposed by the criminal law.

2.21 However, some judges have doubted how effectively the illegality defence can uphold any deterrent effect.[23] This is largely for two reasons. First, many of those entering into transactions involving illegality are unaware of the law. Secondly, even if they are, it could be argued that a rule which acts as a deterrent for one party to a transaction may act as an inducement to the other, should he or she be aware that the illegality defence may result in an unmerited windfall.[24]

2.22 When we asked respondents to CP 160 whether they felt that deterrence was a legitimate rationale behind the illegality doctrine, we received a mixed response. Just over half believed that it was. One provided a realistic example: a man thinking of lending his BMW for a cigarette-smuggling operation may think twice once realising that he could well not have the right to sue if it were lost or damaged.[25] Respondents also suggested that the assertion that the civil law has no deterrent effect is empirically untested; and that to allow a civil claim can have a counter-deterrent effect, by reducing the deterrent effect of the criminal law. However, others thought that deterrence should be left to the criminal law and was not an appropriate policy for the civil law to be pursuing.

---

[20] [1996] CLC 377. The case is discussed in more detail at para 4.11 below.

[21] [1996] CLC 377, 383-384.

[22] P S Atiyah, *An Introduction to the Law of Contract* (5th ed 1995) pp 342-343.

[23] For example, *Tribe v Tribe* [1996] Ch 107, 133-134 by Millett LJ and *Tinsley v Milligan* [1992] Ch 310, 334 by Ralph Gibson LJ.

[24] This point is made by Lord Lowry in *Tinsley v Milligan* [1994] 1 340, 368.

[25] Professor Andrew Tettenborn.

2.23 We believe that deterrence is an important policy behind the illegality doctrine, although it is also clear that its relevance will vary from case to case. For example, it seems more likely to have a bearing on the type of situation envisaged by Lord Millett, where two parties knowingly enter into a transaction designed to defraud another, than in, say, many of the tort situations. When the defendant is the primary instigator of the illegality, the doctrine may even be seen as a benefit, because it enables him or her to escape legal obligations. However provided that it is appropriate on the facts, we agree with the many judicial statements that a policy based on deterrence justifies the application of the illegality doctrine.

5. Maintaining the integrity of the legal system

2.24 Frequent reference is made, particularly in the older case law, to the argument that the proper role of the court is not to provide an arena in which wrongdoers may fight over their spoils.[26] It is suggested there that one aim of the illegality defence is to ensure that the legal system is not abused by being asked to intervene in disputes where the parties have been involved in particularly serious wrongdoing. In the consultation papers we adopted the language used by these cases and referred to this rationale as being the need to uphold the "dignity of the court". Respondents commented that the policy might perhaps be better expressed in updated language – such as the need to uphold the "integrity" of the courts and "maintain public confidence" in the legal system. When we asked respondents to CP 160 whether they believed that this was a legitimate aim, we received an evenly divided response. Half who responded thought that this was a good rationale. The other half argued that it was "pompous" and "outdated".

2.25 The fact that the court will take notice of illegality of its own initiative, regardless of whether or not either party has pleaded it, lends support to the idea that the courts themselves regard the illegality doctrine as having an important function in the way in which they conduct their work. As Mr Justice Colman explained in *Birkett v Acorn Business Machines Ltd*:

> The principle behind the court's intervention of its own motion in such a case is to ensure that its process is not being abused.[27]

---

[26] See, for example, *Everet v Williams* (1725) reported at (1893) 9 *Law Quarterly Review* 197; *Parkinson v College of Ambulance Ltd and Harrison* [1925] 2 KB 1, 13 and *Tappenden v Randall* (1801) 2 Bos & Pul 467, 471; 126 ER 1388, 1390.

[27] [1999] 2 All ER (Comm) 429.

2.26 However, it is also clear that the courts will not simply wash their hands of a case as soon as an issue of illegality is raised by one of the parties. This point was forcefully made in the recent judgment of the Privy Council in *Townsend v Persistence Holdings Ltd.*[28] The claimants sought to exercise their right to terminate an agreement for the sale of land in the British Virgin Islands on the basis that the defendant had failed to satisfy one of the conditions of the sale contract. In argument before the Court of Appeal of the Eastern Caribbean, counsel for the claimants accepted that the agreement had been structured in such a way that the defendant could defraud the revenue of stamp duty owed. At this point the Court of Appeal abruptly stopped the trial, declaring that it refused to entertain any further hearing of the appeal, and entered judgment for the defendant. On appeal, the Privy Council criticised such an approach. Lord Neuberger said that if the transaction were dishonestly structured, the question whether or not that disentitled the claimant from seeking relief was one which plainly called for argument. It would be simply a denial of justice to dismiss the appeal on a point which had not been argued, particularly in relation to illegality, where the law is not straightforward.

2.27 In conclusion, we consider that this rationale does have merit. Indeed it might be regarded as the background to the general test for the application of the illegality defence created by the courts in the late 1980s and early 1990s based on the "public conscience". In a series of cases[29] the courts rejected the technical and inflexible rules that provide when the illegality defence applies. Instead they adopted a general principle that the courts would only refuse to assist the claimant where it would be an "affront to the public conscience if by affording him the relief sought the court was seen to be indirectly assisting or encouraging the plaintiff in his criminal act"[30] – the so-called "public conscience" test. While the use of this test has been rejected by the House of Lords in *Tinsley v Milligan,*[31] the policy that lies behind it has not been questioned.

6. Punishment

2.28 Whether or not punishment can be a legitimate policy underpinning the illegality defence provoked some disagreement amongst the respondents to our two CPs. The large majority thought that punishment was the preserve of the criminal law, and should not be invoked by the civil courts. Certainly it is clear that if punishment were to be regarded as a true rationale, then the rules would need to be carefully applied in order to ensure that any penal effect they produce is proportionate to the unlawful behaviour involved. A minority thought that punishment should not be the sole ground for denying a claim, but suggested that the court should be able to take into account the extent to which it disapproves of the conduct or considers it worthy of punishment.

---

[28] [2008] UKPC 15 (Unreported).

[29] This test was first considered by Hutchison J in *Thackwell v Barclays Bank plc* [1986] 1 All ER 676; and adopted by the Court of Appeal in *Saunders v Edwards* [1987] 1 WLR 1116; *Euro-Diam Ltd v Bathurst* [1990] 1 QB 1; *Howard v Shirlstar Container Transport Ltd* [1990] 1 WLR 1292; and by the majority of the Court of Appeal in *Tinsley v Milligan* [1992] Ch 310.

[30] *Thackwell v Barclays Bank plc* [1986] 1 All ER 676, 687.

[31] [1994] 1 AC 340.

2.29 While we agree with the majority that punishment should not be regarded as an aim underlying the illegality doctrine, the claimant might well regard the successful application of the defence as having exactly this effect. We also agree, therefore, with those respondents who thought that the court should take into account the degree of impropriety of the claimant's actions and the amount which the claimant stands to lose in deciding whether the defence should succeed.

7. Other policies?

2.30 In CP 160 we discussed various other policies that might be regarded as justifying the illegality doctrine. We pointed out that these might simply be alternative ways of looking at those main policies that we have already discussed, and they gained little support from respondents. We noted that several recent cases, particularly in relation to claims brought in tort, have justified the application of the illegality doctrine on the basis that the courts must not "appear to condone" the illegal conduct or "encourage or assist" the claimant in it.[32] At first glance this seems to be no more than an alternative wording of the deterrence rationale. However, it does seem that importance is placed on the "appearance" of the court's behaviour. This has aspects of the "integrity" and "consistency" arguments, and it is not clear that it adds anything further.

2.31 In addition, it has been argued that the illegality defence, particularly as it applies in tort claims, may be justified by the concept of "responsibility". That is, everyone should be treated as being responsible for his or her own acts. So, if a person committed an unlawful act and suffered because of it, then he or she should not be awarded compensation for it. This concept found little support amongst respondents, many of whom felt that the issue of responsibility was better dealt with by the defences of voluntary assumption of risk and contributory negligence.

THE STATUTORY REGIMES FOR CONFISCATION AND CIVIL RECOVERY

2.32 We explained above that an important principle underlying the illegality defence is that a person should not be able to benefit from his or her own wrong. Parliament has enshrined this principle in legislation by providing that in defined circumstances benefits obtained as a result of criminal conduct may be confiscated by the State. Special provisions apply in relation to certain crimes, for example terrorism, but the two main schemes are found in the Proceeds of Crime Act 2002. We have set out the main details of these schemes in Appendix A.

---

[32] See, for example, the decision of the Court of Appeal in *Reeves v Commissioner of Police of the Metropolis* [1999] QB 169, 185; *Cross v Kirkby The Times* 5 April 2000 and *Hall v Woolston Hall Leisure Ltd* [2001] 1 WLR 225, 237.

2.33 The doctrine of illegality must be viewed against this backdrop of legislation for State confiscation and recovery. We have considered at length whether these regimes supersede the need for an illegality defence. In some cases, at least, where the parties are disputing the ownership of property following a transaction tainted by illegality, the State may step in and confiscate the property to itself. However, in many cases the confiscatory or recovery legislation will not be relevant. This may be because there has been no successful criminal prosecution and the case does not meet the criteria in place for civil recovery proceedings. In other cases the amount or property claimed does not represent the proceeds of crime, so the confiscatory regimes are simply not applicable. Yet the legislation is relevant in that it does indicate that it is Parliament's belief that in some cases people should be obliged to forfeit what would otherwise belong to them because of their involvement in unlawful behaviour. We do not believe, however, that the statutory provisions for State forfeiture displace the need for an illegality defence in the civil law. They were enacted against the background of such a defence being available, and there is no suggestion that they were intended to replace it.

CONCLUSION ON THE POLICY RATIONALES

2.34 In our view there are several overlapping policy factors that underlie the illegality defence. Not all will be relevant in every case, but together they show that in some circumstances the claimant's usual rights and remedies should be denied and that the illegality defence is needed. We strongly believe that the courts' decisions should be closely focused on these rationales; and, further, that the claimant's claim should only be denied because of his or her involvement in illegality where that denial can be fully justified by the operation of one or several of them. As we noted at the start of this Part, the illegality doctrine is not aimed at achieving a just result between the parties. Where the defence is successfully raised, the defendant may well end up with a windfall gain, won at the expense of the claimant. Achieving a just result must in illegality cases be weighed against the need to apply the policies that we have considered. In some cases these policies may be found to have overriding importance. Even here we believe that the courts should be concerned that the result is proportionate to the illegality involved.

2.35 **We provisionally recommend that the illegality defence should be allowed where its application can be firmly justified by the policies that underlie its existence. These include: (a) furthering the purpose of the rule which the illegal conduct has infringed; (b) consistency; (c) that the claimant should not profit from his or her own wrong; (d) deterrence; and (e) maintaining the integrity of the legal system.**

PART 3
ILLEGALITY AND CONTRACTUAL ENFORCEMENT

INTRODUCTION

3.1 In this Part we consider when the doctrine of illegality will prevent a party enforcing its rights under a contract. The rules are numerous and complex. In some situations they even appear to be inconsistent. We do not criticise the vast majority of the actual results reached by the courts, but it is difficult to extract the various principles by which they have been decided. The problem is exacerbated by the lack of consensus over how the subject should be structured. Textbook treatments differ markedly. In this Part we set out what we understand the law to be as clearly and as simply as we can, identifying the uncertainties.

3.2 We consider, first, cases in which illegality may act as a defence to a claim for contractual enforcement because of the provisions of a statute or other legislation. These are frequently referred to as cases of "statutory illegality". Next we consider cases where the claim may be unenforceable because of the doctrine of illegality at common law. In a particular case, the court may have to consider both questions. For example, where the contract involves the commission of a statutory crime, the first question the court must consider is whether the legislature has provided that a claim by the relevant party to enforce the contract must be denied. If it has not, there remains a separate question of whether the claim under the contract is unenforceable at common law. Not all authors make this distinction a primary feature of their exposition of the law. We have, however, found it helpful because, as we explain, the nature of the courts' reasoning on the two issues will be different.[1] Finally we look at cases where the courts have awarded damages to the claimant on the basis of a different cause of action.

THE PRESENT LAW

1. Statutory illegality

3.3 A statute (or other legislation) may expressly provide what should be the consequences for a contract that involves the contravention of one of its provisions.[2] However, in many other cases the legislation is silent on the point. Then it will be necessary for the court to interpret the relevant provisions in the ordinary way to determine whether the legislation impliedly renders the contract unenforceable by either or both parties.

---

[1] The distinction is clearly explained in R A Buckley, *Illegality and Public Policy* (2002) p 10. See, also, M P Furmston, "The Analysis of Illegal Contracts" (1966) 16 *University of Toronto Law Journal* 267.

[2] See, for example, Financial Services and Markets Act 2000, ss 26-30 (enforceability of agreements made by unauthorised persons).

3.4 A classic example of this issue is provided by *St John Shipping Corporation v Joseph Rank Ltd*.[3] The claimant had carried grain for the defendants from Alabama to England. In doing so, the claimant had overloaded its ship so that the loadline was submerged. This was a statutory offence, and the claimant was prosecuted and fined for it. The defendants sought to withhold part of the freight due, on the basis that the claimant had carried out the contract in an unlawful manner. The claimant was successful in enforcing the contract. Lord Devlin (then a High Court judge) said that when interpreting the statute two questions were involved. Does the statute mean to prohibit contracts at all? If so, does the contract in question belong to the class which the statute intends to prohibit? Here it was held that the statute did not interfere with the rights and remedies given by the ordinary law of contract.[4]

3.5 This type of "illegality", and the various factors that the courts consider to be relevant in determining the implication of the statute, are described in some detail in CP 154 and need not be repeated here.[5] However, three points are worth emphasising.

3.6 First, where the statute does not expressly provide that the contractual claim is unenforceable, the courts will not be ready to imply that it does so. As Lord Devlin explained:

> I think that a court ought to be very slow to hold that a statute intends to interfere with the rights and remedies given by the ordinary law of contract. Caution in this respect is, I think, especially necessary in these times when so much of commercial life is governed by regulations of one sort or another, which may easily be broken without wicked intent.[6]

3.7 Indeed it has been persuasively argued that, unless the legislation necessarily contemplates the prohibited acts as being done in the performance of a contract, it is artificial to regard the legislation as impliedly prescribing the effect on contractual claims. For example, where a statute penalises the sale of a certain product, it might be permissible to imply that the legislature intended to deny a seller of that product the usual contractual rights. However, where a statute penalises the breaking of road speed limits, it would be artificial to suggest that the statute had anything to say about the enforcement of claims arising out of contracts, the performance of which broke those limits. Such contracts might well be affected by illegality, but under that doctrine as it applies at common law not by virtue of statutory interpretation.[7]

---

[3] [1957] 1 QB 267.

[4] [1957] 1 QB 267, 287-288. See also *Archbolds (Freightage) Ltd v S Spanglett Ltd* [1961] 1 QB 374.

[5] CP 154, paras 2.3 to 2.19.

[6] [1957] 1 QB 267, 288. See also the comments of Sachs LJ in *Shaw v Groom* [1970] 2 QB 504, 523.

[7] R A Buckley, *Illegality and Public Policy* (2002) pp 13-14.

3.8 Secondly, it is not clear from the case law whether a contract that is impliedly prohibited by statute is always unenforceable by both parties, or whether there are circumstances in which only one party will be affected. Many of the cases use terminology that assumes that neither party will be able to enforce an affected contract. The contract is said to be "prohibited" or "void".[8] This has been held to be the case even where one party is innocent of any breach of statutory provision. Thus in *Re Mahmoud v Ispahani*[9] a contract to sell linseed oil to a buyer who did not have the necessary licence was held to be unenforceable by the seller, even though he reasonably and honestly believed that the buyer did have a licence. It was not clear, and according to the majority immaterial,[10] whether the seller as well as the buyer had committed a statutory offence by entering into the contract. This case was followed in the Privy Council decision, *Chai Sau Yin v Liew Kwee Sam*.[11] Clearly this approach can lead to harsh results for the innocent party. On occasion the court has held that the effect on the innocent party would be so severe that the legislature cannot have intended to "prohibit" the contract at all.[12]

3.9 Other cases, however, have suggested that in certain circumstances only the guilty party's contractual claim will be affected by the illegality and the innocent party may be left to his or her usual contractual remedies.[13] Certainly a statute may expressly lay down such an effect. It might, therefore, be better if, instead of deciding whether the contract is "illegal", the court were to ask whether the statute renders the claim being made by the particular claimant unenforceable.

3.10 Thirdly, while in some recent cases the courts have adopted a rather rigid approach towards statutory interpretation in cases involving illegality,[14] in others a more purposive approach has been taken. In *Hughes v Asset Managers plc*[15] investors claimed to recover losses they had made on the stock market. They argued that the contracts they had entered into with the company that managed their investments were void because the relevant representative did not hold the necessary licence required by statute. The claim failed on the basis that on a true interpretation of the relevant legislation[16] the contract was not void. Lord Saville (then a judge of the Court of Appeal) explained:

---

8 For example, see *Phoenix General Insurance Co of Greece SA v Halvanon Insurance Co Ltd* [1988] QB 216, 268 by Kerr LJ: "It is settled law that any contract which is prohibited by statute, either expressly or by implication, is illegal and void".

9 [1921] 2 KB 716.

10 [1921] 2 KB 716, 724 by Bankes LJ and 731 by Atkin LJ.

11 [1962] AC 304.

12 For example, *Hughes v Asset Managers plc* [1995] 3 All ER 669.

13 See *Anderson Ltd v Daniel* [1924] 1 KB 138, 147, and *Marles v Phillip Trant & Sons Ltd* [1953] 1 All ER 645 (reversed but not on this point: See [1954] 1 QB 29.

14 See, for example, *Phoenix General Insurance Co of Greece SA v Halvanon insurance Co Ltd* [1988] QB 216 discussed in CP 154 at para 2.17 and *Re Cavalier Insurance Co Ltd* [1989] 2 Lloyd's Law Rep 430.

15 [1995] 3 All ER 669.

16 Prevention of Fraud (Investments) Act 1958.

As a matter of pure construction, the language used by Parliament does not, to put it at its lowest, clearly indicate that the statute meant to prohibit (that is to say make void) contracts made by unlicensed representatives …Nevertheless, if there were other indications that Parliament intended to strike down deals made by unlicensed representatives, I would not myself regard this point as conclusive, since to do so would be to prefer the form to the substance. In my judgment, however, there really is nothing to indicate that this was the intention of Parliament.[17]

3.11 In reaching the same conclusion, Lord Justice Hirst said that to have allowed the claim to succeed, "would be inimical to public policy, which is the ultimate test to be applied".[18]

2. Illegality under the common law

3.12 Illegality may act as a defence to a claim for contractual enforcement under common law rules. The illegality may be a statutory or a common law wrong and its connection to the claim may take a number of forms. Texts on the subject of illegality adopt different approaches to the best categorisation and classification of the common law rules. This adds to the difficulty of penetrating this complex area of law. Although by no means the only feasible approach, we have found it most helpful to consider the case law under the following three headings:

(a) When the terms of the contract require the commission of a legal wrong;

(b) When the purpose of the contract is to facilitate the commission of a legal wrong; and

(c) When the contract is performed in an unlawful manner.

3.13 As we go through the categories we will see that the law becomes progressively less certain and less transparent.

(1) When the terms of the contract require the commission of a legal wrong

3.14 It is often stated that if the terms of a contract require the commission of a crime then that contract is illegal and unenforceable by either party. Clearly, in the case of a contract to commit a serious crime, such as murder, this must be the case. Such a contract is unenforceable by either party, whether or not he or she was aware that the intended act is contrary to the law.[19]

---

[17] [1995] 3 All ER 669, 673.

[18] See also, *The Estate of Dr Anandh v Barnet Primary Health Care Trust* [2004] EWCA Civ 05; [1995] 3 All ER 669, 675.

[19] *J M Allan (Merchandising) Ltd v Cloke* [1963] 2 QB 340. Where neither party realised that the conduct was unlawful it may be that, following the House of Lords' decision in *Kleinwort Benson v Lincoln City Council* [1999] 2 AC 349, the contract will be void for mistake. Contrast this with the position in relation to contracts that are unlawfully performed. Here, it seems, a party will only be denied contractual remedies if he or she knew that the relevant performance was unlawful (and possibly participated in it). See paras 3.27 to 3.46 below.

> It is settled law that an agreement to do an act that is illegal or immoral or contrary to public policy, or to do any act for a consideration that is illegal, immoral or contrary to public policy, is unlawful and therefore void.[20]

3.15 In theory the common law rules do not explicitly take into account the seriousness of the unlawful conduct at all. As Lord Goff said in *Tinsley v Milligan*, the common law rules on illegality do not distinguish "between degrees of iniquity".[21]

3.16 However it must be doubtful whether the law is really this rigid. There is a vast amount of statutory regulation creating numerous statutory offences which may be committed without any guilty intent and involve misconduct of a fairly trivial nature. To suggest that any contract which necessarily requires the commission of such a minor offence is unenforceable by either party seems questionable.[22] There is curiously little authority on this point. This is probably because most cases involving the breach of a minor statutory provision have been dealt with as cases of statutory illegality. Where the court has found that on its proper interpretation the relevant legislation does not require that the contractual claim should be denied, that has been regarded as the end of the matter. The court has not applied any purported common law rule that a contract which necessarily involves the commission of an offence is unenforceable.

3.17 The validity of the purported rule denying the contractual claims of both parties where a contract is "illegal in its inception" has been questioned by Lord Pearce (then a judge in the Court of Appeal) in *Archbolds (Freightage) Ltd v S Spanglett Ltd*.[23] The defendants carried the claimants' whisky from Leeds to London in a van which, unknown to the claimants, was not licensed to carry goods for reward. The whisky was stolen on route and the claimants sued to recover its value as damages for breach of contract. The Court of Appeal upheld the trial judge's finding that the contract had not specified a particular van for its performance, and was not therefore illegal in its inception. However, Lord Pearce went on to consider what the position would have been if the contract *had* specified the particular van. Having found that the contract of carriage was not impliedly prohibited by the relevant legislation, he looked at the position under the common law. He accepted that a contract which, to the knowledge of both parties could not be carried out without the commission of an unlawful act, would be unenforceable. However, he said that, where one party was ignorant of the circumstances that would produce the illegality, he or she should not be denied relief.[24]

---

[20] *Alexander v Rayson* [1936] 1 KB 169, 182 CA.

[21] [1994] 1 AC 340, 362.

[22] N Enonchong, *Illegal Transactions* (1998) ch 17.

[23] [1961] 1 QB 374.

[24] [1961] 1 QB 374, 387.

3.18   The position in relation to a contract to commit a tort is even less clear. In one early case a contract to beat a third party was held to be illegal,[25] and a contract to print matter known by both parties to be libellous has also been held to be illegal.[26] A contract to indemnify for losses suffered as a result of the deliberate commission of the tort of deceit is unenforceable.[27] There are also suggestions that a contract which to the knowledge of the relevant party requires the breach of another contract is unenforceable by that party, but the matter is not settled.[28]

(2) When the purpose of the contract is to facilitate the commission of a legal wrong[29]

3.19   In some cases, the terms of the contract do not require either party to commit a crime or other wrong, but one or both parties enter into the contract for an unlawful purpose. In this case, a party with an unlawful purpose will not be able to enforce the contract. The intention may be to use the subject matter of the contract for a crime,[30] or even to use the contractual documentation itself for criminal purposes.[31] The contract is unenforceable by a claimant with the unlawful intent, whether or not the defendant shared in it. The effect of the rule may be therefore to allow an equally guilty defendant to reap a windfall benefit.

3.20   There are, however, several points on which the case law is unclear. First, does it matter whether the claimant knew that his or her purpose was unlawful? There are cases which are difficult to reconcile on this point. In *Waugh v Morris*[32] the ship owner had contracted to carry hay from France to London for the defendant. Both parties assumed that the hay would be delivered to a particular dock but this was not stipulated in the charterparty. Unknown to either party it had recently become unlawful to unload French hay into the United Kingdom. When the defendant realised this he unloaded the hay from alongside the ship into another vessel and exported it. However, this caused some delay and the ship owner brought an action for the detention of his ship. His claim succeeded despite the parties' intention to perform in an unlawful manner. Blackburn J explained that in order to avoid a contract which can be legally performed it is necessary to show that there was a "wicked intention" to break the law, and in this case the knowledge of the law is of great importance.

---

[25]   *Allen v Rescous* (1676) 2 Lev 174; 83 ER 505.

[26]   *Apthorp v Neville & Co* (1907) 23 TLR 575.

[27]   *Brown Jenkinson Co Ltd v Percy Dalton (London) Ltd* [1957] 2 QB 621.

[28]   *British Homophone Ltd v Kunz and Crystallate Gramophone Record Manufacturing Co Ltd* (1935) 152 LT 589. See H Lauterpacht, "Contracts to Break a Contract" (1936) 52 *Law Quarterly Review* 494.

[29]   In several of the cases the unlawful purpose has been to commit a fraud on a third party, such as the revenue authorities. Some texts treat these contracts as falling within a discrete heading of public policy. However, we intend to include them here as the principles appear to be the same as when any other unlawful purpose is intended.

[30]   As far as we are aware, the cases have all involved criminal rather than civil law wrongs.

[31]   See, for example, *Alexander v Rayson* [1936] 1 KB 169 where the claimant documented an agreement for lease in such a way that he could defraud the Revenue as to the true rent.

[32]   (1872-73) LR 8 QB 202.

3.21 A later case, *J M Allan (Merchandising) Limited v Cloke*,[33] at first sight appears to contradict this approach. The claimant hired a roulette table to the defendant, together with copies of a book of rules for use in the club. The rules set out a method of playing which was an offence under the Betting and Gaming Act 1960, although neither party appreciated that fact. Despite his innocence, the claimant's attempt to recover rent under the agreement failed. It seems that the Court of Appeal agreed with the trial judge that since it was the intention of both parties when the contract was made that the table would be used in the way described in the rules, the contract could not be performed without involving illegality.[34]

3.22 Secondly, where only one of the parties has any guilty intent, what is the position of the innocent party? If unaware of the other's unlawful purpose, then the innocent party will not be prevented from enforcing the contract.[35] But where he or she has "participated" in the unlawful purpose, it seems that the claim becomes tainted by the illegality and contractual relief will be denied. What amounts to participation? Some cases suggest that mere knowledge of the defendant's unlawful purpose is sufficient for the illegality defence to apply.[36] Other cases require that the claimant has been in some way involved in the unlawful aim, for relief to be denied.[37] In an authoritative review of the relevant case law, the Court of Appeal has recently said that what is important is that the parties "shared the unlawful purpose".[38] A shared purpose could be inferred, for example, from the letting of a flat to a prostitute at a rent beyond any normal commercial rent. It could also be inferred from "active participation", for example, by the supply of goods tailored to an unlawful purpose. However, even where participation is required, what is the necessary degree of involvement is not clear.[39]

3.23 Thirdly, as with contracts that require the performance of an illegal act, there is a question as to whether the rule applies to all minor illegality.

---

[33] [1963] 2 QB 340.

[34] See Toulson LJ's helpful discussion of these cases in *Anglo Petroleum Limited v TFB (Mortgages) Limited* [2007] EWCA Civ 456, (2007) BCC 407.

[35] See, for example, *Fielding & Platt Ltd v Najjar* [1969] 1 WLR 357 where a seller of machinery agreed to give the Lebanese buyer an invoice in the form requested by the buyer. The buyer intended to use the invoice to deceive the Lebanese authorities. The seller was entitled to sue on the sale contract because he neither knew of the buyer's unlawful object nor actively participated in it.

[36] For example, *Langton v Hughes* (1813) 1 M & S 593; 105 ER 222. The seller's knowledge that the buyer intended to use the subject matter of the contract in the unlawful brewing of beer was sufficient to defeat the seller's action for goods sold and delivered. In *Anglo Petroleum Limited v TFB (Mortgages) Limited* [2007] EWCA Civ 456, (2007) BCC 407 Toulson LJ said that the distinction between the seller's knowledge and his participation was not raised in the arguments and it would be wrong therefore to read too much into the judgments on this point.

[37] For example, *Hodgson v Temple* (1813) 5 Taunt 181; 128 ER 656. The claimant sold spirits to the defendant knowing that he intended to use them in an illegal manner. Despite his knowledge, the claimant was able to recover their price. See also *Holman v Johnson* (1775) 1 Cowp 341.

[38] *Anglo Petroleum Limited v TFB (Mortgages) Limited* [2007] EWCA Civ 456, (2007) BCC 407.

[39] See the examples given in *Pearce v Brooks* (1865-66) LR 1 Ex 213.

3.24 The fourth area of uncertainty relates to the closeness of the contract to the unlawful purpose. At some point the illegality must be too remote to be relevant. However it is not clear when this should be. The case law does not appear to be entirely consistent. In *21st Century Logistics Solutions Ltd v Madysen Ltd*[40] Mr Justice Field found for the claimants on the basis that the fraudulent intent at the time of the contract was too remote from the contract itself. The case involved a form of VAT fraud known as "missing trader" or "carousel" fraud. A company had been set up specifically to buy high value goods from abroad without VAT and to sell them on within the UK with VAT added. The main purpose and profit from the deal was to gain the VAT, pocket the money and disappear without paying anything to Customs and Excise. The company imported the goods and agreed to sell them to the defendant. However, after the company had delivered the goods to the defendant, the defendant became suspicious and alerted the relevant authorities before paying any money. The company went into liquidation and the liquidator brought a claim to enforce the debt against the defendant. The court held that the sale contract was enforceable as the company's illegal purpose was too remote to have any effect on it.

3.25 This case is difficult to square with the earlier Court of Appeal decision in *Alexander v Rayson*.[41] Here the claimant had agreed to grant a lease to the defendant at an annual rent of £1,200 and to perform certain services in connection with the property. The claimant sent the defendant two documents. One was a lease with the benefit of the services at a rent of £450 pa. The other was an agreement for virtually the same services for a fee of £750 pa. The claimant had documented the arrangement in this way in order to defraud the local rating authority by representing that the total rent was only £450 pa. It was held that this fraudulent scheme prevented the claimant from enforcing the contract. As in the *21st Century Logistics Solutions Ltd* case, the contract did not require either party to do anything unlawful and both contracts could have been performed without any fraud. However, in *Alexander v Rayson* the fraudulent purpose prevented the lessor from enforcing the lease, whereas in *21st Century Logistics Solutions Ltd* the fraudulent purpose was found to be too remote to have any effect on the contract.

3.26 A final area of uncertainty relates to the time at which the unlawful purpose is held. Does it make a difference at what time the party (or parties) had the illegal purpose? On the one hand, if at the outset a party intended to use the contract for an illegal purpose, but has subsequently changed its mind, is it still prevented from enforcing the contract? On the other hand, is an illegal purpose that was only formed later relevant? It is not easy to find authority on the point, although as we shall go on to see, in cases involving illegal performance the time at which the illegal intention was formed can be crucial to the outcome of the case.

---

[40] [2004] EWHC 231(QB), [2004] 2 Lloyds Rep 92.
[41] [1936] 1 KB 169, CA.

(3) When the contract is performed in an unlawful manner

3.27 In some circumstances a contract that does not require the commission of any unlawful act, and which was not entered into in order to facilitate an unlawful purpose, is nevertheless *performed* in an unlawful way. The effect that this unlawful performance has on the parties' contractual rights is very unclear.[42] Of course where the unlawful conduct involves the breach of a statutory provision, there will be a question of statutory interpretation as to whether the legislature expressly or impliedly prohibited the contract.

3.28 At common law, historically a distinction has been drawn between cases where the guilty party intended from the time of entering into the contract to perform it unlawfully, and cases where the intention to perform unlawfully was only made subsequently.

(i) where one or both parties intended to perform in an unlawful manner from the outset

3.29 It is often stated that a party who intends to perform the contract in an unlawful manner from the outset will not be able to enforce it. So, in *St John Shipping Corporation v Joseph Rank Ltd* Lord Devlin (then a High Court judge) said that had the shipper intended to overload his ship when he entered into the contract, then he would not have been able to enforce it.[43] Where both parties shared this illegal intention, neither will be able to enforce it. It is never made clear in the case law why the time at which the intention to perform illegally is formed should be crucial to determining the outcome. In some cases, this has led to a convoluted examination of the evidence.[44]

3.30 There is one exception. If both parties intended to perform the contract in an unlawful manner, but provided that they did in fact perform it lawfully, they will be able to enforce it.[45] This is established at least where the parties were unaware that the intended method of performance was illegal because they did not know of a recent change in the law. However, there seems no reason why the same principle should not apply if the parties knew that what they intended to do originally would be unlawful, and simply thought better of it.

3.31 However, it clearly cannot be in every case that a contract is unlawfully performed, even where this was the original intention, that the offending party loses his or her remedies. Such a proposition would result in the widespread forfeiture of contractual remedies as a result of minor and incidental transgressions. Although there is general agreement on this point amongst academic commentators, there is surprisingly little authority.[46]

---

[42] For a different analysis of the effect of unlawful performance on contractual rights, see N Enonchong, "Illegal Transactions: The Future?" [2000] *Restitution Law Review* 82.

[43] [1957] 1 QB 267, 287-288. For the facts of the case see para 3.4 above.

[44] For example, *Skilton v Sullivan, The Times*, March 25, 1994.

[45] *Waugh v Morris* (1873) LR 8 QB 202.

[46] N Enonchong, *Illegal Transactions* (1998) ch 17; R A Buckley, *Illegality and Public Policy* (2002) paras 3.12 to 3.17.

(ii) Where one or both parties subsequently decided to perform in an unlawful manner

3.32 The law in relation to cases where the decision to perform unlawfully is not made until after the contract is formed is even less clear. There are certainly cases decided on the basis that the mere commission of an unlawful act in the course of carrying out a contract would not at common law affect enforcement. This is illustrated by *Wetherell v Jones*.[47] The claimant succeeded in an action for the price of goods delivered, despite his unlawful performance in providing an irregular statutory invoice. Lord Tenterden CJ said: "Where the consideration and the matter to be performed are both legal, we are not aware that a plaintiff has ever been precluded from recovering by an infringement of the law, not contemplated by the contract, in the performance of something to be done on his part".[48]

3.33 But this principle is subject to at least four possible exceptions. First, the unlawful act may turn the contract into one that is expressly or impliedly forbidden by statute. Secondly, in at least some cases, the illegal performance will turn the contract into one which is not enforced at common law. Thirdly, the forfeiture rule may prevent recovery. Fourthly, recovery may not be permitted where the claimant has to "rely" on his illegality in order to prove his or her claim. We look at these four exceptions below.

(a) first exception: statutory illegality

3.34 The first exception is merely an example of statutory illegality. This seems to be the best interpretation of *Anderson v Daniel*.[49] The claimant agreed to sell "salvage" (the sweepings from the holds of ships that had carried certain chemical cargoes) to the defendant for use as fertiliser. The Fertilisers and Feeding Stuffs Act 1906 required that the vendor of fertiliser imported from abroad should give the purchaser an invoice setting out its chemical contents. This would have been impractical in the case of salvage, and, in accordance with the custom of the trade, the claimant did not do so. In an action by the claimant for the price, the purchaser argued that since the claimant had failed to supply the required invoice, he had committed a statutory offence in the performance of the contract which rendered the contract illegal and the price could not therefore be recovered. The Court of Appeal accepted this argument. It was not necessary for the purchaser to show that the contract was illegal when it was entered into in order to avoid it. It was sufficient to show that the claimant failed to perform it in the only way in which the statute allowed it to be performed.

---

[47] (1832) 3 B & Ad 221. See also, *A L Barnes Ltd v Time Talk (UK) Ltd* [2003] EWCA Civ 402; [2003] BLR 331 at [11].

[48] (1832) 3 B & Ad 221, 226; 110 ER 82, 84.

[49] [1924] 1 KB 138. See Devlin J's comments on this case in *St John Shipping Corporation v Joseph Rank Ltd* [1957] 1 QB 267, 284. Devlin J said that the case did not proceed on the basis that in the course of performing a legal contract an illegality was committed, but on the narrower basis that the way in which the contract was performed turned it into the sort of contract that was prohibited by the statute.

(b) second exception: illegal performance "turns the contract into one which is not enforced at common law"

3.35 The second exception is very unclear in its scope. In some cases the courts have held that illegality in the course of performance may turn the contract into one that is forbidden by the common law[50] and is thus unenforceable, at least by a "guilty" party. This departure from previously accepted principles was based on the decision in *Ashmore, Benson, Pease & Co Ltd v Dawson*,[51] where the court considered whether the claimant had "participated" in the unlawful performance of the other party and having done so was unable to enforce the contract. The claimants employed the defendants to carry equipment on an articulated lorry The defendants used a lorry that was not suitable to carry such a heavy load. This constituted an offence. The lorry toppled over onto the verge during its journey and was damaged. The claimants claimed damages for breach of contract. A majority of the Court of Appeal held that, even if the contract was lawful when made, the claimants had participated in its unlawful performance, and were therefore unable to claim.

3.36 The principle has been extended into employment contract case law where courts are frequently asked to decide whether an employee's claim under an employment contract is unenforceable where the employer has performed the contract unlawfully. Indeed, the cases have assumed without further discussion that the employer will be unable to enforce the contract.[52] Rather, the argument has turned on whether the employee is sufficiently implicated in the illegality to lose his or her contractual rights too. We look at these cases in some detail below. However, it must be clear that it is not every unlawful act in the course of performing an employment contract that will prevent even the guilty party from enforcing it. Otherwise, every lorry driver who breaks the speed limit, or employee who takes home office stationery, would be unable to enforce their employment contracts. As Lord Justice Waller explained in *Colen v Cebrian (UK) Limited*,[53] the question is "whether the common law would say that a contract has by its illegal performance been turned into an illegal contract".

---

[50] *Colen v Cebrian (UK) Limited* [2003] EWCA Civ 1676, (2004) ICR 568.

[51] [1973] 1 WLR 828.

[52] *Newland v Simons and Willer (Hairdressers) Ltd* [1981] IRLR 359.

[53] [2003] EWCA Civ 1676, (2004) ICR 568.

3.37   Over the last few years, the issue of illegal employment contracts has been considered in numerous cases before the Employment Appeal Tribunal and the Court of Appeal.[54] Some employment cases have dismissed illegality in the course of performance as irrelevant if there was no intention to act unlawfully at the time the contract was made.[55] However there is now a significant number of cases in which the court has held that, where the contract has in fact been performed in an unlawful manner, an employee who knows of and participates in that illegality is unable to enforce the contract. This means that the employee will be unable to claim unpaid wages or compensation for unfair dismissal.

3.38   The illegality in question typically involves some form of tax fraud committed by the employer. The cases concern the claim of an employee who knows that his or her employer is failing to pay tax and national insurance, but who only makes half-hearted efforts to regularise the position. The courts appear to have vacillated between holding that mere knowledge of the fraud renders the contract unenforceable by the employee, and allowing the employee to claim unless he or she has further participated in the scheme. In *Newland v Simon & Willer (Hairdressers) Ltd*[56] the Employment Appeal Tribunal held that the applicant could not claim unfair dismissal because she had known that her employers were engaged in a fraud on the Inland Revenue when she received her P60. However, in *Hall v Woolston Hall Leisure*[57] the *Newland* decision was doubted. Although not decisive to the outcome of the case,[58] the Court of Appeal in *Hall* reviewed the existing case law on unlawful performance in employment contracts. It reaffirmed that knowledge alone will not prevent the employee's claim, and that the employee must have also participated in some way for relief to be denied. Lord Justice Peter Gibson said:

> In cases where the contract of employment is neither entered into for an illegal purpose nor prohibited by statute, the illegal performance of the contract will not render the contract unenforceable unless in addition to knowledge of the facts which make the performance illegal the employee actively participates in the illegal performance. It is a question of fact in each case whether there has been a sufficient degree of participation by the employee.[59]

---

[54]   S Forshaw and M Pilgerstorfer, "Illegally Formed Contracts of Employment and Equal Treatment at Work" (2005) 34 *Industrial Law Journal* 158.

[55]   *Coral Leisure Group v Barnet* [1981] ICR 503, and *Rosan Heims plc v Duke* EAT 10 Dec 2002, 2002 WL 32067886.

[56]   [1981] ICR 521.

[57]   [2001] 1 WLR 225.

[58]   The relevant claim was compensation for sex discrimination under the Sex Discrimination Act 1975. The Court of Appeal confirmed the decision in *Leighton v Michael* [1995] ICR 1091 that the illegality of the contract is not necessarily fatal to a discrimination claim.

[59]   [2001] 1 WLR 225, 234.

3.39   The Court of Appeal considered its earlier decision in *Hewcastle Catering Ltd v Ahmed and Elkamah.*[60] The employers had been engaged in a VAT fraud. The claimant waiters had known about the fraud and taken part in it by the method of invoicing customers. Having acted as witnesses in the prosecution of their employers, they were dismissed. They complained to the Employment Tribunal alleging unfair dismissal. The employer argued that because of the unlawful performance, the employment contracts were not enforceable. The waiters' claim was allowed. The Court of Appeal looked at various factors in deciding that public policy should not preclude their claim. These were that the obligation to make VAT returns fell upon the employer only; that the contract of employment was not one by which the employee was engaged to assist in the fraud; and that to deny an employee the right to claim compensation could discourage the disclosure of such fraudulent schemes to the relevant authorities.[61]

3.40   However more recent comments made by the Court of Appeal suggest a stricter test. That is, that unless there are exceptional circumstances, the employee will be denied relief simply as a result of knowing about the arrangements which formed the employer's unlawful performance and acquiescing in it. In *Wheeler v Quality Deep Ltd*[62] the employee had received only two payslips from her employer during the course of her three year employment. She had requested more and was told the matter would be "straightened out", but heard nothing further. She received no documentation from the Inland Revenue. The Employment Tribunal found that the employer was failing to deduct tax and national insurance from the employee's earnings, that the employee must have realised this, and that as a result the employee was unable to enforce her employment contract. The Court of Appeal quashed this decision on the grounds that the applicant had only limited knowledge of the English language and of English tax provisions. There was no evidence that she knew of her employer's fraud. However, Lord Justice Hooper stressed that this was a "very unusual case" and that "had she not had that limited knowledge, she may well not have succeeded".

---

[60]   [1992] ICR 626.

[61]   Although this case was decided using the "public conscience" test which was later rejected by the House of Lords in *Tinsley v Milligan* [1994] 1 AC 340, the Court of Appeal has subsequently confirmed that the list of factors are proper considerations to be taken into account in determining whether the defence of illegality should prevail: *Hall v Woolston Hall Leisure Ltd* [2001] 1 WLR 225.

[62]   [2004] EWCA Civ 1085, [2005] ICR 265.

3.41 Two recent decisions have considered whether the employee is unable to enforce an employment contract where he or she knew of the relevant facts concerning the unlawful arrangement and had participated in that arrangement, but did not know that it was unlawful. In the context of a payment arrangement devised by the employee, the Employment Appeal Tribunal found that mere knowledge of the relevant facts is sufficient to render the contract unenforceable. Knowledge of the law is irrelevant.[63] However, in two subsequent joined cases the Court of Appeal held that there must have been some misrepresentation of the true facts to the Inland Revenue. Otherwise quite legitimate arrangements which are difficult to categorise correctly for tax purposes would be rendered unenforceable.[64]

3.42 The courts have never explained why different and stricter treatment seems to be given to unlawful performance in the context of an employment contract as opposed to contracts of other types. It may stem from the long-term nature of the contractual relationship between the parties. It makes even less sense, in this context, for the outcome of the case to turn on whether the illegal performance was intended prior to entering into the contract or only formed later. Or it may be because the cases have largely been concerned with a type of illegality that the court takes very seriously – tax fraud. Even within the context of tax fraud, the court appears to take a harsher line in relation to income tax as opposed to VAT fraud. This may be on the basis that the employee can sometimes see a benefit from PAYE fraud in the form of increased pay. However, there has been no express statement that the principle is limited by either of these factors, and therefore the extent of this second exception remains very unclear.

(c) third exception: the forfeiture rule

3.43 The third exception is based on the forfeiture rule. The forfeiture rule stems from the principle already discussed that no person may benefit from his or her own unlawful conduct. It seems that in a case where the unlawful performance constitutes a very serious criminal act, then versions of that rule may prevent a party from enforcing a contractual right which would allow him or her to benefit directly from the crime. The classic application of this principle is illustrated in *Beresford v Royal Insurance Company Limited*.[65] The personal representatives of a man who had shot himself sought to recover on life insurance policies that the deceased had taken out with the defendants. There was no suggestion that the insurance contracts were illegal, but the House of Lords held that the personal representatives were unable to recover, because if they could do so the estate would be benefiting from the deceased's suicide, and, at the time, suicide was a crime. Lord Atkin said:

---

[63] *Daymond v Enterprise South Devon* EAT 6 June 2007, 2007 WL 1685234.

[64] *Enfield Technical Services Ltd v Payne* and *BF Components Ltd v I Grace* [2008] EWCA Civ 393, [2008] IRLR 500.

[65] [1938] AC 586.

> ... no system of jurisprudence can with reason include amongst the rights which it enforces rights directly resulting to the person enforcing them from the crime of that person.[66]

3.44 In the *St John Shipping* case, it was doubted whether this principle applies to all statutory offences.[67] In any event, it was held that it did not affect the claim in that case because it could not be shown that the freight claimed was directly due to the overloading. That is, it could not be shown that it was the defendants' cargo that had caused the overloading.

3.45 However, it is easy to imagine facts on which the benefit claimed would flow directly from the crime committed. Then it is necessary but difficult to establish the scope of the rule. Probably it applies only to serious crimes that were committed intentionally.[68]

(d) fourth exception: the reliance principle

3.46 As we shall see in Parts 5 and 6, the reliance principle is the test used by the courts to determine whether a property right has passed under an illegal transaction. The general rule is that the claimant will be able to enforce his or her usual property rights despite the involvement of illegality at some point in the transaction, provided that he or she does not have to "rely" on that illegality to prove the claim. This principle has been much criticised for its arbitrariness and, indeed, later in this report, we provisionally recommend its legislative reform in the context of equitable interests. It is only infrequently referred to in the contractual case law. However, in some cases, particularly those involving illegal performance, it has been suggested that the claimant would not be able to enforce the contract if he needed to "rely on his illegal action in order to succeed".[69] It is not at all clear when the claimant would have to rely on his illegal action in a contract case. If the claimant has performed his or her side of the bargain in an unlawful manner, then on a broad interpretation the claimant will always be relying on the illegality to prove that he or she has already fulfilled the contractual obligations.

---

[66] [1938] AC 586, 596.

[67] [1957] 1 QB 267, 292.

[68] The forfeiture rule has been applied in cases in which a party has committed a deliberate crime and has then claimed on an insurance policy (*Gray v Barr* [1971] 2 QB 554) or has claimed an indemnity or damages from another party whose fault was alleged to have caused the claimant to commit the crime (*Askey v Golden Wine Co Ltd* [1948] 2 All ER 35 and *Meah v McCreamer (No 2)* [1986] 1 All ER 943). It was not applied to insurance claims in "motor manslaughter" cases, on the basis that the crime was not deliberate (*Tinline v White Cross Insurance* [1921] 3 KB 327).

[69] For example, *Archbolds (Freightage) Ltd v S Spanglett Ltd* [1961] 1 QB 374, 388; *Colen v Cebrian (UK) Limited* [2003] EWCA Civ 1676, [2004] ICR 568 at [23]. Which party was required to "rely" on the illegality of a minimum purchase requirement entered into in breach of Article 81 EC Treaty in order to plead their case was a source of considerable disagreement in *Byrne v Inntrepreneur Beer Supply Co Ltd* [1999] 2 EGLR 145.

3. Damages for a different cause of action

3.47   Even where the court is not prepared to enforce a contract which involves illegality, the claimant may be able to claim damages for a different cause of action albeit one that is based on the unenforceable contract. For example, in some cases the claimant has been allowed to bring an alternative claim in tort. In *Shelley v Paddock*[70] the defendants, who were resident in Spain, agreed to sell property there to the claimant, who was resident in England. The claimant paid the purchase price to the defendants, who fraudulently misrepresented that they were acting on behalf of the owners of the property. However, the claimant, ignorant of the requirement, had failed to obtain Treasury permission to remit money overseas as then required. When it transpired that the defendants were unable to make good title to the property and had, in fact, defrauded the claimant, she brought an action in the tort of deceit to recover her money. The defendants argued that the sale contract was illegal and unenforceable. The Court of Appeal allowed the tortious claim. Lord Denning MR said that the defendants were "guilty of a swindle" and concluded that it was "only fair and just that they should not be allowed to keep the benefit of their fraud".[71]

3.48   However it is clear that the courts will not permit the claimant to bring an alternative claim in every case. For example, in *Parkinson v College of Ambulance Ltd and Harrison*,[72] the secretary of a charity fraudulently misrepresented to the claimant that in return for a large donation, he or the charity was in a position to ensure that the claimant would receive a knighthood. After making the donation but not receiving the knighthood, the claimant brought an action claiming, inter alia, damages for deceit. The Court held that the claim failed despite the defendant's fraud. The claimant's involvement in a scheme of such turpitude ruled out not only his contractual claim to enforce the contract but also a tort claim for deceit.

3.49   In other cases, the courts may be prepared to imply the existence of a collateral contract between the parties which is untainted by the illegality of the primary contract. The main example here is *Strongman (1945) Ltd v Sincock*.[73] The claimants were builders who had undertaken certain work on the defendant's premises. Under regulations then in force, licences were required to cover the work. The defendant, an architect, promised that he would obtain them, but failed to do so. On completion, the defendant sought to avoid payment, relying on the illegality. The Court of Appeal held that the builders could not sue on the building contract itself, which was illegal and unenforceable, but that the defendant's assurance amounted to a collateral contract by which the architect promised that he would get the necessary licences, or if he failed to do so, that he would stop the work. The claimants were allowed to recover, as damages for breach of that promise, exactly the sum due to them under the unenforceable building contract.

---

[70]   [1980] QB 348.

[71]   [1980] QB 348, 357. See also *Saunders v Edwards* [1987] 1 WLR 1116.

[72]   [1925] 2 KB 1.

[73]   [1955] 2 KB 525.

PROBLEMS WITH THE PRESENT LAW

3.50 We do not suggest that the present law in relation to illegality and contracts is producing manifestly unjust decisions. On the whole the case law illustrates the judges tracing a careful path through the various rules in order to reach an outcome that most would regard as "fair" between the parties involved.

3.51 Only occasionally do we see cases where one might argue that the claimant has been harshly penalised.[74] These mainly occur in relation to unlawful performance. In particular, where an employee has participated in an employer's PAYE fraud, and as a result loses employment rights far more valuable than the gain, if any, that the employee enjoyed from the fraud.[75]

3.52 However, we do argue that the present law is unnecessarily complex, uncertain, arbitrary and lacks transparency. This largely results from the fact that the illegality rules have to cover a huge variety of cases. The unlawful conduct in question may range from the heinous to the trivial, and its connection to the claim may be inextricably close or merely incidental. To expect one set of detailed and ostensibly rigid rules to cater for all circumstances that may be encountered is overly ambitious.

1. Complexity

3.53 As our overview of the present law has shown, the crude application of the general contractual illegality rules could lead to unnecessarily harsh decisions. So how have the courts successfully avoided this potential for injustice in relation to the dispute before them? This has been achieved largely by the use of two methods. The first is by the creation of the numerous exceptions to the application of the general rules. One example is the development of relief for an innocent party in the cases involving a contract entered into with an illegal purpose. After some initial wavering the courts seemed set on denying relief to a claimant who was simply aware of the other party's illegal purpose,[76] but have now swung back round to requiring some form of shared purpose before relief is denied.[77]

---

[74] For example, *Brown Jenkinson & Co Ltd v Percy Dalton (London) Ltd* [1957] 2 QB 621, 638 where Pearce LJ said: "I share the reluctance that any court must feel to find in favour of defendants whose behaviour and whose defence are so lacking in merit". A recent example is *Birkett v Acorn Business Machines Ltd* [1999] 2 All ER (Comm) 429 (CA). The defendant agreed to hire a photocopier to the claimant. However, the defendant persuaded the claimant to falsify their contractual documentation by substituting details in relation to a fax machine. The purpose of the substitution was to defraud a third party finance company which would provide finance only in relation to telecommunications equipment and not photocopiers. Because the contract between the claimant and the defendant thereby became one which had as its object an illegal act, the claimant, having performed his side of the bargain, was subsequently unable to enforce it. The defendant was able to avoid its contractual obligations by relying on its own unlawful scheme. Sedley LJ said that "this is one of those cases where (at least in my view) law and justice part company".

[75] For example, *Hyland v JH Barker (North-West) Ltd* [1985] IRLR 403.

[76] See, for example, *Mason v Clarke* [1955] AC 778.

[77] See the Court of Appeal's recent judgment, *Anglo Petroleum Limited v TFB (Mortgages) Limited* [2007] EWCA Civ 456, (2007) BCC 407.

3.54   The second method of avoiding harsh decisions is seen in the way in which the application of the relevant rules can be strained in order to meet the justice of the particular case. One example of this is shown by the House of Lords' decision in *Mason v Clarke*.[78] The claimant had paid for shooting rights over a landowner's estate. On payment, he accepted a receipt which stated that the consideration was paid "towards bailiff's wages". In a dispute between the claimant and a tenant farmer of the same land, the question arose whether the agreement for shooting rights was enforceable, or whether the acceptance of this receipt fixed the claimant with knowledge of the landowner's fraudulent tax scheme thereby rendering the agreement unenforceable. Reversing the decision of the Court of Appeal, the House said that, even if fraudulent intention in the form of the receipt had been established, the claimant was not made aware of it simply by accepting the receipt. Several commentators suggest that the receipt could hardly have been invoiced in the way that it was except for some unlawful purpose, and any person accepting the receipt must have realised this. The real problem was that barring a claim merely because the claimant has knowledge of another's unlawful scheme can be an unduly harsh rule. In order to circumvent the rule's consequences in this case, the court adopted a very generous view of the facts.[79]

3.55   Overall, the result has been a complex body of case law with technical distinctions that are difficult to justify.[80] As one respondent to CP 154 noted, illegality disputes are often adjudicated by lay arbitrators to whom the complexities and uncertainties, not to mention the contradictions, of the present law can present a formidable obstacle to its understanding, and which can therefore impede a fair resolution of the dispute.[81]

2. Uncertainty

3.56   Uncertainty in the present law was a frequent complaint from the respondents to CP 154. The law was described as "notoriously unclear", and as a "small jungle of rules and precedents" that have an "unpredictable and unreliable effect". Litigants and their advisers are clearly finding it difficult to predict how a contractual dispute with an element of illegality will be decided. The cause of the uncertainty seems to be twofold.

3.57   First, in some areas, it is not possible to state clearly what the relevant rules are. This is particularly true in relation to unlawful performance. We know that in some instances unlawful performance (or participation in the other party's unlawful performance) that was not intended at the time the contract was made will be sufficient to deny a party his or her contractual rights. However, it is not at all clear when this will be the case. To date, it is apparently limited to cases involving employment contracts and some form of revenue fraud, but there is no suggestion that the rule is only applicable here or why this situation has been singled out.

---

[78]   [1955] AC 778.

[79]   See R A Buckley, *Illegality and Public Policy* (2002) para 4.04.

[80]   Professor Enonchong describes it as a "baffling entanglement of rules": N Enonchong, *Illegal Transactions* (1998) p 20. All the major texts on the illegality defence criticise its complexity.

[81]   The Law Society.

3.58 Secondly, even where the law is clear, there is uncertainty as to how it will be applied. For example, where there are two possible rules governing the case, the courts sometimes only look at one and apparently disregard the other. This is particularly true in relation to statutory illegality. Here the courts often look at the question whether the statute impliedly renders the claim unenforceable, and, if not, then ignore the issue as to whether it might be unenforceable at common law. However, they do not always adopt this approach.[82]

3. Arbitrariness

3.59 At certain points, the rules relating to illegality and contract appear to draw arbitrary distinctions, the importance of which is never explained. For example, the time at which one of the parties decided on its unlawful performance (before or after the contract was made) can be determinative of the case. This leads to a detailed examination of the evidence to decide exactly when the intention was created. Yet it is never made clear why this issue should be so important.[83]

4. Lack of transparency

3.60 The complexity and uncertainty of the present law sometimes mean that it is impossible to analyse why the claim was allowed or denied. Why did the court choose one line of authority rather than another? In effect the court is able to select the analysis or rule that produces what it considers to be the right result in the circumstances of the dispute before them. There is very seldom any open discussion in the judgments of what considerations the court has followed in order to reach its decision.

ILLEGALITY IN OTHER JURISDICTIONS

3.61 Having considered how the present illegality rules operate in our jurisdiction and the problems which they invoke, we now look at how they work overseas. We look briefly in turn at other European legal systems, the United States Restatement, and the New Zealand legislative provisions. We go on to consider the compatibility of our system of rules with first, European Union law, and secondly, the European Convention on Human Rights.

1. The Illegality doctrine in other European legal systems

3.62 All European legal systems take notice when a contract involves an illegality,[84] although their individual approaches can be quite different.

---

[82] For example, in *Shaw v Groom* [1970] 2 QB 504 the court decided that failure to supply a rent book containing all the details required by legislation did not make the contract unenforceable as a matter of implied statutory illegality under the Rent Acts. It did not go on to consider whether the landlord's intention to perform the lease in this unlawful manner should make it unenforceable at common law. However, in *Ashmore Benson Pease & Co Ltd v A V Dawson* [1973] 1 WLR 828 the Court of Appeal considered the effect of common law illegality rules on a contract which was performed in a manner which contravened statutory provisions and denied the claimant relief.

[83] See, for example, *Skilton v Sullivan* (CA) *The Times,* 25 March 1994 and the discussion about exactly when the defendant decided to provide inaccurate invoices.

[84] Different legal systems use different terminology, although the underlying concept is similar.

The French Code Civil[85]

3.63 The French *Code Civil* sets out its broad policy regarding illegality in contracts in Article 6, which states that "statutes relating to public policy and morals may not be derogated from by private agreements". This concept covers agreements which will conflict with statutory provisions, but also those which will offend public order or good morals. In constructing a contract, the *Code Civil* requires both an "*objet*" and a "*cause*" of the agreement. The *objet* is the agreed act or acts themselves, whereas the *cause* is the reason or motivation for entering into the agreement.

3.64 The *Code Civil* places limitations on the nature of both the *objet* and the *cause*, with the intention of prohibiting illegal agreements. The *objet* can only be a thing that may be the subject matter of legal transactions between private individuals.[86] Similarly, an obligation without *cause*, or with a false or unlawful cause, cannot have any effect.[87] The code also defines "unlawful" in this context, being where it is "prohibited by legislation, where it is contrary to public morals or to public policy".[88]

3.65 The effect of these provisions is that, under the *Code Civil*, an illegal contract is void from the very start and is of no effect.[89] The parties cannot expressly ratify it, nor can they voluntarily perform the obligation to make the agreement valid. The practical application of these provisions of the *Code Civil* to illegal contracts tends to be straightforward, and raises few problems. Despite this, it has been criticised at times for being overly rigid and unable to take into account the nuances of different cases.[90]

The German Bürgerliches Gesetzbuch[91]

3.66 The German civil code, the *Bürgerliches Gesetzbuch,* approaches illegality in contract in a similar way to English and French law, in that it can cover acts which are in breach of statutory provisions as well as acts which offend good morals and good faith.

---

[85] English translation available at http://www.legifrance.gouv.fr/html/codes_traduits/code_civil_textA.htm (last visited 16 Jan 2009).

[86] Article 1128.

[87] Article 1131.

[88] Article 1133.

[89] Article 1172: "Any condition relating to an impossible thing, or contrary to public morals, or prohibited by law, is void, and renders void the agreement which depends upon it". See also *Croizé v Veuax* S. 1931. I. 49, 52: An agreement "declared null as contrary to *ordre public* cannot… produce any legal effect either for the future or for the past".

[90] See, for example, N Enonchong, "Illegality in French and English Law" *International and Comparative Law Quarterly* Vol 44, Jan 1995, 196.

[91] English translation available at http://bundesrecht.juris.de/englisch_bgb/index.html (last visited 16 Jan 2009).

3.67 With regard to the breach of statutory provisions, §134 of the *Bürgerliches Gesetzbuch* states that "a legal transaction that violates a statutory prohibition is void, unless the statute leads to a different conclusion". The application of this article depends on the specific wording of the statute – only where the statute prohibits the final result of the transaction, or where it uses imperative words such as "cannot", will an agreement be voided under §134. Conversely, where a statute contains provisions relating to merely circumstantial matters (for example, restricting shop opening hours) or does not use imperative words such as "ought not", then a breach will not mean an agreement would fall within the scope of §134. Although the usual effect of §134 is that the contract is void, in some circumstances the court may instead vary the offending terms of the agreement and allow the transaction to continue.[92]

3.68 In addition to the prohibition on agreements which are contrary to statutory provisions, the *Bürgerliches Gesetzbuch* also states that "a legal transaction which is contrary to public policy is void".[93] This is clearly wider than §134, and is aimed at contracts which have the potential to exploit an unequal bargaining position between the parties.[94]

The Principles of European Contract Law[95]

3.69 The Principles of European Contract Law (the "PECL") were published between 1995 and 2003 by the Commission on European Contract Law in conjunction with a body of lawyers, under the chairmanship of Professor Ole Lando. Although not legally binding, the principles have attempted to bring together aspects of European contract law into a single code, and may in the future form a basis for the European Common Frame of Reference.[96] Parties can expressly include the principles into their contract, subject to any overriding applicable law (the 'applicable law').[97]

---

[92] For example, where a statute sets maximum prices for certain goods, if parties enter into a contract at a higher price, then the court may simply reduce the price to within the specified limit – see *BGHZ* 51, 174.

[93] §138(1).

[94] §138(2): "in particular, a legal transaction is void by which a person, by exploiting the predicament, inexperience, lack of sound judgement or considerable weakness of will of another, causes himself or a third party, in exchange for an act of performance, to be promised or granted pecuniary advantages which are clearly disproportionate to the performance".

[95] The Commission on European Contract Law, *Principles of European Contract Law* (2000 (Parts I and II) and 2003 (Part III)).

[96] The European Common Frame of Reference is a long-term project intended to provide the European Commission, the European Council and the European Parliament with a handbook, containing fundamental principles, key concepts and definitions of contract law to be used when reviewing existing legislation, or developing new legislation.

[97] Article 1:103.

3.70 The PECL do not deal with the complex task of defining *when* a contract, or its performance, will be deemed to be illegal. This is left to the applicable law. Rather, they deal with the subsequent implications of that illegality, the most significant of which being that an illegal contract can be held to be "ineffective", either wholly or in part.[98] This could include an otherwise valid contract if its enforcement would necessarily involve an illegality.

3.71 A contract may be deemed ineffective if a term is found to be contrary to a fundamental principle, or infringes a mandatory rule of law. Where a contract is found to be contrary to a fundamental principle (for example, in breach of the European Community Treaty or the European Convention on Human Rights), the court has no discretion and it must find that the agreement is of no effect to the extent of the conflict.[99] Conversely, where the contract infringes a mandatory rule of law, one of two approaches may be taken, depending on the circumstances.[100] If the rule which is infringed expressly prescribes the consequences of that infringement, then those consequences shall apply.[101] If there is no such express provision, then the court has the discretion to declare that the contract shall either have full effect, some effect, or no effect, or alternatively the court may modify its terms.[102]

3.72 When exercising this discretion, the court must reach an "appropriate and proportionate" decision, taking into account all of the relevant circumstances. A number of factors to be considered are specifically identified. These are: the purpose of the rule which has been infringed; the category of persons for whose protection the rule exists; any potential sanctions provided by the rule itself; the seriousness of the infringement; whether the infringement was intentional; and the proximity between the infringement and the contract.[103]

2. The United States

3.73 The Restatement (Second) of Contracts,[104] §178(1) states that:

---

[98] Article 15:103.

[99] Article 15:101: "A contract is of no effect to the extent that it is contrary to principles recognised as fundamental in the laws of the Member States of the European Union".

[100] Article 15:102.

[101] Article 15:102(1).

[102] Article 15:102(2).

[103] Article 15:102(3).

[104] The American Restatements of Law are published by the American Law Institute. They are intended to "address uncertainty in the law through a restatement of basic legal subjects that can tell judges and lawyers what the law was". The Restatements are frequently cited and given great authority in American judicial decisions: American Law Institute: http://www.ali.org (last visited 16 Jan 2009).

A promise or other term of an agreement is unenforceable on grounds of public policy if legislation provides that it is unenforceable or the interest in its enforcement is clearly outweighed in the circumstances by a public policy against the enforcement in such terms.[105]

3.74 This policy is based on two principal considerations – first, that refusing to enforce such an agreement may act as a deterrent; and secondly, that enforcing an illegal agreement would be an inappropriate use of the court's resources.

3.75 Instances of statutory restriction are becoming more common, and a number of these expressly deal with the issue of contractual enforcement. Most, however, do not, and the court is then required to weigh the policy indicated by the statute against the policy of enforcing contracts. A court may find that the penalty prescribed in the legislation is adequate, making it unnecessary to impose the additional sanction of loss of contractual rights.[106]

3.76 In many other situations, the objection to the agreement will be on the basis of public policy rather than statute. In this case, the court has a high degree of flexibility in determining whether the agreement is enforceable. According to the Restatement (Second) of Contracts, account will be taken of the parties' justified expectations, any forfeiture that would result if enforcement were denied, and any special public interest in the enforcement of that term in weighing up the interest in enforcing the term.[107] Similarly, the strength of the policy argument, the likelihood that refusal will further that policy, the seriousness and deliberateness of the conduct, and the connection between the conduct and the term, will all be factors which support a finding that the term is unenforceable.[108]

3.77 There are also ways for the court to mitigate the effects of this rule. If it can be shown that one party was excusably ignorant of the prohibition, and the other was not, then the excusably ignorant party may claim damages.[109] Alternatively, the court has the power to enforce the rest of the agreement in favour of a party who did not engage in serious misconduct provided that the unenforceable part is not an essential element.[110]

---

[105] A similar approach can be found in *Sternamen v Metropolitan Life Insurance Co* 62 N.E. 763 (N.Y. 1902): "The power to contract is not unlimited. While as a general rule there is the utmost freedom of action in this regard, some restrictions are placed upon the right by legislation, by public policy, and by the nature of things. Parties cannot make a binding contract in violation of law or of public policy".

[106] *Daynard v Ness, Motley, Loadholt, Richardson and Poole* 188 F. Supp. 2d 115 (D. Mass 2002). For more detail on the American case law, see E A Farnsworth, *Contracts* (2004) ch 5.

[107] Restatement (Second) of Contracts, §178(2).

[108] Restatement (Second) of Contracts, §178(3).

[109] Restatement (Second) of Contracts, §180.

[110] Restatement (Second) of Contracts, §184(1).

3. The New Zealand Illegal Contracts Act

3.78 Following a report from the Contracts and Commercial Law Reform Committee,[111] the New Zealand legislature enacted the New Zealand Illegal Contracts Act 1970[112] which comprehensively provides for the effect of illegality on "illegal contracts". The Act does not attempt to set out what constitutes an illegal contract. This is left to the common law. Section 3 of the Act provides:

> "Illegal contract" defined – Subject to section 5 of this Act, for the purposes of this Act the term "illegal contract" means any contract governed by New Zealand law that is illegal at law or in equity, whether the illegality arises from the creation or performance of the contract; and includes a contract which contains an illegal provision, whether that provision is severable or not.

3.79 The Act does however limit the scope of the Act in relation to contracts that are illegal at common law only because of the manner is which they are performed. Section 5 of the Act provides:

> Breach of enactment – A contract lawfully entered into shall not become illegal or unenforceable by any party by reason of the fact that its performance is in breach of any enactment, unless the enactment expressly so provides or its object clearly so requires.

3.80 The central provisions of the Act are focused on the effect that the illegality has on the contract, once the court has found it to be "illegal" under the common law rules. A radical approach is adopted – all illegal contracts are unenforceable and void. However, the court is given a discretion to grant relief to any party to the contract (or person claiming through such party) in whatever way the court thinks just. Special protection is granted to a purchaser acting in good faith.

> 6. Illegal contracts to be of no effect – (1) Notwithstanding any rule of law or equity to the contrary, but subject to the provisions of this Act and of any other enactment, every illegal contract shall be of no effect and no person shall become entitled to any property under a disposition made by or pursuant to any such contract:
>
> Provided that nothing in this section shall invalidate-
>
> (a) Any disposition of property by a party to an illegal contract for valuable consideration ... if the person to whom the disposition was made was not a party to the illegal contract and had not at the time of the disposition notice that the property was the subject of, or the whole or part of the consideration for, an illegal contract and otherwise acts in good faith.

---

[111] Report of the Contracts and Commercial Law Reform Committee of New Zealand, Illegal Contracts (1969).

[112] The 1970 Act was amended by the Illegal Contracts Amendment Act 2002.

7. Court may grant relief – (1) Notwithstanding the provisions of section 6 of this Act, but subject to the express provisions of any other enactment, the Court may in the course of any proceedings, or on application made for the purpose, grant to –

(a) Any party to an illegal contract; or

(b) Any party to a contract who is disqualified from enforcing it by reason of the commission of an illegal act in the course of its performance; or

(c) Any person claiming through or under any such party –

such relief by way of restitution, compensation, variation of the contract, validation of the contract in whole or part or for any particular purpose, or otherwise howsoever as the Court in its discretion thinks just.

3.81 The operation of a discretion in this area has been widely heralded as a success.[113] It has not created the deluge of litigation that was feared by some commentators.[114] This model of reform, with slight variations, has been recommended by the law reform bodies of several other Commonwealth jurisdictions.[115]

THE INTERACTION BETWEEN THE RULES ON ILLEGALITY AND RIGHTS GRANTED UNDER EUROPEAN UNION LAW

3.82 Several recent cases have considered the question of how far illegal conduct may deprive claimants of rights granted to them under European Union law. This issue is important, because some contractual rights are now granted by EC Directives. For example, the right to equal pay granted by the Equal Pay Directive[116] is implied as a term into the employment contract. In other cases, such as the Sale of Consumer Goods Directive,[117] European Union law provides remedies that depend on there being a contract between the parties. Where the national illegality law prevents a party from enforcing that contract, it is effectively making it impossible for the party to enforce those rights. Is such an approach acceptable under European Union law?

[113] D W McLauchlan, "Contract and Commercial law Reform in New Zealand" (1984-1985) 11 *New Zealand Universities Law Review* 36, 41 and B Coote, "The Illegal Contracts Act 1970" in the New Zealand Law Commission, Contract Statutes Review (1993) ch3.

[114] It has been reported that in the first fifteen years of its operation, some 20 cases were decided under it: D W McLauchlan, "Contract and Commercial law Reform in New Zealand" (1984-1985) 11 *New Zealand Universities Law Review* 36, 41.

[115] See, for example, Law Reform Committee of South Australia (37th Report Relating to the Doctrines of Frustration and Illegality in the Law of Contract, 1977); Law Reform Commission of British Columbia (Report on Illegal Transactions, 1983); the Ontario Law Reform Commission (Report on the Amendment of the Law of Contract, 1987) and Law Reform Committee of the Singapore Academy of Law (Relief from Unenforceability of Illegal Contracts and Trusts, 2002).

[116] Directive 75/117/EEC.

[117] Directive 99/44/EC.

3.83 The interaction between European Union rights and national rules on illegality arose in the context of the beer tie agreements which gave rise to so much litigation in the 1990s. Some breweries had let public houses on condition that the tenants either placed a minimum order for beer and other drinks with the brewery, or did not purchase such drinks elsewhere. These contracts were found to be unenforceable because the ties breached article 81 (previously article 85) of the European Community Treaty (which prevents the restriction of competition). The question then arose whether the fact that the claimant had been a party to an arrangement which breached article 81 should bar him or her from claiming damages for losses suffered against the other party? Initially the Court of Appeal rejected the idea that a party to a beer tie which breached article 81 could claim damages against the other party when the claim was based on the illegality. As Lord Justice Peter Gibson put it in *Gibbs Mew Plc v Gemmell*:

> In my judgment English law does not allow a party to an illegal agreement to claim damages from the other party for loss caused to him by being a party to the illegal agreement.[118]

3.84 However in *Courage Ltd v Crehan*,[119] the Court of Appeal referred the question to the European Court of Justice. Did European Union law preclude a rule of national law which denied a person the right to rely on his own illegal actions to obtain damages? In its judgment, the European Court of Justice recognised that an illegality doctrine may affect rights under European Union law. It stated in *Crehan*:

> Community law does not preclude national law from denying a party who is found to bear significant responsibility for the distortion of competition the right to obtain damages from the other contracting party. Under a principle which is recognised in most of the legal systems of the member states and which the court has applied in the past … a litigant should not profit from his own unlawful conduct, where this is proven.[120]

3.85 However, the European Court of Justice was clearly unhappy with the idea that national courts may deprive citizens of their rights under European Union law through the application of formalistic tests that bear little relationship to considerations of fairness or public policy. In *Crehan*, the Advocate-General argued that it was not at all clear that being a party to an illegal agreement "amounts automatically in all circumstances to a wrong". The rule was "too formalistic and [did] not take account of the particular facts of the individual cases". It failed to distinguish between parties who were genuinely responsible for the wrongdoing and parties who were "too small to resist the economic pressure" imposed by more powerful undertakings. The Court agreed. It spelled out that the test must take account of the economic and legal context in which the parties find themselves and their respective bargaining power and conduct.

[118] [1999] 1 EGLR 43, 49.

[119] [1999] ECC 455.

[120] Case C-453/99 [2001] ECR 1-6297

3.86   Issues regarding the interrelationship between the illegality doctrine and European Union rights have also arisen in relation to rights granted by the Equal Treatment Directive.[121] In *Hall v Woolston Hall Leisure Ltd*,[122] the Court of Appeal was asked to consider whether national illegality rules could prevent an employee who had been discriminated against on the grounds of her sex from claiming compensation under the Sex Discrimination Act 1975 as interpreted in the light of the wording and purpose of the Equal Treatment Directive. The Court held that on the facts of the particular case, national illegality rules did not prevent a claim. It therefore did not have to decide whether it was permissible for the illegality rules to derogate from the rights granted under the Directive. However, Lord Mance (then a judge of the Court of Appeal) doubted whether this was the case. He suggested that it was improbable that a national court would be expected to afford a remedy for sex discrimination where the very essence of the employment was illegal, for example employment as part of a hit-squad or by a company known to have been established to carry out bank robberies or to launder stolen money. However, he said:

> Any limitation of this nature in the protection in respect of sex discrimination afforded by the Directive must be derived from the wording and purpose of the Directive. It cannot be determined by any rule of domestic public policy, especially one which is not a principle of justice and may operate indiscriminately.[123]

3.87   This part of Lord Mance's judgment was cited by the Employment Appeal Tribunal in *Rosan Heims plc v Duke*[124] in the context of the interrelationship between national illegality rules and the Acquired Rights Directive.[125] It had been argued that employment contracts which are void because of illegality should not be taken into account when assessing whether there is an economic entity in the hands of the transferor for the purposes of deciding whether the Acquired Rights Directive applied. In fact, the relevant employment contracts were found not to be unenforceable as a matter of national law. However, the Employment Appeal Tribunal suggested that any restriction as to the factors which a Tribunal could consider when determining whether or not an economic entity exists must be found in the framework of the Directive and not principles of English public policy.

3.88   A similar question arose in an employment context in *Vakante v Addey & Stanhope School*[126] regarding the interrelationship between the illegality rules and the Race Directive.[127] However, here, the Court of Appeal held that the alleged acts of racism were carried out before the Directive came into force and the matter did not therefore need to be decided.

---

[121] Directive 76/207/EEC.

[122] [2001] 1 WLR 225.

[123] [2001] 1 WLR 225, 244.

[124] EAT 10 Dec 2002, 2002 WL 32067886

[125] Directive 77/187/EEC.

[126] [2004] EWCA Civ 1065, [2004] 4 All ER 1056.

[127] Council Directive No 2000/43/EC.

3.89 None of these cases involved the direct enforcement of a contractual obligation. However, many European Union rights, particularly in the consumer context, depend on there being a contract between the parties. We suspect that the European Court of Justice would not be content with a system of domestic illegality rules which prevented the enforcement of those contractual rights, and thereby negated the European Union rights, where that system consisted of formalistic rules that did not allow for a consideration of the particular facts. Instead the European Court of Justice would require a proportionate balancing exercise to be carried out in each case based on clear principles of public policy.

THE INTERACTION BETWEEN THE RULES ON ILLEGALITY AND RIGHTS GRANTED UNDER THE EUROPEAN CONVENTION ON HUMAN RIGHTS

3.90 As we pointed out in CP 154,[128] any national rules on illegality must comply with the European Convention for the Protection of Human Rights and Fundamental Freedoms (ECHR) as incorporated into UK domestic legislation by the Human Rights Act 1998. Of particular relevance is a person's right to a fair trial (Article 6) and entitlement to the peaceful enjoyment of his possessions (Article 1 of the First Protocol).

3.91 The interaction between the rules on illegality and rights granted under the ECHR was raised in *Soteriou v Ultrachem Ltd*.[129] The claimant sought damages for wrongful dismissal before the High Court. In earlier litigation the Employment Appeal Tribunal had found that the claimant was not able to enforce his employment contract against his employer because of fraudulent representations that the claimant had made to the contributions agency regarding his employment status. In the later High Court proceedings, the claimant argued that the domestic illegality doctrine breached several articles of the ECHR.

---

[128] CP 154, para 1.22

[129] [2004] EWHC 983 (QBD), (2004) IRLR 870.

3.92   His first submissions related to Article 6 which provides that in the determination of his civil rights and obligations, everyone is entitled to a fair hearing.[130] He argued that insofar as a finding of illegality results in the dismissal of a claim without further enquiry as to the merits, it provided a procedural ban on the hearing of his case which breached Article 6. The Court disagreed. It held that this part of the law relating to illegality was part and parcel of the substantive law of contract. As it applied in this case it is to be categorised not as an exclusionary rule or an immunity depriving the claimant of access to the Court, but as a means of determining whether there is an enforceable contract so as to found a claim. It is not therefore a "procedural" bar so as to engage Article 6. And, even if Article 6 were in play, the illegality rules pursued legitimate objectives and were proportionate in their application.[131]

3.93   The claimant's second submissions related to Article 1 of the First Protocol of the ECHR.[132] He argued that the domestic illegality doctrine was inconsistent with his right to the peaceful enjoyment of his possession, namely his right of action in damages. The Court disagreed. The claim for breach of contract was not a "possession" so as to engage Article 1, and even if it were, the claimant had not been "deprived" of it. Furthermore, even if Article 1 were engaged, it was not reasonably arguable that the illegality rules did not fulfil a legitimate purpose of considerable importance. Nor would the unenforceability of the contract be a disproportionate response.[133]

3.94   The claimant's final submissions related to Article 14 which provides that the Convention rights and freedoms should be secured without discrimination.[134] He argued that the doctrine of illegality unjustifiably discriminated against him as a litigant bringing a claim for damages. Again the Court disagreed. Even if there were relevant provisions of the Human Rights Act to which Article 14 could attach, there had been no discrimination. The claimant failed to show that there was any different treatment between himself and other persons in an analogous position put forward for comparison.

---

[130] Article 6(1) provides: "In the determination of his civil rights and obligations ... everyone is entitled to a fair and public hearing within a reasonable time by an independent and impartial tribunal established by law".

[131] HH Judge Altman specifically distinguished other cases of illegality, in particular as they applied in a *Tinsley v Milligan* situation. The Court also rejected a claim that the raising of the defence of illegality amounted to a criminal charge for the purposes of Article 6(2) and Article 6(3).

[132] Article 1 provides: "Every natural or legal person is entitled to the peaceful enjoyment of his possessions. No one shall be deprived of his possessions except in the public interest and subject to the conditions provided by law".

[133] The Court relied heavily on the Court of Appeal's earlier judgment in *Al-Kishtaini v Shanshal* [2001] EWCA Civ 264, [2001] 2 All ER (Comm) 601.

[134] Article 14 provides: "The enjoyment of the rights and freedoms set forth in this Convention shall be secured without discrimination on any grounds such as sex, race, colour, language, religion, political or other opinion, national or social origin, association with a national minority, property, birth or other status".

3.95 This case shows that there is considerable doubt whether the application of the illegality defence in a contractual context could infringe any rights protected by the ECHR. However, if, and to the extent that it might, it is quite clear that the defence would have to be applied flexibly in order to satisfy the requirement of legitimacy and proportionality.

REFORM: STATUTORY ILLEGALITY

1. Our proposals on consultation and reaction to them

3.96 In CP 154 we said that where a statute expressly lays down what should be the consequences for a contract that involves a breach of the statute's provisions we would not recommend any legislative reform. We believed that it would constitute an unacceptable undermining of Parliamentary Sovereignty if our reform proposals were to allow the courts to override such express statutory provisions.[135] We noted that this differed from the New Zealand approach. There the Illegal Contacts Act 1970 does allow the courts to apply their discretion to validate a contract even if a statute specifically states that the contract should be of no effect.[136]

3.97 We remain of the view we expressed in CP 154 and the vast majority of those responding to this issue agreed with our approach. However, several suggested that our proposals had not gone far enough. We had proposed that our legislative reform should apply unless another statute *expressly* provided for the consequences for a contract. However, it was forcefully pointed out to us that it is not sensible to attempt to distinguish between the express and implied meaning of legislative words and that, in any event, equal weight should be given to both.

3.98 As one respondent[137] clearly explained:

> When does a statute "expressly" lay down consequences? The line between express and implied meaning of words is (I think) very difficult and probably impossible to draw. It is easy to imagine a statute that clearly (though not expressly) indicates the intention that the contract should not be enforced, eg a statute that prohibits subdivision of land without planning permission. In such a case surely the contract should not be enforceable, or the decision of the planning authorities could be circumvented by the discretion of every judge.

---

[135] CP 154, paras 7.94-7.102.

[136] Illegal Contracts Act 1970 as interpreted in *Harding v Coburn* [1976] 2 NZLR 577.

[137] Professor Stephen Waddams.

2. The way forward

3.99   We accept these arguments. In disputes relating to contracts involving the breach of a legislative provision, the courts should continue to look first at the legislation itself in order to determine whether it *expressly or impliedly* provides how the contractual claim is affected. When Parliament enacted the legislation, it will have been able to consider at length and in context, the policies behind the prohibition imposed. Where the legislation provides what should be the effect on a contract, we think that it would be wrong to give the court a power to "second guess" this, without the benefit of all the time and information that would have been before Parliament.

3.100   However, we believe that it will be only in rare cases that the answer can be found as a matter of statutory interpretation. When Parliament makes conduct a crime, it rarely expressly provides what should be the consequences for a contractual claim that involves that criminalised conduct. We think that it will only be in an unusual case that it would be possible to say that it has impliedly done so.

3.101   We applaud the approach to statutory illegality adopted by the Court of Appeal in *Hughes v Asset Managers plc*.[138] When determining whether the relevant statutory provisions impliedly provided for the effect which the regulatory breach had on contractual rights, the court focused not only on the wording of the legislation but also on its purpose. We venture to suggest that it might be helpful if the court also considered the possibility that statute might affect the contractual rights of the guilty party only, leaving the innocent party unaffected. That is, it could ask whether the particular claim is prohibited by the legislation, rather than the contract itself. This approach might have assisted the Court of Appeal to avoid its "unfortunate" conclusion that the contracts of insurance were unenforceable even by the innocent party in *Phoenix Insurance v Helvanon Insurance*.[139] The relevant statute[140] prohibited an unlicensed insurer not only from "effecting contracts of insurance" but also from "carrying out" such contracts. In (non-binding) commentary, the Court of Appeal said that this phraseology led to the conclusion that the insurance contracts were illegal and void, and therefore could not be enforced even by the innocent insured party.[141] Had the Court considered whether only one party's contractual rights might be affected, it might have been able to avoid this conclusion.

---

[138] [1995] 3 All ER 669.

[139] [1988] QB 216.

[140] Insurance Companies Act 1974. The relevant provisions were subsequently amended to enable the insured, but not the insurer, to enforce the insurance contract: section 132 of the Financial Services Act 1986. See now section 28 of the Financial Services and Markets Act 2000.

[141] See *Re Cavalier Insurance Co Ltd* [1989] 2 Lloyd's Rep 430 for the same interpretation.

3.102 Accordingly, we do not recommend any legislative reform in relation to "statutory illegality". We consider that the courts are confidently managing to interpret any relevant provisions using their general rules of interpretation, and that this applies both to the express and implied meaning of the legislation. Where problems have arisen, these have often stemmed from the particular wording of the statue, rather than the courts' approach.

3.103 We now therefore turn to the separate question of how illegality may affect contractual rights under the common law.

REFORM: ILLEGALITY UNDER THE COMMON LAW

1. Our proposals on consultation and reaction to them

3.104 In CP 154 we provisionally proposed that the law should be reformed by the adoption of a discretionary approach to decide the effect which the involvement of illegality should have on contractual rights. We considered that given the wide variety of circumstances in which illegality might interact with a contract and the range of possible offences, a discretionary approach was the only way forward. It would allow the court openly to take into account such important factors as the seriousness of the illegality involved, the innocence or guilt of the claimant, and the purpose of the rule which the unlawful conduct has infringed. We had not found it possible to devise a new regime of "rules" which could cater for all the circumstances in which illegality might be involved in a contractual dispute.[142]

3.105 We also proposed that such reform would have to be introduced by way of legislation. We argued that following the rejection of the public conscience test by the House of Lords in *Tinsley v Milligan*[143] any possibility of wholesale judicial reform appeared to be blocked. Although the courts would be able to refine the present rules to the particular case before them, in doing so they would not have the opportunity to assess the structure of the illegality rules as a whole. Such tinkering at the edges was likely to result only in further complexity and uncertainty.[144]

3.106 On consultation the large majority (eighty percent) of those considering these two proposals agreed with them. They agreed for the reasons that we had set out in CP 154. Those who disagreed with the need for legislation did so on the basis that they did not consider that wholesale reform was warranted. They thought that a better way forward would be for development, as and where needed, through the common law.

---

[142] CP 154, Part VII.

[143] [1994] 1 AC 340.

[144] CP 154, para 5.10.

3.107   The minority who disagreed with the introduction of a discretion did so largely on three grounds. The most frequently voiced concern was that a discretion would produce greater uncertainty than the present set of rules. It was suggested that it would become very much more difficult for contracting parties to know at the time they enter into contracts what the effect of any illegality might be upon their rights and liabilities. Secondly, such broad reform was felt to be unnecessary because the present law does not result in numerous examples of injustice. Finally it was suggested that the proposed scheme might add to the law's complexity rather than detract from it.

2. A new approach – difficulties with the proposed statutory discretion

3.108   Despite the wide support for our provisional proposals to introduce a statutory discretion, we no longer advocate such an approach. In revising our thinking we have derived great assistance from the responses we received to CP 154. In particular, those who disagreed[145] with what we proposed raised cogent arguments supporting their point of view. They pointed out that the scope of our proposals was unclear and as a result would introduce further uncertainty into this already complex area of the law. We also found, in attempting to draft our proposals into legislation, that we encountered many difficulties of definition. While these problems might not have been insurmountable, they led us to look further at other options for reform. An additional reason for no longer supporting a statutory discretion is that, even if the statutory scheme could be made to work satisfactorily, it would deliver less than we had hoped. This is as a result of our revised thinking on statutory illegality. We explain this further below, before going on to consider the objections based on difficulties of scope and definition. We were not persuaded against a discretion by disagreement based on uncertainty. We were not convinced that the statutory discretion would have created any greater uncertainty than currently exists under the present system of "rules" and "exceptions".

(1) Reduced scope of the proposed statutory scheme

3.109   In the proposals set out in CP 154 we had envisaged that, unless the legislation *expressly* declared its effect on the contractual claim, the case would be decided under the proposed statutory discretion. As explained above, we are now persuaded that this is not the correct approach and that the court should also be required to consider whether the legislation had any express *or implied* effect on the claim being made. If adopted, the proposed statutory discretion would not therefore be the sole determinant in a case involving the breach of a legislative provision. The court would first be required to go through the difficult process of statutory interpretation in order to establish whether the legislature had impliedly provided that the claim is unenforceable. In effect, the proposed discretion would only displace the "common law" illegality rules. Given that it would not be able to remedy all the difficulties that are present in this area of law, we are no longer convinced that such sweeping legislative reform is justified.

---

[145] This group largely consisted of barristers and a few academics. In particular, Professors Andrew Tettenborn and Sir Guenter Treitel wrote very persuasive responses against the CP proposals. Most academics, solicitors and the judiciary agreed with the main CP proposals.

(2) Difficulties of scope and definition

3.110   In addition, we accept the force of the arguments that our provisional legislative proposals were not sufficiently clear. In particular, respondents pointed out to us that the precise scope of the legislative discretion which we proposed in CP 154 was uncertain. What we proposed was very broad. We suggested that the discretion should apply "where the formation, purpose or performance of the contract involves the commission of a legal wrong (other than the mere breach of the contract in question)".[146] It was quite rightly pointed out to us that this would catch situations that were not intended to be within its scope. For example, every contract that is induced by fraud involves a legal wrong in its formation. There are very clear rules dealing with contracts induced by fraud, and it was never intended that these should be displaced by a statutory discretion. It might be possible to narrow down the scope of any discretion more precisely so as to include only those cases intended to be within its remit. However there are other problems relating to the scope of the scheme that are more difficult to solve.

3.111   One problem relates to the unlawful performance of a contract. As we have seen, under the present law the mere fact that an illegal act has been committed in the course of performance does not make the contract unenforceable because of illegality. If it did, large numbers of contracts would be brought within the doctrine: for example, taxi drivers who exceed the speed limit would forfeit their right to the fare. Indeed it is frequently said that illegality in the course of performance is irrelevant unless it was intended from the outset to perform in an illegal manner. This is not wholly accurate, but illegality in the course of performance seems only to be relevant in fairly exceptional cases and the point will not normally be taken. Yet under the CP 154 proposals all cases of unlawful performance would be included within the discretion. A much greater number of contractual claims would therefore fall within the scope of the discretion than would presently be affected by the illegality doctrine.[147] No doubt a court would seldom refuse to enforce them, but there would be scope for considerable uncertainty and the law could be used opportunistically as a delaying tactic.

3.112   We have considered simply excluding cases of "illegal performance" from the scope of the proposed legislative discretion. Of course if the unlawful behaviour is in breach of a statutory provision, then the statute may expressly or impliedly render the claim unenforceable. However, we do not believe this to be the proper approach. It seems to us that there may be some serious cases of this type where enforcement should not be permitted. It may be stretching the doctrine of implied statutory illegality too far to suggest that it could cater for all possible scenarios. Moreover it would require the court to draw a sharp distinction between cases where the illegality is a purpose or object of the contract (which would be within the discretion) and cases where it is simply a matter of performance only (which would fall outside the discretion). It seems to us that it is not sensible, or necessarily always possible, to make such a distinction.

---

[146] CP 154, para 7.10.

[147] For criticism on the breadth of the proposals in CP 154, see N Enonchong, "Illegal Transactions: The Future?" [2000] *Restitution Law Review* 82.

3.113   Another problem relates to the difficulty of defining "illegality". In CP 154 the proposed scheme drew a distinction between contracts that involve the commission of a "legal wrong" and contracts that are "otherwise contrary to public policy". The discretion would apply only to the former and not to the latter. We explained that we thought it necessary to exclude the latter because one cannot separate here the question as to whether the contract is contrary to public policy from the idea of giving the courts a discretion to refuse to enforce the contract as against the public interest. These are two sides of the same coin. In deciding whether or not a contract is contrary to public policy, the court already effectively is asking the question – would it be against public policy to enforce the contract?

3.114   However, fewer than half of respondents were content with this approach. The most common objection was that it is hard to draw a distinction between on the one hand contracts that involve a legal wrong and on the other those that are contrary to public policy only. For example, a contract that involves illegality under a foreign law is usually regarded as being "contrary to public policy" rather than "illegal". It was also pointed out that drawing the distinction might produce odd results, since a court might decide that conduct which is lawful renders the contract unenforceable as a matter of public policy but, where it was unlawful, the court might decide that the contract should be enforced nevertheless.

3.115   There are also difficulties simply in defining what is meant by a "legal wrong". Clearly it would include a crime and a tort, but what about an infringement of a statute, not involving a criminal penalty? An example is provided by article 81 (previously article 85) of the European Community Treaty, which prohibits agreements, decisions and concerted practises that "have as their object or effect the prevention, restriction or distortion of competition within the Common Market". The Court of Appeal has said that a contract that infringes this article is "illegal"[148] and yet no criminal penalty is imposed. It is doubtful whether this applies to every act forbidden by statute but not made a crime, and yet it would be very hard to determine which cases would fall within the scheme. What about wrongs such as breaches of fiduciary duty? We think that it would cause great uncertainty to introduce a statutory discretion that applied to legal wrongs without defining exactly what was included.

[148] *Gibbs Mew v Gemmell* [1999] 1 EGLR 43, 49.

3.116 Many of these problems of definition could be avoided by adopting a different form of statutory scheme, such as that set out in the New Zealand Illegal Contracts Act 1970.[149] As we have seen, this does not provide clear guidance as to which contracts fall within its scope, defining an "illegal contract" as a contract that is illegal at law or in equity.[150] The complex common law rules on classification therefore survive. This approach has been criticised in the academic literature,[151] although it has also been described as "deliberately minimalist" on the basis that whether a contract should be illegal is as much a matter of judicial policy as of public policy, or of the policy of the legislature.[152] As one member of the New Zealand Contracts and Commercial Law Reform Committee, whose report[153] gave rise to the 1970 Act, explained: "The urgent need was to reform the law as to the results flowing from illegality. It seemed wiser to press on with this than to delay to tackle the difficult and contentious task of prescribing which contracts are to be regarded as illegal."[154]

3.117 A review of the recent New Zealand case law provides several instances of cases where a dispute has arisen in relation to the correct scope of the Act.[155] It is not unusual for the court to declare that the contract is not an "illegal contract" within the scope of the Act, but that even if it were the relief granted under the judicial discretion would be the same. In some cases involving the breach of a statutory provision, the legislature has made its position clear by specifically providing within that legislation that a breach of one of its provisions does or does not render a contract "illegal" within the definition of the Illegal Contracts Act 1970.

---

[149] See para 3.78 above. A similar approach to legislative reform has been recommended by the Law Reform Commission of British Columbia (Report on Illegal Transactions, 1983); the Law Reform Committee of South Australia (37th Report Relating to the Doctrines of Frustration and Illegality in the Law of Contract, 1977) and the Ontario Law Reform Commission (Report on Amendment of the Law of Contract, 1987).

[150] New Zealand Illegal Contracts Act 1970, section 3.

[151] M P Furmston, "The Illegal Contracts Act 1970 – An English View" (1972) 5 New Zealand Universities Law Review 151, 154; D McLauchlan, "Contract and Commercial Law Reform in New Zealand" (1984) 11 New Zealand Universities Law Review 36, 41; and New Zealand Commenatry on Halsbury's Laws of Engalnd (4th ed) ch 34.

[152] B Coote, "The Illegal Contracts Act 1970" in Contract Statutes Review (1993) NZLC R 25, 173.

[153] Illegal Contracts Report of the Contracts and Commercial Law Reform Committee of New Zealand (1969).

[154] D F Dugdale, "Procul Este Bonanzas – A Note on the Illegal Contracts Act 1970" (1971) New Zealand Law Journal 209, 210.

[155] For example, Dawson v Chief Executive, Ministry of Social Development [2005] NZHC 191; Contributory Mortgage Nominees Ltd v Harrison [2005] NZHC 294; Money Managers Ltd v National Mortgage Brokers Ltd [2005] NZHC 359; Sure Developments Ltd v Northshore Taverns Ltd [2006] NZHC 276; South Pacific Tyres NZ Ltd v Persland (NZ) Ltd Civ 2008-485-427; and Stirling v Parke [2008] NZHC 936.

3.118　We do not consider that a model based on the New Zealand Act is the best way forward. It would not solve any of the problems relating to the complexity of the present law or its lack of transparency. Under such an approach the court would still have to struggle through the tangled mess of current rules in order to decide whether it is dealing with an "illegal contract" and thus whether the discretion applied. To base a statutory regime on such insecure foundations would seem likely to lead to more rather than less confusion.

(3) Arguments against a statutory discretion based on uncertainty: some uncertainty inevitable

3.119　Even if its scope could be satisfactorily defined, a number of respondents objected to the introduction of a statutory discretion on the ground that it would give rise to unnecessary uncertainty in its operation. In CP 154 we realised that this would be a criticism of a discretionary approach and attempted to reduce any uncertainty by setting out a list of factors that the court would be required to consider in reaching its decision.[156]

3.120　However, not all respondents were persuaded. The Commercial Bar Association commented that it did not "find the proposed 'structure' any form of reassurance in reducing uncertainty. The factors which will be permissible under the structured discretion are of a very wide nature, and still leave the problem of prediction almost as difficult as it would be without the structure". We received similar comments from the Bar Council:

> On the whole, we consider that the substitution of a discretion per se is not going to resolve the difficulties in this area, in the sense that it will not make it easier for lawyers to advise their clients with confidence.

3.121　We believe that some element of uncertainty is unavoidable in this area. The range of possible illegalities and the variety of different ways by which a contract may be affected mean that a set of exact rules is simply impossible. It is clear from our review of the case law that, despite ostensibly applying a set of rules and exceptions, the courts already hold a considerable degree of flexibility in this area of law. We are not, therefore, persuaded that introducing a statutory discretion would add to uncertainty. However, whether or not this is articulated in the form of a discretion, we consider that, if the decisions of the courts were openly based on the guiding principles that underlie the illegality defence, it would be easier for the parties and their advisers to predict how future disputes might be decided. Uncertainty would thereby be reduced. We go on to explain how this might be achieved below.

3.122　**We no longer recommend that the law on illegality and contract should be reformed by way of the introduction of a statutory discretion.**

---

[156] These included the seriousness of the illegality; the knowledge and intention of the claimant; whether denying relief would act as a deterrent; whether denying relief would further the purpose of the prohibiting rule; and proportionality: CP 154, paras 7.27 to 7.43.

3. The way forward

3.123 Having decided no longer to pursue our original proposals for a legislative statutory discretion, we must consider what is the best way forward now. In CP 154 we suggested that, following the House of Lords' decision in *Tinsley v Milligan*,[157] reform of illegality by way of case law development was out of reach of the judiciary.[158] As we explain in Part 6, we continue to believe that this is the case in relation to the application of the illegality defence to equitable interests – the matter at issue in the *Tinsley* case. However, recent cases in other areas of the law involving illegality have shown that, whatever "test" is apparently used by the courts, they do in fact take into consideration a variety of factors relevant in deciding whether a defence based on public policy should succeed. In particular, in the contract cases, the courts have made only passing reference to the reliance principle laid down in *Tinsley*, and it has not proved to be the indiscriminate decisive factor that we feared it might become when we prepared CP 154.

3.124 Without being able to point to a number of actual or potential unjust decisions resulting from *Tinsley v Milligan* that will bind the hands of the lower courts, we believe that any reform that is needed in this area can be safely left to incremental case law development. A major advantage of this type of approach is that it can be a much more sensitive instrument than a one-off statutory provision. The exactness required by legislative drafting necessarily involves a certain bluntness that is not wholly suited to this area of the law. As we have explained, our attempts to define precisely the exact scope of any statutory discretion to apply to all contractual claims proved fraught with difficulties.

3.125 We have already explained that we do not criticise the present law for reaching unjust results. Rather, the courts have managed to find a path between the myriad complex rules to reach what might be regarded as the "right" conclusion in the vast majority of cases. How has this been achieved? It seems that despite often referring to the illegality doctrine as being one which may operate indiscriminately and apparently applying a set of rules, the courts do in fact take into consideration a whole variety of factors which ensure that relief is only denied where it is a fair and proportionate response to the claimant's conduct. These factors are tied to the policies that underlie the illegality doctrine. The so-called "rules" are in fact more in the way of guidance that show how these policies often operate, but they are no more than guidance. What matters is how the relevant factors apply to each particular case. We believe that it would be beneficial if these considerations that already underlie the judgments could be brought to the fore and openly weighed and considered. We look at what we consider some of these factors to be below.

---

[157] [1994] 1 AC 340.

[158] CP 154, para 5.10.

(1) Whether allowing the claim would undermine the purpose of the prohibiting rule

3.126   The most important factor that the courts appear to take into account is whether allowing the claim would undermine the purpose of the rule which renders the relevant conduct unlawful. The importance of this factor has been highlighted in recent years in the cases involving breaches of statutory provisions. The court will look at the policy of the legislator in enacting the provisions in order to determine whether that policy would be frustrated by allowing the claim. This was emphasised in the Court of Appeal's decision in *Hughes v Asset Managers plc.*[159] As we have seen,[160] the question in this case was whether insurance contracts entered into by unlicensed agents were rendered void as a result of the statutory offence. Having considered the precise wording of the relevant provisions, Lord Saville (then a judge of the Court of Appeal) looked at the purpose of the Prevention of Fraud (Investments) Act 1958 and said:

> I readily accept that the purpose of the 1958 Act was to protect the investing public by imposing criminal sanctions on those who, as principals or agents, engaged in the business of dealing in securities without being duly licensed. Parliament clearly intended to provide the investing public with the safeguard of the approval and licensing of professional dealers by the Board of Trade. However, I can see no basis in either the words the legislature has used or the type of prohibition under discussion, or in considerations of public policy (including the mischief against which this part of the 1958 Act was directed), for the assertion that Parliament must be taken to have intended that such protection required (over and above criminal sanctions) that any deals effected through the agency of unlicensed persons should automatically be struck down and rendered ineffective. On the contrary, it seems to me that not only is there really no good reason why Parliament should have taken up this stance, but good reason why Parliament should have held the contrary view.[161]

---

[159] [1995] 3 All ER 669.

[160] See para 3.10 above.

[161] [1995] 3 All ER 669, 673.

3.127   The idea of looking at the purpose of the prohibiting rule is also important to the doctrine of illegality at common law. Although not transparently argued, we can see it in play in the reasoning of the Court of Appeal's decision in *Marles v Philip Trant*.[162] In this case seed merchants had sold some wheat seed to a farmer, but inadvertently failed to supply him with a statement in writing showing that the seed satisfied the requirements as to purity and germination laid down by the Seeds Act 1920. The seed had in fact been tested and was pure. The farmer sued for breach of warranty because the seed had been sold to him as spring wheat when it was in fact winter wheat. He recovered damages from the merchants. The merchants sued their supplier because he had also sold them the wheat as spring wheat. The supplier had no defence to this breach of warranty, but he argued that the merchants could not recover as damages the amount which they had had to pay to the farmer, because those were damages awarded against them in breach of an illegal contract (the illegality being the failure to supply the statement about purity and germination). By majority and on differing grounds, the Court of Appeal rejected this defence. Whatever their different reasoning, it is quite clear that allowing the claim would not have undermined the purpose of the1920 Act.

3.128   The difficulty encountered by the Court of Appeal in reaching this conclusion was caused by the supposed "rule" laid down in its own previous decision in *Anderson Ltd v Daniel*.[163] As we have seen, in that case the vendor of "salvage" had failed to supply the required invoice detailing the exact components of the salvage. This was because the cost of testing salvage to analyse its make-up would outweigh its value. The vendor was not permitted to recover the contract price from the purchaser after delivering the goods because of this unlawful performance. However, here there was a thriving trade in salvage which by custom was not subjected to the required analysis, and the vendor was deliberately breaking the law. As the Court noted, the statute may well have been intended to prevent people dealing at all in artificial manure where for some reason it was impossible to have an analysis. The facts were therefore far removed from the *Marles* case where the purity of the seed had been tested, and the vendor had merely inadvertently failed to provide the particulars. Yet in the *Marles* case, the Court felt obliged to apply convoluted reasoning to explain why it was not following the "rule" laid down in *Anderson*. Had the court instead looked at the policies underlying that decision, it would have immediately been distinguishable.

---

[162] [1954] 1 QB 29.
[163] [1924] 1 KB 138.

(2) The seriousness of the offence

3.129 Secondly, we consider the courts take into account the seriousness of the offence involved. In some cases this is openly expressed. For example, in *Hall v Woolston Hall Leisure Ltd*[164] it was doubted whether the Equal Treatment Directive was intended to confer any protection in relation to employment the essence of which was illegal, such as employment as part of a hit squad or by a company known to have been established to carry out bank robberies or to launder stolen money.

3.130 In other cases the court does not specifically refer to the seriousness of the offence, but it does appear to affect the way which the courts approach the case altogether. This can be illustrated by the different approach that it is taken to statutory illegality and the common law rules. When looking to see whether a statute has impliedly rendered a claim unenforceable, the seriousness of the offence is central to the decision. If the court decides that the criminal penalty provides an adequate deterrence, it is likely to conclude that the statute has nothing to say about the enforceability of the contract. By contrast, the common law rules do not explicitly take into account the seriousness of the conduct at all. Professor Buckley points out that this could lead to absurd results. In *St John Shipping*,[165] for example, it might be sensible to allow a shipowner who overloads his vessel to recover his freight. It is difficult to believe, however, that the same rules would apply to a shipowner who, realising that he would incur penalties for late delivery, deliberately ordered his ship to plough through a yachting regatta, drowning many of the participants.[166] Where the offence is minor in nature, the courts achieve the desired outcome by simply ignoring the common law rules.[167]

(3) The causal connection between the claim and the illegal conduct

3.131 Thirdly, it seems that the court considers, although not necessarily explicitly, how closely the unlawful conduct is connected to the particular claim. So, for example, under the present law where the object of the contract is an unlawful act, then the contract cannot be enforced by either party. The reason for this apparently rigid rule might be that, where the commission of the illegality is the very purpose of the contract, the claim is likely to be very closely connected to it. Yet a contract, which is unlawful in performance only, is generally enforceable. Here the reason could be that the illegality is more likely to be incidental to the claim.

---

[164] [2001] 1 WLR 225, 244 by Mance LJ.

[165] [1957] 1 QB 267.

[166] R A Buckley, *Illegality and Public Policy* (2002) para 3.13.

[167] For example, *Shaw v Groom* [1970] 2 QB 504.

3.132   The problem with these rigid divisions is that they do not take into account the particular circumstances of the facts before the court. In some cases it may be difficult to decide whether the illegal act is an object of the contract, or simply the method by which the contract is performed.[168] For example, as we have seen, in *Archbolds (Freightage) Ltd v S Spanglett*[169] the defendant agreed to transport the claimant's goods. The defendant did so, but in a lorry that did not have the necessary licence for this particular task. In doing this, the defendant committed an offence, but it is not clear at what stage it decided to use this particular van, and whether the claimant was ever aware of the issue. Due to the defendant's negligence, the goods were stolen on route. The relevant issue here appears to be that the lack of licence had no bearing on the defendant's failure to take care. That is, there was no causal connection between the illegality and the breach of contract. Given that the court found that the purpose of the relevant statutory provisions was to promote an efficient road transport network, allowing the claim for failure to take care would not appear in any way to encroach on its purpose. The question whether using a van that did not have the necessary licence was a purpose of the contract, or merely the way in which it was performed, would not seem to have any bearing on the right outcome to the case. The court did allow the claim, but was forced to fit its reasoning within the boundaries of rigid rules, and did not openly concentrate on those factors that appear to be most relevant to the policies that underlie the illegality defence.

3.133   The importance of the connection between the illegality and the claim was brought to the fore in *Marles v Philip Trant*. The Court was at pains to point out that the omission to deliver the particulars did not make any practical difference in this case. The merchants had tested the purity of the wheat and the failure to supply the required particulars was an inadvertent slip that was not connected with the basis of their claim for breach of warranty.[170]

---

[168] For example, in *Birkett v Acorn Business Machines Ltd* [1999] 2 All ER (Comm) 429 the trial judge regarded the case as one of illegal performance, whereas the Court of Appeal judges treated it as a case of illegal purpose.

[169] [1961] 1 QB 374.

[170] [1954] 1 QB 29, 38.

(4) The conduct of the parties

3.134   Fourthly it seems that the courts do consider the comparative guilt of the parties. This is most obviously illustrated in those cases of illegal purpose and performance where the courts have denied relief only if the claimant has in some way "participated" in the illegality. This may explain why the courts take a particularly harsh line in the PAYE fraud cases compared with that taken in the VAT fraud cases. Recent judicial statements suggest that, if the employee is aware of the employer's illegal scheme and takes no further action, he or she will have sufficiently participated in it to be refused relief. Although not explicitly stated in their reasoning, this may be because the income tax fraud is a mutual benefit to the employee and employer, and would not be possible without at least some participation or omission on the part of the employee. The VAT fraud cases present a more lenient view. One such example is *Hewcastle Catering Ltd v Ahmed and Elkamah.*[171] While not explicitly stating that the court was comparing the guilt of the employer and employee, this does seem to have been a very relevant factor in the decision. It is not at all clear that any less would satisfy any European requirement to take into account the economic and legal context in which the parties find themselves and their respective bargaining power and conduct.

(5) The proportionality of denying the claim

3.135   Finally it appears that the court may consider the consequences of denying the claim. That is, it considers the value of the claim at stake compared to the seriousness of the illegality involved. One example is found in the decision in *St John Shipping Corporation v Joseph Rank Ltd.*[172] As we have seen, here the claimant had carried grain for the defendants from Alabama to England. In doing so, the claimant had overloaded its ship so that the loadline was submerged. This was a statutory offence and the claimant was fined for it. However, when the defendants sought to withhold part of the freight due, on the basis that the claimant had carried out the contract in an unlawful manner, the claimant was successful in enforcing the contract. The Court pointed out that to hold otherwise would mean that a shipowner who accidentally overloaded his ship by a fraction of an inch would not be able to recover from any of the shippers or consignees a penny of the freight.[173]

---

[171] [1991] IRLR 473. For the facts, see para 3.39 above.

[172] [1957] 1 QB 267.

[173] [1957] 1 QB 267, 282.

4. Conclusion

3.136   Overall, what seems to be happening in the case law is that in practice the courts have considerable flexibility to enforce the particular claim or not, as seems appropriate given the particular circumstances. However, this flexibility is disguised in a series of so-called rules which may in fact contradict each other or do not tell the whole truth. Because the courts are at least purportedly bound to apply the rules, there can be little or no open discussion in the judgments of some of the underlying issues. We believe that it would be enormously helpful to litigants and their advisers if it were recognised that the rules are more in fact in the nature of guidance and that what matters is whether any of the policy issues that underlie the illegality defence justify its operation in the case before the court.

3.137   In the late 1980s and early 1990s the courts recognised the failings of the common law rules and developed a general principle that the courts would only refuse to assist the claimant where it would be an "affront to the public conscience to grant the plaintiff the relief which he seeks because the court would thereby appear to assist or encourage the plaintiff in his illegal conduct or to encourage others in similar acts".[174] This became known as the "public conscience test". Under this test the court was required to take into account all the circumstances of the case and then "weigh, or balance, the adverse consequences of granting relief against the adverse consequences of refusing relief".[175] Those rules which were previously regarded as laying down when the illegality defence would apply and what were the exceptions to its application were to be regarded as no more than valuable guidelines. The ultimate decision called for a value judgment. On the one hand, allowing the claim might encourage illegal conduct or be an inappropriate use of the court system. On the other hand, it is generally in the public interest to protect the expectations of contracting parties.

3.138   The most graphic application of the public conscience test can be found in *Howard v Shirlstar Container Transport Ltd*.[176] The claimant, a pilot, agreed for a fee to retrieve the defendant's aircraft which was being detained in Nigeria. This operation was contrary to the wishes of the Nigerian military authorities, and involved the claimant and his wireless operator in considerable personal danger. As a result, they left Lagos airport without obtaining permission from the air traffic control, which, under Nigerian law, constituted a criminal offence. The defendant sought to avoid paying the claimant's fee by relying on his unlawful performance. However the pilot was allowed to enforce the contract. There would be no affront to the public conscience in allowing his claim since the offences committed by the claimant were designed to free himself and his wireless operator from pressing danger.

---

[174] *Euro-Diam Ltd v Bathurst* [1990] 1 QB 1, 35-36, by Kerr LJ.

[175] *Tinsley v Milligan* (CA) [1992] Ch 310, 319, by Nicholls LJ.

[176] [1990] 1 WLR 1292.

3.139 However, when the House of Lords heard *Tinsley v Milligan* both the majority and minority rejected the public conscience test as having an application in English law. Lord Browne-Wilkinson said that the consequences of being a party to an illegal transaction cannot depend on such an "imponderable factor" as the extent to which the public conscience would be affronted.[177] Lord Goff said that the test was inconsistent with numerous binding authorities; it was by no means self-evidently preferable to the present strict rules; and if there were to be reform it should only be attempted by legislation after a review by the Law Commission.[178]

3.140 We agree that the public conscience test was vague. However, we believe that it was useful in suggesting that the present rules should be regarded as no more than guidance that help the court to focus its attention on particular features of the case before it. What lies behind these "rules" is a set of policies. This is why the courts are sometimes required to "bend" the rules (if possible) to give better effect to the underlying policies as they apply to the facts of the case before them. It would be preferable if the courts were to base their decisions transparently on these policies.[179] They could then accept that existing authority helps, but only insofar as the case law illustrates the various policies to be applied.

3.141 If this approach were adopted, we consider that the illegality defence would succeed in only the most serious of cases. That is, we believe that the policy issues underlying the defence would have to be overwhelming before it would be a proportionate response to deny the claimant his or her usual contractual rights.

3.142 **We provisionally recommend that the courts should consider in each case whether the application of the illegality defence can be justified on the basis of the policies that underlie that defence. These include: (a) furthering the purpose of the rule which the illegal conduct has infringed; (b) consistency; (c) that the claimant should not profit from his or her own wrong; (d) deterrence; and (e) maintaining the integrity of the legal system. Against those policies must be weighed the legitimate expectation of the claimant that his or her legal rights will be protected. Ultimately a balancing exercise is called for which weighs up the application of the various policies at stake. Only when depriving the claimant of his or her rights is a proportionate response based on the relevant illegality policies, should the defence succeed. The judgment should explain the basis on which it has done so.**

---

[177] [1994] 1 AC 340, 369.

[178] [1994] 1 AC 340, 362-364.

[179] Similar arguments are put forward by R A Buckley, "Social Security Fraud as Illegality" (1994) 110 *Law Quarterly Review* 3.

3.143   We also consider that it would be helpful if, rather than simply asking whether the contract is illegal – a term which itself is vague and confusing – the courts were to ask whether the particular claimant, in the circumstances which have occurred, should be denied his or her usual relief in respect of the particular claim. This focus on the particular claimant and particular claim are important. As we have suggested, one of the most important factors bearing on the case will be the closeness of the connection between the claim and the unlawful conduct. It may well be the case that it would be a proportionate response to deny the claimant relief in respect of one of the defendant's obligations, where this is closely linked to the claimant's unlawful actions, but not to any other.

3.144   **We provisionally recommend that the courts should consider whether illegality is a defence to the particular claim brought by the particular claimant, rather than whether the contract is "illegal" as a whole.**

3.145   In one recent case Lord Walker openly recognised the flexibility of the illegality doctrine. In *Bakewell Management Ltd v Brandwood and Others*[180] the House of Lords allowed the acquisition of an easement by long uninterrupted use based on access that was criminal. Lord Walker said that the judgment did not amount to a reintroduction of the "public conscience test". Rather, he said:

> It is merely a recognition that the maxim *ex turpi causa* must be applied as an instrument of public policy, and not in circumstances where it does not serve any public interest.[181]

3.146   The approach that we are advocating would, we believe, most clearly satisfy the requirements of EC law, and, to the extent that it might be applicable, ECHR law. As we have seen, there was concern in the European Court of Justice's judgments in the beer tie litigation that the English national illegality rules were not sufficiently flexible to take into account all the relevant circumstances of the case. An approach which explained the court's decision by focusing on those factors that interact with the policies underlying the illegality defence would undoubtedly meet any legitimacy and proportionality requirements. The resultant transparency would provide greater guidance for parties in attempting to know their legal rights and remedies.

---

[180] [2004] UKHL 14, [2004] 2 AC 519.

[181] [2004] UKHL 14 at [60], [2004] 2 AC 519, 549.

3.147   In particular we do not think that it is helpful to import the reliance principle laid down in *Tinsley v Milligan* into the case law on contractual enforcement. As we have seen, this arbitrary principle is seldom given more than a passing reference in cases concerning claims to enforce an executory contract.[182] We do not think that it has any useful role to play in this area of the law.

3.148   **We provisionally recommend that the courts should not use the reliance principle to determine whether the claimant can succeed in a case involving the enforcement of an executory contract.**

---

[182] See para 3.46 above.

PART 4
ILLEGALITY AND THE REVERSAL OF UNJUST ENRICHMENT

INTRODUCTION

4.1 Where the claimant has conferred benefits on the defendant under a contract which later turns out to be unenforceable because of the involvement of illegality, the question arises whether those benefits (or their value) can be reclaimed. In this Part we examine the two different roles that illegality plays in the present law of unjust enrichment. First, illegality can act as a defence to what would otherwise be a standard restitutionary claim. Secondly, in one particular circumstance, it arguably acts as the very ground upon which the claim in unjust enrichment is based. Finally, we also look at how illegality may affect one of the main defences to a claim for unjust enrichment, the defence based on change of position.

4.2 In each case we consider the problems with the present law, and any reform that is needed.

ILLEGALITY AS A DEFENCE TO A CLAIM FOR THE REVERSAL OF UNJUST ENRICHMENT

1. The present law

4.3 As we explained in CP 154,[1] one might have expected to find that illegality has little role to play as a defence to a claim for the restitution of benefits conferred under a contract that is unenforceable because of illegality. After all, the claimant is seeking to "undo" the contract rather than execute it. However, after a more liberal start, the courts adopted a much tougher stance, and in cases involving illegality, the traditional approach is to apply the Latin maxim "*in pari delicto, potior est conditio defendentis*" (when the parties are equally blameworthy, the defendant has the stronger position). The restitutionary remedy will only be allowed where the claimant is the "less blameworthy" party.

---

[1] CP 154, para 2.34.

4.4 Furthermore, the courts have been inflexible in balancing the guilt of the parties. Rather than enquiring into the facts of the particular case, a more formal, technical approach is adopted. A claimant will only be regarded as less blameworthy - and therefore recovery allowed - where he or she falls into one of three main categories. That is where the claimant (i) was induced to enter into the contract as a result of the duress of the other party; (ii) was ignorant of a fact or, probably, law that rendered the contract illegal; or, possibly, (iii) belonged to a vulnerable class protected by statute. This means that illegality generally acts as a defence to claims based on failure of consideration, but not to claims based on other grounds such as duress, mistake or vulnerability. We look at each of these in turn. We then look at the difficult Court of Appeal case, *Mohamed v Alaga*.[2] This suggests a possible relaxation in the courts' approach, although its full ramifications are not yet clear.

(1) A preliminary point: a claim in unjust enrichment will not be permitted where granting it would have the same effect as enforcing an unenforceable contract

4.5 While looking at the effect illegality may have on a claim for unjust enrichment it is important to bear in mind a wider principle that may also prevent recovery in this area. That is, that the court will not award restitution where the award would have the same effect as the enforcement of a contract which the common law or statute refuses to enforce. This principle applies not only where a contract is unenforceable for illegality, but whenever an unjust enrichment claim is brought in respect of benefits conferred under a contract that is unenforceable for whatever reason, such as incapacity or lack of formality.[3] To allow the restitutionary claim would otherwise make a nonsense of the law's refusal to enforce the contract.[4] The point is forcefully made in the House of Lords' decision in *Boissevain v Weil*.[5]

4.6 The defendant, a British subject resident in enemy occupied territory, had borrowed French francs from the claimant, a Dutch subject, agreeing to repay it in England at the end of the war. When the defendant failed to repay, the claimant sought either to enforce the agreement or to recover the sums loaned. The House of Lords held that the loan contravened the Defence (Finance) Regulations 1939 and was therefore unenforceable. However, the House also rejected the claim in unjust enrichment, even on the assumed basis that it was the defendant who had committed the relevant offence and the parties were not to be treated as "equally blameworthy". Lord Radcliffe said:

---

[2] [2000] 1 WLR 1815.

[3] For example, *Dimond v Lovell* [2002] 1 AC 384 and *Wilson v First County Trust Ltd (No 2)* [2003] UKHL 40, [2004] 1 AC 816 (improperly executed consumer credit agreements).

[4] P Birks, "Recovering Value Transferred Under an Illegal Contract" (2000) 1 *Theoretical Inquiries in Law* 155.

[5] [1950] AC 327.

If this claim based on unjust enrichment were a valid one, the court would be enforcing on the [defendant] just the exchange and just the liability, without her promise, which the Defence Regulation has said that she is not to undertake by her promise. A court that extended a remedy in such circumstances would merit rather to be blamed for stultifying the law than to be applauded for extending it.[6]

4.7 In an influential article,[7] Professor Birks analysed the illegality defence as being simply one manifestation of this broader "stultification" defence. In some cases, he wrote, allowing the claim would give the claimant substantially the same performance as he or she would have had under the illegal contract. However, even where this is not the position, he suggested that in illegality cases, to allow the routine action in unjust enrichment would provide a lever to compel performance and a safety net in case that indirect compulsion failed. This would stultify the law's refusal to enforce the contract. The unjust enrichment claim is therefore refused unless the claimant can show that the lever and safety net arguments are not applicable. These arguments might not be applicable where, for example, the claimant only became involved in the illegality because of pressure or because of a mistake that concealed the illegality. Professor Birks wrote:

> Almost all cases in which illegality appears to defeat a restitutionary claim are cases in which to allow the non-contractual claim would stultify the law and, in particular, the law's refusal to allow action on the contract itself.

4.8 However, in *Mohamed v Alaga*,[8] the Court of Appeal has taken a more flexible attitude to this question of "stultification" and suggested that in some cases allowing restitution in respect of a contract that is unenforceable for illegality does not make a nonsense of the law. We will examine this case in more detail, after looking at how the illegality defence generally applies to different claims for unjust enrichment.

4.9 The House of Lords has signalled a return to a more orthodox approach in *Dimond v Lovell*[9] and *Wilson v First County Trust Ltd.*[10] Both cases involved improperly executed consumer credit agreements which were unenforceable by virtue of the Consumer Credit Act 1974 (although not illegal). The House of Lords held that Parliament had clearly intended that the agreement should be unenforceable and that the debtor should not have to pay the lender. It would be contrary to Parliament's intention to allow the unjust enrichment claim. It therefore followed that the borrowers' enrichment was not unjust, but simply what Parliament intended.

---

[6] [1950] AC 327, 341.

[7] P Birks, "Recovering Value Transferred Under an Illegal Contract" (2000) 1 *Theoretical Inquiries in Law* 155.

[8] [2000]1 WLR 1815.

[9] [2002] 1 AC 384.

[10] [2003] UKHL 40, [2004] 1 AC 816.

(2) Failure of consideration

4.10 Illegality generally acts as a defence to a claim for unjust enrichment based on a failure of consideration. Without more, the courts will regard the parties as equally blameworthy, and the claim disallowed. The leading case here is *Parkinson v College of Ambulance Ltd and Harrison*.[11] The claimant had made a large donation to charity on the basis of the charity secretary's fraudulent misrepresentation that the charity would procure a knighthood for him. When the honour was not forthcoming, the claimant sought to recover his donation. Although there had been a total failure of consideration, his claim failed. A contract for the sale of honours was contrary to public policy. The claimant knew this and therefore, despite the charity secretary's fraud, the parties were held to be equally blameworthy and recovery denied.[12]

4.11 It might also be right to include the case of *Taylor v Bhail*[13] in this section, although the basis on which the claimant made his claim in unjust enrichment is not clear. The defendant was a headmaster. He agreed to employ the claimant builder to repair storm damage to his school roof provided that the claimant falsely inflated his £12,480 cost estimate by £1,000. The defendant intended to increase his insurance claim by this amount and pocket the difference for himself. Most of the repair work having been done, the defendant paid the claimant builder £7,400 but refused to pay anything more. The claimant claimed alternatively damages for breach of contract or a *quantum meruit* for the work for which he had not been paid. The Court of Appeal refused both claims. As Lord Millett (then a judge of the Court of Appeal) pointed out, the result of the decision was "perhaps fortuitously" not altogether unfair. The claimant would be some £5,000 out of pocket, and the defendant, being unable to claim on his insurance, would be some £7,400 out of pocket.

---

[11] [1925] 2 KB 1.

[12] Other cases that show illegality acting as a defence to a claim for unjust enrichment based on a failure of consideration include *Berg v Sadler and Moore* [1937] 2 KB 158, and possibly, although the ground for the claim was not clearly identified, *Awwad v Geraghty and Co* [2001] QB 570.

[13] [1996] CLC 377. The case is noted by F D Rose, "Confining Illegality" 1996 (112) *Law Quarterly Review* 545.

(3) Mistake

(a) Mistake of fact

4.12 By contrast, where the claimant has entered into a contract on the basis of a mistake of fact which leaves him or her ignorant of any illegality, an unjust enrichment claim is allowed. Even where the defendant is also mistaken, so that one could argue that the parties are "equally innocent", the illegality defence cannot be raised. This is clearly shown by the facts of *Oom v Bruce*.[14] The claimants had paid insurance premiums as agent of a Russian subject for a contract of insurance for goods on a ship sailing from Russia to England. Unknown to the claimants, war had already broken out between Russia and England, making the insurance contract illegal and unenforceable. The claimants sought to recover the premiums paid on the basis of mistaken liability. They were allowed to do so. The defence based on illegality failed. Lord Ellenborough CJ said:

> The plaintiffs had no knowledge of the commencement of hostilities by Russia, when they effected this insurance; and, therefore, no fault is imputable to them for entering into the contract; and there is no reason why they should not recover back the premiums which they have paid.

(b) Mistake of law

4.13 Where the mistake involved is one of law rather than fact, it is well established that recovery will be allowed where the relevant law was made for the protection of persons in the claimant's position. In such a case the claimant is not regarded as being "equally blameworthy". Indeed, prior to its removal by the House of Lords' decision in *Kleinwort Benson Ltd v Lincoln City County*,[15] this category was accepted as an exception to the general rule that there was a bar on recovery for mistakes based on law rather than fact. The leading case here is *Kiriri Cotton Co Ltd v Dewani*.[16] The claimant tenant had paid a premium to the defendant landlord on taking up the sublease of a flat. Unknown to either party, the payment of such a premium was contrary to the Uganda Rent Restriction Ordinance. The claimant, after going into occupation, sought the return of the premium. The Privy Council upheld his claim.

---

[14] (1810) 12 East 225; 104 ER 87.

[15] [1999] 2 AC 349.

[16] [1960] AC 192.

4.14   However, where the purpose of the law that is mistaken is not the protection of one party from the other, the courts traditionally took a much stricter position. Recovery was not allowed even where the claimant's mistake of law had been caused by the negligent misrepresentation of the other party.[17] This is shown by the facts of *Harse v Pearl Life Assurance Co*.[18] An innocent claimant who had paid premiums on an illegal contract of life insurance attempted to recover what she had paid on the ground that the defendant insurance agents had misrepresented to her that the transaction was legal. The court denied her claim. The defendants' misrepresentation was not fraudulent. The parties were therefore equally blameworthy and the claimant could not recover.

4.15   It may be, however, that the House of Lords' abrogation of the mistake of law bar in the *Kleinwort Benson* case will have the effect of assimilating claims for mistake of law with those for mistake of fact so that, whatever the basis of the claimant's mistake, so long as it made him or her unaware of any illegality, the claim will be successful. As we have seen, recovery seems always to be allowed where the claimant's mistake of fact means that he or she is unaware of the illegality, whatever the state of mind of the defendant. If the same approach were to be adopted in cases involving mistakes of law concealing the illegality, recovery would have been permitted in *Harse v Pearl Life Assurance Co*.[19]

(4) Duress

4.16   Illegality does not operate as a defence to unjust enrichment claims based on duress. The duress makes the claimant innocent of the illegality so that the parties cannot be regarded as "equally blameworthy". In *Davies v London and Provincial Marine Insurance Co*[20] friends of an employee of the defendant insurance company were led to believe that the employee was about to be prosecuted by the company for embezzlement. In order to prevent the prosecution taking place, they agreed to replace the sums allegedly missing. It subsequently transpired that charges could not have been brought for embezzlement in any event, and the friends sought to recover the money which they had paid to the company. The company defended the claim on the basis that what had occurred constituted an attempt to compound a felony and the illegality defence therefore applied. The High Court allowed the claim because, although the contract was illegal, the friends had paid under duress.

[17] Where the misrepresentation is fraudulent, recovery will be allowed on the basis that the parties are not equally guilty: *Hughes v Liverpool Victoria Friendly Society* [1916] 2 KB 482.

[18] [1904] 1 KB 558.

[19] [1904] 1 KB 558.

[20] (1878) 8 Ch D 469.

4.17 The same principle was applied in a number of earlier cases where the claimant had been induced to pay money to one of several creditors by that creditor's threat to sue. Recovery was allowed on the basis that the agreement was illegal as a fraud on the other creditors and the claimant had paid the sums under duress.[21]

(5) Statutory class protection

4.18 There is also a number of cases in which the claimant has been permitted to recover benefits conferred on the defendant in breach of a statutory provision, where the object of that provision is the protection of a vulnerable class of which the claimant is a member.[22] It would seem here that the unjust enrichment claim is based on the vulnerability of the claimant, and, because of this vulnerability, it is assumed that the parties are not "equally guilty" and the illegality defence does not apply.

4.19 Lord Mansfield clearly explained the basis of the principle in *Browning v Morris*.[23] He said:

> Where contracts or transactions are prohibited by positive statutes, for the sake of protecting one set of men from another set of men; the one, from their situation and condition, being liable to be oppressed or imposed upon by the other; there, the parties are not in pari delicto; and in furtherance of these statutes, the person injured, after the transaction is finished and completed, may bring his action and defeat the contract.[24]

---

[21] See, for example, *Smith v Cuff* (1817) 6 M & S 160; 105 ER 1203 and *Atkinson v Denby* (1862) 7 H & N 934; 158 ER 749.

[22] See also *Re Cavalier Insurance Co Ltd* [1989] 2 Lloyd's Rep 430. *Kiriri Cotton Co Ltd v Dewani* [1960] AC 192 might be relevant here as Lord Denning included elements of class-protection reasoning in his judgment. However, the Privy Council seems to have regarded the main ground for the unjust enrichment claim as mistake, and so we have dealt with the case on that basis.

[23] (1788) 2 Cowp 790.

[24] (1788) 2 Cowp 790, 792.

4.20   The scope of this claim based on statutory class protection is far from settled. It appears not to be lightly invoked by the courts. For example, in *Green v Portsmouth Stadium*,[25] the Court of Appeal refused the bookmaker's claim for the recovery of course charges which he had paid to the defendant in contravention of the Betting and Lotteries Act 1934. For the purposes of the case it was assumed that the claimant knew that he had paid more than the lawful charge, and it was not argued that he had paid the money under a failure of consideration, because he had been allowed to conduct his business on the track. The Court held that it was a question of the true interpretation of the statute whether an action lay to recover the overcharge. Here the statute was not enacted for the purpose of protecting bookmakers, but for the purpose of regulating racecourses. The mode of regulation was by means of the criminal rather than the civil courts, and no recovery was therefore allowed.

(6) Mohamed v Alaga[26]

4.21   This review of the present law leads us onto the decision of the Court of Appeal in *Mohamed v Alaga*. A Somalian translator had agreed with a firm of solicitors that he would introduce clients to the firm, translate for them and help in preparing cases. In return he would receive half the solicitors' fees. After making many referrals and carrying out work, the translator sought to enforce the agreement or alternatively a reasonable price for the translation and other work he had undertaken. The solicitors attempted to strike out the claim on the basis that the agreement was illegal and unenforceable and that the alternative claim in restitution was not maintainable. They were successful before Mr Justice Lightman.[27] The Court of Appeal agreed that the contract contravened the Solicitors' Practice Rules 1990 on two grounds – first because it involved payment for introductions, and secondly because it involved sharing profits. The Rules had the force of legislation. The contract was therefore unenforceable. However, deciding the strike out application on the assumption that the translator was unaware of any illegality, the Court of Appeal held that the claim for a *quantum meruit* for reasonable remuneration for services rendered could be properly pursued.

4.22   The decision of Lord Bingham to allow the *quantum meruit* claim to proceed was based on two grounds. First, he did not think that the claimant was seeking to recover any part of the consideration payable under the unlawful contract, but simply a reasonable reward for services rendered. Secondly, the parties were not in a situation where their blameworthiness was equal. The solicitors' firm should reasonably be assumed to know what the rules are and to comply with them. By contrast the claimant, on the assumption made, was ignorant of them.[28]

---

[25]   [1953] 2 QB 190.

[26]   [2000] 1 WLR 1815. For criticism of the decision see N Enonchong, "Restitution Following Illegal Fee-Sharing Agreement with a Solicitor" [2000] *Restitution Law Review* 241.

[27]   [1998] 2 All ER 720. For the purposes of deciding the case, the court assumed that the alleged agreement had been made and that the claimant was unaware of the illegality.

[28]   [2000] 1 WLR 1815, 1825.

4.23 Lord Justice Robert Walker was seemingly of the view that it would be sufficient for the claimant to establish at trial that "he was not culpable, or was significantly less culpable than the defendant solicitors".[29]

4.24 The case is difficult to interpret because it is never made clear on what basis the claimant was making his unjust enrichment claim. If the correct basis is failure of consideration, then it arguably introduces a considerable flexibility in the availability of relief that did not exist before. The Court of Appeal's reasoning suggests that it might be prepared to enquire into the facts of the particular case to determine whether the claimant was "less blameworthy" than the defendant. The claimant would not be required to show that he fell within one of the established class of claimants to whom relief is permitted. This understanding of the decision would appear to be endorsed by comments made by Lord Justice Longmore in a subsequent case. Although not necessary for deciding the case before him, he remarked that:

> If the contracts were illegal there would be much to be said for the view that a claim can be made by the less culpable party to a reasonable fee for services rendered, as the Court of Appeal thought was arguable in *Mohamed v Alaga*.[30]

4.25 However, an alternative analysis of *Mohamed v Alaga*[31] is that the correct basis for recovery is mistake of law. If this is right, then the case shows that, as we have suggested, recovery for mistakes of law that leave the claimant unaware of the illegality will be permitted without the need for a finding that the purpose of the particular legislation infringed was to protect the interests of the claimant. If the claimant's mistake is crucial to the claim, the case would not introduce any flexibility in the failure of consideration case law.

4.26 In any event, the *Mohamed* case was not followed by the Court of Appeal in *Awwad v Geraghty*.[32] Here the claimant solicitor had entered into a type of conditional fee arrangement with her client which the Court of Appeal held to be contrary to public policy and therefore unenforceable. When the client failed to pay his costs, as an alternative to enforcing the agreement, the solicitor claimed to recover her fees on a *quantum meruit* basis. The claim was not allowed. In a broad statement, Lord Justice Schiemann said "If the court, for reasons of public policy refuses to enforce an agreement that a solicitor should be paid it must follow that he cannot claim on a *quantum meruit*".[33] The position in the *Mohamed* case was said to be totally different. In that case, the claimant interpreter was blameless and no public policy was infringed by allowing him to recover a fair fee for interpreting; the public policy element in the case only affected fees for the introduction of clients.

---

[29] [2000] 1 WLR 1815, 1827.

[30] *A L Barnes Ltd v Time Talk (UK) Ltd* [2003] EWCA Civ 402, [2003] BLR 331.

[31] [2001] 1 WLR 1815.

[32] [2001] QB 570.

[33] [2001] QB 570, 596.

4.27 Judicial comments in a subsequent decision of the High Court, *Dal Sterling Group Plc v WSP South & West Limited*,[34] have approved the restrictive approach adopted in *Awwad*. The claimant had agreed to provide assistance to the defendant in its claims against a third party. After the defendant had successfully brought court proceedings against the third party, it refused to pay the claimant on the basis that their agreement was champertous and therefore contrary to public policy and unenforceable. In fact the High Court found that the terms of the agreement were not champertous and therefore could be enforced. However, it considered whether the claimant could have recovered a sum on a *quantum meruit* basis if the contract had been unenforceable. Following *Awwad v Geraghty*, the Court said not. Where services are provided under a champertous agreement the public policy which prevents the enforcement of the agreement prevents any alternative means of, in effect, enforcing the agreement. The circumstances of *Mohamed* were described as being "rather special".

4.28 It is not clear whether these two cases represent a backtracking on the apparent broadening of the availability of relief that the *Mohamed* case had suggested. Certainly the facts were very different in that the claimant in *Awwad* was the person on whom the responsibility to comply with the relevant law fell. This would not seem necessarily to be the case in *Dal Sterling Group Plc v WSP South & West Limited*.[35]

2. Problems with the present law

4.29 We do not have any criticism of the present rules on illegality where the claimant is able to base his or her claim for unjust enrichment on the grounds of mistake, duress or statutory class protection. In these situations the courts have acknowledged that the claimant is the less guilty party and, since he or she is seeking to undo the effects of the illegal transaction rather than enforce it, the claim is allowed. However, the position is different in relation to claims based on a failure of consideration. Here, it seems that an unmeritorious defendant may rely on the illegality defence. This is because a technical approach is taken to deciding whether the parties are "equally guilty". In such cases little weight would appear to be given to the fact that the claimant is seeking to reverse rather than exploit the illegal contract, and that the result of allowing the illegality defence may be to leave the defendant with an undeserved windfall.

4.30 Professor Rose brought together the criticisms of many academics when he wrote:

> It is ... commonly accepted that the rules denying relief to a plaintiff who has been involved in illegality are crude and capricious, generally fail to discriminate between the relative demerits of the parties and may penalise a plaintiff disproportionately to the relevant wrongdoing.[36]

---

[34] [2002] TCLR 20.

[35] [2002] TCLR 20.

[36] F D Rose, "Gratuitous Transfers and Illegal Purposes" (1996) 112 *Law Quarterly Review* 386, 388.

4.31 In addition, in some cases it is hard to see how the courts have reached their decisions. In order to avoid unwarranted results, the courts are forced to extend the rules to the facts of the particular case to reach the desired outcome. For example, in *Mohamed v Alaga*,[37] the Court of Appeal accepted that one of the bases on which relief was denied in *Taylor v Bhail*[38] was that the claimant builder would have to "rely" on his illegal contract. This he was not permitted to do. Yet in *Mohamed v Alaga* it was accepted that the claim could be made out without any reference to the agreement at all. The claim was allowed to proceed. While not necessarily criticising the outcome in either case, it is hard to see how a distinction can be made between the two claimants on this ground.

4.32 The strict application of the illegality defence to claims for restitution based on a failure of consideration has been further criticised because of the disparity that results between the personal claim for unjust enrichment and proprietary claims for the return of the claimant's property. On very similar fact situations, the court must reach opposite results. We shall go on to consider the proprietary claim in Parts 5 and 6, but it is clear that in almost every case here, despite the involvement of illegality, the claim will succeed.

4.33 An example of the different treatment that is afforded to these two claims based on broadly similar factual situations is given by *Anzal v Ellahi*.[39] The claimants originated from Pakistan and spoke no English. They became friendly with the defendant, a prominent member of their local community and relied on him for advice. When the claimants received a large cheque for the compulsory purchase of their home, the defendant advised them to endorse it over to him rather than pay it into their bank account so that they could continue to claim social security benefits. This the claimants did, falsely telling the Department of Social Security that the proceeds of their home had been spent on repaying debts and remitting the money back to Pakistan. The defendant subsequently refused to return the money to them. His attempt to dismiss their action against him was rejected by the Court of Appeal. It held that the proper legal analysis of the situation was not that there had been any contract for the repayment of the money by the defendant. The claimants had not lent the money to the defendant for him to use or to be free to use, but later to repay. Rather they gave him the money for him to keep for them. The claim was therefore that the defendant was wilfully retaining the fund which was the property of the claimants under a resulting trust. The illegality case law showed that a distinction had to be drawn between the assertion of contractual rights and the assertion of property rights. A claim to the property rights would be enforceable under the illegality rules. It is implicit from the reasoning that, had the court found there to be a contract of loan between the parties, the opposite conclusion would have been reached. It is doubtful whether such a distinction can be justified simply by a slightly different analysis of the facts.

---

[37] [2000] 1 WLR 1815.

[38] [1996] CLC 377.

[39] 1999 WL 819140.

3. Our proposals and reaction to them

4.34 In CP 154 we suggested that many of the criticisms of the present law might be solved by the adoption of the same discretionary approach that we provisionally recommended should apply in relation to the enforcement of a contract involving a legal wrong.[40] That is, the court should be given a statutory discretion to decide whether or not illegality should be recognised as a defence to a standard claim for the reversal of unjust enrichment in relation to benefits transferred under a contract which is unenforceable for illegality.

4.35 We proposed that the fact that the defendant, as a result of the unenforceability of the contract, would otherwise retain a benefit would not, in itself, be sufficient to justify a claim based on unjust enrichment.[41]

4.36 The large majority of respondents who considered our proposals in relation to unjust enrichment claims agreed with them. Those who disagreed tended to do so on the basis that our proposals did not go far enough. That is, they argued that a claim for unjust enrichment should be the primary remedy available when a contract is unenforceable for illegality, and indeed some argued that the court should generally have a discretion to award restitutionary relief in order to undo the effect of an illegal contract, whether or not a standard claim for restitutionary relief could have been made out on the facts. A few disagreed with the proposal because they disagreed with the introduction of a discretion generally. One thought that the law should lean against allowing unjust enrichment claims.

4. The way forward now

4.37 We remain of the view that the illegality defence should not automatically succeed in relation to claims based on a failure of consideration pursuant to an illegal contract. This is on the basis that we believe the policies that underlie the illegality defence are less likely to come into play where the parties are attempting to undo, rather than carry out, their illegal contract. We believe that, as in the case of contractual enforcement, it would be helpful if the courts were to base their decisions directly on these policies in deciding whether the particular claim should be allowed. That is, for example, the courts should ask whether disallowing this particular unjust enrichment claim would deter others from entering into illegal contracts, or whether allowing the claim would undermine the purpose of the invalidating rule. Such an approach may indeed be the basis on which claimants outside the established categories have been refused relief, but the reasoning of the courts does not openly explain this.

4.38 And even where the policies that underlie the defence are relevant, the court must balance these against the objective of achieving a just result between the parties. In assessing this, the court must take into account factors such as the relative merits of the parties and the proportionality of denying the claimant's relief. In the end, the court is required to carry out a balancing exercise to assess whether the illegality defence can be justified.

---

[40] CP 154, paras 7.17 to 7.22.

[41] CP 154, para 7.20.

4.39　We do not agree with the few respondents who suggested that the illegality defence should simply be abolished in relation to claims for unjust enrichment. They argued that the policy of deterrence was just as likely to be fulfilled by allowing restitution to a claimant who has been tainted by illegality as denying it. As we have explained, we do consider that there is merit in the deterrence argument, although we think that the court should consider whether it actually applies to the facts of the case before it. Other principles underlying the illegality defence may be relevant. Indeed, among those putting forward this argument, it was generally accepted that some discretion would need to be retained to deny relief in cases of extreme turpitude.

4.40　We also continue to believe that it would not be right for us to propose legislation to introduce a general right to restitution on the failure of an illegal contract. As we said in CP 154, there is not generally any right to claim relief on the failure of a contract. The claimant must show that he or she falls within the accepted grounds for an unjust enrichment claim. There appears to be no compelling reason to provide greater relief in the illegality cases. This does mean that, without more, the claimant will not be able to obtain a remedy in every case where justice would seem to require one. Our approach is predicated on the basis that, illegality apart, the claimant would have an unjust enrichment claim. Under the present law, where the claimant is seeking the return of money paid in advance under a contract which has failed for any reason, he or she can only do so where there has been a *total* failure of consideration. In CP 154 we suggested that the law was moving in the direction of allowing restitution for a partial failure of consideration. However, this prophecy is as yet unfulfilled, so that a claimant who has prepaid under a contract and received some, but not all, of the goods or services for which he bargained, is unable to claim in unjust enrichment for the return of the money and must rely on contractual remedies. We do not think that it would be right for us to single out one reason for the contractual failure - illegality - and provide a distinct remedy for partial failure of consideration. Although now firmly established, the law relating to unjust enrichment claims is still being developed, and it would appear to us that it would be better left to move forward as a whole, rather than through piecemeal statutory intervention.

4.41　In contrast to the provisional proposals we made in CP 154, we no longer propose to recommend legislative reform in this area for the introduction of a statutory discretion. This is for two main reasons. First, to a large degree our drive for legislative reform in relation to unjust enrichment claims was linked to our proposals for legislative reform in relation to the enforcement of contracts tainted by illegality. It appeared to us unbalanced to have a statutory discretion for the one and not the other. However, we have now abandoned any proposals for statutory intervention in the enforcement cases. This issue, therefore, no longer arises.

4.42 Secondly, we believe that the courts are beginning to show a more flexible approach in illegality cases. The removal of the bar to relief for a mistake based on law rather than fact has opened up the possibility of an "innocent" claimant obtaining relief in a much wider range of circumstances. The only difficult case, therefore, seems to arise where both parties are aware of the illegality involved in the transaction, but arguably the defendant bears more responsibility for the illegal involvement than the claimant. This might be because he or she is the instigator of the illegal plan, or because he or she is the person on whom compliance with the law is imposed. Unless the claimant can show duress or vulnerability sufficient to found a claim for unjust enrichment, or that he or she is a member of a class protected by statute, the claimant will be forced to base his or her claim on the failure of consideration. This is where the illegality defence has traditionally been strictly applied. Even here the Court of Appeal decision in *Mohamed* seems to bring more flexibility to the law than was the case when we made our provisional proposals in CP 154. A claimant may now be allowed restitution when he or she is substantially less at fault than the defendant. This will be the case where the claimant can show that he or she falls within one of the categories listed in paragraph 4.4 above. It will also be the case in a standard claim based on a failure of consideration where the claimant is the less blameworthy party and allowing relief will not undermine the policy of the relevant prohibiting rule. Such a development should, we believe, be encouraged. By focusing on the nature of the illegality, which party was most responsible for it, and the conduct of the claimant, the court can establish whether the principles that underlie the illegality defence require its application in the case before them.

4.43 Such an approach, we believe, is likely to result in an increase in the number of claims for unjust enrichment that are allowed following the failure of a contract for illegality. This will have the advantage of bringing this area of the law into line with that which exists where the claimant seeks to protect a proprietary interest. As we shall go on to see in the Parts that follow, this is nearly always permitted. Allowing a greater number of personal restitutionary claims will produce more symmetry in these two situations.

4.44 **We provisionally recommend that the courts should consider in each case whether the application of the illegality defence to the unjust enrichment claim can be justified on the basis of the policies that underlie that defence. In reaching its decision the court will need to balance the importance of these policies against the objective of achieving a just result, taking into account the relative merits of the parties and the proportionality of denying the claim. Whenever the illegality defence is successful, the court should make clear the justification for its application.**

ILLEGALITY AS A GROUND TO A CLAIM FOR RESTITUTION FOR UNJUST ENRICHMENT: "THE TIME FOR REPENTANCE"

1. The present law

4.45 We have just considered how, under the present law, illegality may act as a defence to a claim for unjust enrichment. We now go on to look at how, in one particular circumstance, illegality may act as the very ground on which the unjust enrichment claim is based.[42] That is, illegality aside, the claimant would not have any basis on which to bring his or her claim. These are cases where the claimant is seeking to withdraw from an illegal contract during "the time for repentance". In many cases the courts use the Latin terminology, "*locus poenitentiae*".

4.46 The policy behind this rule appears to be that it discourages illegality by allowing parties to abandon illegal contracts. Thus, the claimant is allowed to withdraw from an illegal contract during "the time for repentance" and recover benefits conferred even though the defendant is ready, willing and able to perform his or her side of the bargain. The precise boundaries of this doctrine are very unclear. The courts originally adopted a fairly relaxed approach, but at the turn of the twentieth century imposed tight boundaries on the relief. However, most recent cases, in particular the Court of Appeal's decision in *Tribe v Tribe*,[43] suggest a less strict approach. Two features are particularly uncertain. First, can the claimant withdraw at any stage of the contract? Secondly, need the claimant genuinely repent of his or her illegal purpose? We look at both of these issues below.

(1) Up to what point is withdrawal allowed?

4.47 Early case law suggested that withdrawal would be allowed up until a late stage in the performance of the contract, provided that the illegal purpose had not been fully achieved. It did not matter that the claimant had performed the whole of his or her side of the bargain. For example, in *Taylor v Bowers*,[44] the claimant had handed over certain goods to his nephew in an attempt to deceive his creditors about the value of his assets. One of the creditors was the defendant who was found to be a party to the intended fraud. Before any settlement with the creditors had been concluded, the nephew, without the consent of the claimant, assigned the goods to the defendant. The claimant successfully sued to recover the value of the goods detained by the defendant. Lord Justice Mellish, with whom Lord Justice Baggally agreed, said:

---

[42] Not all commentators agree that illegality is acting as a ground for the unjust enrichment claim. See, for example, G Virgo, *The Principles of the Law of Restitution* (2nd ed 2006) p 352 where it is argued that the real basis is failure of consideration. Such an approach is also supported by Professor Birks: P Birks, "Recovering Value Transferred under an Illegal Contract" [2000] 1 *Theoretical Inquiries in Law* 155.

[43] [1996] Ch 107.

[44] (1876) 1 QBD 291.

> If money is paid or goods delivered for an illegal purpose, the person which had so paid the money or delivered the goods may recover them back before the illegal purpose is carried out, but if he waits till the illegal purpose is carried out, or if he seeks to enforce the illegal transaction, in neither case can he maintain an action; the law will not allow that to be done.[45]

4.48   Later cases suggested that the withdrawal had to be made at an earlier stage for the unjust enrichment claim to succeed. In *Kearley v Thomson*[46] the claimant, the friend of a bankrupt, had unlawfully paid the fees owed to the defendants, a petitioning creditor's solicitors. These fees were due to be paid out of the bankrupt's estate, but had not been paid owing to want of assets. In return, the defendant solicitors agreed not to appear at the bankrupt's public examination, nor to oppose his discharge. The solicitors accordingly did not appear, and the bankrupt passed his public examination. However, before the bankrupt had applied for his discharge, the claimant sued the solicitors for the return of the money that he had paid them. The Court of Appeal dismissed his claim. Lord Justice Fry questioned the withdrawal principle laid down in *Taylor v Bowers*. Even if it did exist, he said that it could not be used here, because too many steps had already been taken towards the fulfilment of the unlawful purpose.[47]

4.49   But full circle may have been reached by the Court of Appeal's decision in *Tribe v Tribe*.[48] This case concerned the withdrawal doctrine as it applies to illegal trusts, and we discuss it in some detail in Part 6. However, Lord Millett (then a judge of the Court of Appeal) was clear that he intended his reasoning to apply to all claims for restitutionary relief. A liberal approach was adopted towards the time by which withdrawal must occur. A father, the claimant, had transferred shares in his company to his son, the defendant, in order to hide them from his creditors. The plan was that once an agreement had been reached with the creditors, the son would retransfer the shares to his father. In the event, the feared liability never arose, and the father asked for the shares back. The son refused, and argued that his father could not enforce the illegal agreement. The Court of Appeal allowed the father's claim. The withdrawal was in time because, although the shares had been transferred, no creditors had in fact been deceived.

---

[45] (1876) 1 QBD 291, 299-300. It is not entirely clear from the reported case exactly what the agreement between the claimant and his nephew was. James LJ (and arguably Grove LJ) held that the claimant could recover because he could prove his title independently of the illegal transaction.

[46] (1890) 24 QBD 742.

[47] (1890) 24 QBD 742.

[48] [1996] Ch 107.

(2) Need the claimant "repent"?

4.50 A second point on which the law is uncertain is whether the claimant needs genuinely to have repented of his or her illegality, or is withdrawal allowed where the illegal purpose has been frustrated or is simply no longer needed? Again, the courts seem to have gone from taking a fairly liberal approach, to a stricter requirement, and now reverted back in *Tribe*. Certainly in the early case, *Taylor v Bowers*,[49] the fact that the illegal scheme had been frustrated by the defendant's actions did not prevent the claimant from recovering.

4.51 However, particular emphasis was placed on the need for repentance in the decision in *Bigos v Bousted*.[50] The defendant had attempted to contravene the Exchange Control Act 1947 by arranging for the claimant to supply Italian currency to his wife and daughter in Italy. As a security for the loan, the defendant had deposited a share certificate with the claimant. When the claimant reneged on the agreement, the defendant sought to recover the certificate, arguing that the contract, although illegal, was executory and he should be allowed to withdraw from it. His claim failed on the basis that he had not withdrawn because he repented of the illegality, but rather because the illegal contract had been frustrated by the claimant's breach of it. The Court reached its conclusion with reluctance – the merits of the case being entirely with the defendant. The claimant's behaviour was described as being "despicable in the extreme". Not only had she failed to return the share certificate, she had also commenced an action to recover the money which she falsely claimed to have lent.

4.52 The need for genuine repentance was, however, rejected by the Court of Appeal in *Tribe v Tribe*. Lord Millett explained: "Justice is not a reward for merit; restitution should not be confined to the penitent. I would also hold that voluntary withdrawal from an illegal transaction when it has ceased to be needed is sufficient. It is true that this is not necessary to encourage withdrawal, but a rule to the opposite effect could lead to bizarre results". On the other hand, he said that the claimant must withdraw voluntarily, and not because he or she had been forced to do so because the illegal plan had been discovered.[51]

(3) A further limit on recovery?

4.53 One further limitation on recovery that is supported by early authority is that a claim for unjust enrichment based on withdrawal will not be allowed if the transaction is so obnoxious that the court should not have anything to do with it. In *Tappenden v Randall*, Mr Justice Heath said:

---

[49]   (1876) 1 QBD 291.

[50]   [1951] 1 All ER 92.

[51]   [1996] Ch 107, 135.

"Undoubtedly there may be cases where the contract may be of a nature too grossly immoral for the Court to enter into any discussion of it; as where one man has paid money by way of hire to another to murder a third person".[52]

2. Problems with the present law

4.54 There has been much criticism of the reasoning adopted by the Court of Appeal to justify its decision in *Tribe v Tribe*,[53] although the outcome has generally been accepted as fair. Two points in particular have been highlighted. First, it is hard to see how one could say that the illegal purpose of the claimant had not been carried out, unless one adopts a particularly restrictive view of what that purpose was. Indeed it could be argued that the judgment of the court in fact fulfilled the illegal purpose by returning the shares to the father once any perceived threat from creditors had passed.

4.55 Secondly, by allowing the claim without the need for repentance but simply once the risk has passed, it is no longer possible to justify the policy on which this ground for the unjust enrichment claim is based as being the encouragement of withdrawal from illegal transactions. The case is another example of the court striving to adapt the relevant rules to meet the facts of the case before it in order to reach a desired result.

3. Our proposals and reaction to them

4.56 In CP 154 we provisionally proposed that legislation should provide the court with a discretion to allow a party to withdraw from an illegal contract and to have restitution of benefits conferred under it, where allowing the party to withdraw would reduce the likelihood of an illegal act being completed or an illegal purpose being accomplished. We said that in exercising this discretion the court should consider (i) whether the claimant genuinely repents of the illegality; and (ii) the seriousness of the illegality. We argued that the justification for the doctrine of withdrawal was twofold. The first justification is based on deterrence. The second is based on repentance.[54]

4.57 There was little comment in relation to our proposal to put the right to withdraw on a statutory footing.[55] Most respondents agreed. Some thought that this was unnecessary in view of their arguments for a wider right to restitutionary relief after the failure of an illegal contract generally.

[52] (1801) 2 B&P 467, 471; 126 ER 1388, 1390.

[53] [1996] Ch 107. See, for example, F D Rose, "Gratuitous Transfers and Illegal Purposes" (1996) 112 *Law Quarterly Review* 386 and G Virgo, "Withdrawal from Illegal Transactions – A Matter for Consideration" [1996] *Cambridge Law Journal* 23.

[54] For fuller details of our proposals and the reasoning behind them, see CP 154, paras 7.58 to 7.69.

[55] A few respondents queried the need to look for repentance, suggesting that it was a needless complication that would be difficult to apply in practice.

4. The way forward now

4.58　Given that we are no longer advocating legislative reform in relation to the role that illegality plays as a defence to claims for unjust enrichment, we do not intend to propose legislative reform here. Although it is possible to criticise the reasoning in some of the cases that use illegality as a cause of action, few criticise the outcomes.[56] Legislative reform in this area alone does not, therefore, seem warranted. We do believe, however, that it would be helpful for potential litigants if the courts were to explain more fully the basis on which the withdrawal is allowed. As we explained in CP 154,[57] we do not think that repentance by itself can justify permitting a claim in unjust enrichment where one would not otherwise be available. Where the illegality is of a minor technical nature, a greater injustice may be invoked by allowing the claimant to renege on a contract which the defendant remains ready, willing and able to perform. Following *Tribe v Tribe*,[58] repentance would no longer seem to be a requirement for the remedy to be available. Rather, the withdrawal doctrine is based on deterring illegality. That is, the claim should be allowed where the claimant can show that his or her withdrawal will reduce the likelihood of the illegal conduct taking place.[59] We believe that any future refinement of the law in this area can be best left to the incremental development of the case law.

4.59　**We do not recommend any legislative reform to the use of illegality as a ground for a claim for the reversal of unjust enrichment.**

---

[56]　Although the decision in *Bigos v Bousted* [1951] 1 All ER 92 does seem harsh, following its criticism in *Tribe v Tribe* [1996] Ch 107 it is unlikely that it would be decided in the same way today.

[57]　For a fuller discussion see CP 154, paras 7.58 to 7.69.

[58]　[1996] Ch 107.

[59]　Although this was the reasoning adopted in *Tribe v Tribe* [1996] Ch 107, it is difficult to see how the case can be supported on that ground. Rather, the withdrawal doctrine was there used as an artificial device to avoid the effects of the illegality doctrine and the reliance principle. We discuss this principle, and our proposed reforms, in Part 6 below.

ILLEGALITY AND THE DEFENCE OF CHANGE OF POSITION

4.60   In *Barros Mattos Junior v MacDaniels Ltd*,[60] the court was called upon to consider how illegal behaviour may affect the availability of the defence of change of position. The defendants had received several million dollars which had been stolen from the claimants, a Brazilian bank, by third party fraudsters. For the purposes of the claim for summary judgment it was assumed that the defendants were innocent recipients of this money, with no knowledge of its illicit source. Following instructions from the fraudsters, the defendants had changed the money into Nigerian currency and distributed the majority of it according to the fraudsters' instructions. Both sides accepted that unless the defendants could rely on a defence of change of position, the claimants had a valid claim in unjust enrichment for the return of the money. The claimants argued that because the defendants' handling of the money was illegal under Nigerian law, they could not rely on it. Mr Justice Laddie accepted this argument. He rejected the defendants' arguments that the court should have any discretion in the matter. Subject to the possibility that in some cases the illegality will be so minor as to be ignored on the de minimis principle, there was no room for the exercise of any discretion by the court in favour of one party or the other. If the recipient's actions of changing position are treated as illegal, the court cannot take them into account.[61]

---

[60]   [2004] EWHC 1188, [2005] 1 WLR 247.

[61]   [2004] EWHC 1188, [2005] 1 WLR 247 at [43].

4.61   The principle established in *Barros Mattos Junior v MacDaniels Ltd*[62] has been the subject of criticism as being unduly harsh.[63] Unless it falls within the proposed de minimis exception, the breach of a minor technical regulation may result in a completely disproportionate denial of the change of position offence. While not criticising the outcome of the decision in that case, we suggest that the principle on which it relies is unnecessarily broadly stated. In other areas of the law of unjust enrichment we have urged that the courts should adopt greater flexibility in the way that it deals with illegality. We suggest that they should do the same here. This would be more in line with the approach adopted by the House of Lords in *Bakewell Management Ltd v Brandwood*, where Lord Walker said the illegality defence "must be applied as an instrument of public policy, and not in circumstances where it does not serve any public interest".[64]

4.62   **We provisionally recommend that the courts should disallow the defence of change of position because the defendant has been involved in some unlawful conduct only where the disapplication of that defence can be firmly justified by the policies that underlie the existence of the doctrine of illegality.**

---

[62]   [2004] EWHC 1188, [2005] 1 WLR 247.

[63]   Lord Goff of Chieveley and G Jones, *The Law of Restitution* (7th ed 2007) para 40-006; M Halliwell, "The Effect of Illegality on a Change of Position Defence" [2005] *The Conveyancer and Property Lawyer* 357; A Tettenborn, "Bank Fraud, Change of Position and Illegality: The Case of the Innocent Money- Launderer" [2005] *Lloyd's Maritime and Commercial Law Quarterly* 6.

[64]   [2004] UKHL 14, [2004] 2 AC 519 at [60]. This case decided that if an easement over land could be lawfully granted by the landowner, then that easement could be acquired by prescription even where the use relied on was illegal rather than simply tortious.

PART 5
ILLEGALITY AND THE RECOGNITION OF CONTRACTUALLY TRANSFERRED, CREATED OR RETAINED LEGAL PROPERTY RIGHTS

INTRODUCTION

5.1   In this Part we examine how the courts have dealt with contracts which purport to transfer or create legal interests in property, but the contract is in some way tainted by illegality. So, for example, we examine whether the court will recognise the transfer of goods under an executed contract, even if, because of the illegality, it would not have enforced the contract had the transfer not already taken place. We look at what happens where the transferor has transferred or created only a limited legal interest, such as a lease or bailment, under a contract tainted by illegality. We ask whether the court will recognise and protect that limited interest in the hands of the transferee. We also consider whether the transferor can enforce his reversionary interest on the termination of the limited interest?

5.2   Traditionally the case law has adopted a different approach in relation to the transfer or creation of equitable interests under transactions tainted by illegality, and these are therefore examined in the following Part.

THE PRESENT LAW

1. Property passes under an illegal contract

5.3   After some initial confusion, it is now clear that where a legal interest in property is transferred pursuant to a contract then ownership of the interest does pass, notwithstanding the involvement of illegality and the fact that, if executory, the court would not have assisted in the enforcement of the contract. This is certainly the case as against a third party who wrongly interferes with the property acquired under the illegal contract.[1] But it seems also to be the case as against the other party to the contract if the property has been delivered.

---

[1]   *Belvoir Finance Co Ltd v Stapleton* [1971] 1 QB 210. See also *Webb v Chief Constable of Merseyside* [2000] QB 427. Money obtained from illegal drugs dealings is held by the vendor under a possessory title which the court will protect. The money cannot be confiscated by the police except under specific statutory power.

5.4 In *Singh v Ali*[2] the defendant sold and transferred a lorry to the claimant, but, pursuant to a scheme between the parties to defraud the Malayan licensing authorities, registered the lorry in his own name. This enabled the defendant to obtain a permit to operate the lorry which, under statutory regulations then in force, the claimant would not have been able to obtain for himself. The defendant later detained the lorry without the claimant's consent and refused to return it to him. The Privy Council held that property in the lorry had passed to the claimant, notwithstanding the illegality of the contract for sale, and that the claimant could therefore maintain an action against the defendant for the return of the lorry or its value. Lord Denning said:

> Although the transaction between the plaintiff and the defendant was illegal, nevertheless it was fully executed and carried out; and on that account it was effective to pass the property in the lorry to the plaintiff. … The reason is because the transferor, having fully achieved his unworthy end, cannot be allowed to then turn round and repudiate the means by which he did it – he cannot throw over the transfer.[3]

5.5 As well as recognising that full legal title may pass under a contract that involves illegality, it is clear that the court will recognise that a limited legal interest may also pass. So, for example, if the lessor of premises under an illegal lease forcibly ejects the lessee before the expiry of the term, the court will assist the lessee in regaining possession.[4]

5.6 In summary, subject to the two exceptions explained at paragraphs 5.12 to 5.13 below, the true picture in relation to the transfer or creation of a legal interest seems to be that the court simply ignores the illegality.

2. The recovery of property in which a limited interest has been created – the reliance principle

5.7 As we have just seen, where only a limited legal interest is created the court will recognise and protect that limited interest in the hands of the transferee. We consider now whether the transferor can enforce his reversionary interest on the termination of the limited interest. The traditional answer given by the courts seems to be "yes", provided that he or she can establish the reversionary interest without "relying" on the illegal contract.

---

[2] [1960] AC 167.

[3] [1960] AC 167, 176.

[4] *Feret v Hill* (1854) 15 CB 207; 139 ER 400.

5.8 What exactly does this mean? The leading case on the application of this "reliance" principle is usually cited as the Court of Appeal's decision in *Bowmakers Ltd v Barnet Instruments Ltd.*[5] The defendants hired machine tools from the claimant finance company under three separate hire purchase agreements. The agreements were part of an arrangement that contravened statutory regulations relating to pricing and it was assumed that they were therefore "illegal". After making some of the payments due under the agreements, the defendants refused to pay anything further. They sold the machine tools hired under the first and third agreements to third parties and refused to deliver up on demand the tools subject to the second agreement.

5.9 The Court of Appeal found the defendants liable to the claimant for conversion in respect of all the machine tools. Lord Justice Du Parcq said:

> In our opinion, a man's right to possess his own chattels will as a general rule be enforced against one who, without any claim of right, is detaining them or has converted them to his own use, even though it may appear from the pleadings, or in the course of the trial, that the chattels in question came into the defendant's possession by reasons of an illegal contract between himself and the plaintiff, provided that the plaintiff does not seek, and is not forced, either to found his claim on the illegal contract or to plead its illegality in order to support his claim.[6]

5.10 This case has been criticised on the basis that it is hard to see how the claimant could make out its claim, in particular with regard to the machine tools hired under the second agreement, without relying on the illegal contract.[7] The defendants' sale of the tools under the first and third agreement may have amounted to a repudiatory breach which would automatically terminate the defendants' interest in them. This does not explain, however, how the claimant was able to enforce its claim in respect of the tools under the second agreement which the defendants simply kept. It may be that the second contract specifically provided that non-payment of hire should amount to a repudiatory breach or gave an option to the claimant to terminate the agreement.[8] In either case, it is hard to see how that claimant could establish this without relying on the contract. The result is that a sharp distinction is drawn between cases where goods are transferred under hire purchase terms, where the threat of recovery may compel payment, and cases where goods are transferred under other forms of credit agreement which the courts would not enforce.[9]

---

[5] [1945] KB 65.

[6] [1945] KB 65, 71.

[7] B Coote, "Another Look at *Bowmakers v Barnet Instruments*" [1972] *Modern Law Review* 38 and C J Hamson, "Illegal Contracts and Limited Interests" (1949) 10 *Cambridge Law Journal* 249.

[8] The terms of the hire purchase agreements are not set out in the reported case.

[9] The difficulties with the decision are noted by several commentators. See, for example, Professor GH Treitel, *The Law of Contract* (12th ed 2007) paras 11-139-11-140 *Chitty on Contracts* (29th ed 2004) para 16-174 and B Coote, "Another Look at *Bowmakers v Barnet Instruments*" (1972) 35 Modern Law Review 38.

5.11   As with the transfer or creation of legal interests under an illegal contract, the true picture seems to be that the courts simply ignore the illegality. Once executed, the illegal contract is regarded as "past history". Indeed in the leading House of Lords' decision on the treatment of equitable interests under illegal trusts, Lord Browne-Wilkinson explained that at law a person may rely on the illegal contract for the purpose of "providing the basis of his claim to a property right".[10] Professor Enonchong has argued that, "the often-repeated assertion that a title claim will succeed only where there is no reliance on the contract or its illegality is more illusory than real".[11]

3. Exceptions

5.12   It seems that there are at least two exceptions to the proposition that the courts ignore the illegality for the purpose of determining the transfer or creation of legal property interests. The first of these comes from judicial remarks in two cases which suggest that where the goods claimed are of such a kind that it is unlawful for the defendant to transfer them to the claimant or for the claimant to be in possession of them at all, the court would not intervene. Examples were given of obscene books,[12] controlled drugs or illegal weapons.[13]

5.13   Secondly, the court will not recognise that legal property has passed under a contract which contravenes a legislative provision and that legislative provision is interpreted to provide that the contract should be of no effect. This would appear to be one of two grounds for the Privy Council's decision in *Amar Singh v Kulubya*.[14] The lessor of "mailo" lands was allowed to evict the lessee from them. The lease had been entered into in contravention of legislation which provided that it was an offence for a landowner to lease mailo lands to a non-African and for a non-African to take such lands on lease without the consent of the Governor.

---

[10] *Tinsley v Milligan* [1994] 1 AC 340, 370.

[11] N Enonchong, "Title Claims and Illegal Transactions" (1995) 111 *Law Quarterly Review* 135.

[12] *Bowmakers Ltd v Barnet Instruments Ltd* [1945] KB 65, 72.

[13] *Costello v Chief Constable of Derbyshire Constabulary* [2001] EWCA Civ 381; [2001] 1 WLR 1437, 1451.

[14] [1964] AC 142.

PROBLEMS WITH THE PRESENT LAW

5.14 In CP 154 we argued that the greater protection given by the present law to property rights transferred or created under an illegal contract over that given to personal rights might be regarded as out-moded. One could argue that the same rules should apply in both cases. The disparity between the treatment given to property rights and contractual rights is clearly illustrated by the judicial commentary in *Choudhry v United Bank Ltd*.[15] The claimant was a resident of Pakistan. A bank account in his name was opened with the defendant in the UK. The claimant's brother carried on business in the UK, and used the bank account in order to avoid tax liabilities. In reliance on a letter of lien bearing the forged signature of the claimant, the defendant transferred sums from the claimant's bank account to itself. The claimant sought the return of this money. The Court held that the claimant was not the true account holder and therefore there was no contract between the claimant and defendant. However, even if there had been, that contract would have been unenforceable due to the illegal purpose of avoiding tax. It was accepted that had the claimant been asserting a *proprietary* right, he would have been able to do so because he could have brought the claim without making reference to the illegal purpose. However, here he was seeking a mere contractual right and his claim would have been vitiated by the illegal purpose of the contract.

5.15 In addition, in CP 154 we criticised the application of the "reliance principle". We suggested that even if, frequently, the courts ignore its application, the mere fact that the courts pay lip service to such a principle is a cause of confusion. If the truth is that the illegality is simply being ignored, it would be far more satisfactory for the court to state this openly. Such an approach tends to give priority to procedural issues over those that seem to us to be the most relevant factors – ensuring that the policies of the rule giving rise to the illegality are upheld. Where, for example, the rule that is infringed is statutory, unless it is possible to argue that the statute itself provides the consequences for the property rights, the reliance principle provides no opportunity for the court to consider the underlying policy of the legislation and determine whether this would be undermined by allowing the claim.

5.16 We do not suggest that there will be many cases where it would be appropriate to disallow a claimant who has carved a limited interest out of his or her property to recover the property at the end of that temporary interest. However, to decide whether or not he or she can do so on the basis of the need to "rely" on any illegality seems arbitrary. As Professor Treitel has written:

> [The reliance rule is] ... open to the objection that it ignores the crucial question: whether to allow the owner to recover his property would tend to promote or to defeat the purpose of the rule of law which makes the contract illegal.[16]

---

[15] Unreported, 18 November 1999.

[16] G H Treitel, *Law of Contract* (12th ed 2007) p 549.

5.17   He points out that on the facts of *Bowmakers,* allowing recovery was unlikely to defeat the purposes of the rule making the contracts illegal, since these were aimed at preventing profiteering and regulating the allocation of scarce resources in wartime. In addition, the owners made an involuntary error. He wrote: "The position would have been different if the owners had been guilty of a deliberate violation of a regulation made for the purpose of protecting hirers".[17]

5.18   In CP 154 we also pointed out that there are some points of uncertainty in relation to the present law. For example, it is not clear what rules would be applied to property that has never been delivered to the claimant under the illegal contract, particularly if the claim was for non-delivery against the other party to the contract rather than against a third party for some kind of wrongful interference. In *Belvoir Finance Co Ltd v Stapleton*[18] the Court of Appeal held that property could pass under an illegal contract notwithstanding the fact that here the vendor transferred the relevant goods directly to a third party and the purchaser never took possession of them. The claimant finance company bought three cars from dealers and, without taking possession of them, let them out on hire purchase to the defendant. The Court of Appeal held that the claimant could sue the defendant for conversion when it fraudulently sold the cars to innocent purchasers. However, this case was concerned only with the position between the purchaser and a third party. It cannot be used to support the proposition that a purchaser to whom property in goods has passed under an illegal contract can claim them, or damages for their conversion, from a vendor who has not delivered them. Such a claim would not differ in substance from claims, which would not be directly enforced, for the delivery, or damages for non-delivery, of the goods under the illegal contract.

5.19   In addition, there is some doubt as to what point in time the courts recognise that ownership of the property has passed under an illegal contract.[19] The cases refer to the "execution" of the contract, but it is not clear what this means. Does it require that both parties should have performed their side of the bargain? Such an approach might be regarded as more equitable, since it is less likely to result in the unjust enrichment of the transferee, but it would, on the other hand, give the transferee an incentive to perform the illegal contract.

5.20   It is also not at all clear how the reliance principle operates in relation to an illegal lease. We have seen that an illegal lease does vest a term of years in the tenant, and the court will act to protect that. However, what if the tenant fails to pay the rent? The landlord will presumably be neither able to enforce the lease nor to demand back the property since the failure to pay rent does not automatically terminate a lease. In *Alexander v Rayson*[20] the Court of Appeal suggested that the tenant would effectively be able to live in the leased property rent free.

---

[17]   G H Treitel, *Law of Contract* (12th ed 2007) p 549.

[18]   [1971] 1 QB 210.

[19]   For a full discussion, see A Stewart, "Contractual Illegality and the Recognition of Proprietary Interests" (1986) 1 *Journal of Contract Law* 134, 144-149.

[20]   [1936] 1 KB 169, 186.

OUR PROPOSALS ON CONSULTATION AND REACTION TO THEM

5.21 In CP 154 we provisionally proposed that the same statutory discretionary approach which we provisionally recommended in relation to contractual enforcement should apply in relation to the recognition of contractually transferred or created legal property rights. We suggested that a great merit of this proposal would be the abandonment of the "reliance principle". However, in order to provide security and protect third parties, we also proposed that illegality should not invalidate a disposition of property to a third party purchaser for value without notice of the illegality.[21]

5.22 This provisional approach was supported by a majority (60%) of those who responded on this issue. These respondents largely agreed with our reasoning. Some respondents objected to the introduction of a discretion because they did not want any discretionary reform in relation to illegality. The principal concern of others was that a discretion in this area would cause unacceptable uncertainty in relation to legal property rights. Indeed there was notably less support for the introduction of a discretion in relation to the recognition of property rights than there was in relation to claims to enforce contractual rights or for unjust enrichment. It was argued that there remains a very real difference between property rights and contractual rights, and that it would *not* be arbitrary to provide greater protection for the former than the latter. It was suggested that to leave property rights in limbo would lead to "an inherently unstable situation". The need for certainty was thought to be more important than the policy issues which point towards the special treatment of parties in a situation which involves illegality. Given the powers that the courts have to confiscate the proceeds of crime,[22] it was felt unnecessary and indeed undesirable for the courts to replicate this confiscation with the use of the civil illegality rules.

5.23 There was also concern in relation to the protection which we had proposed for third party purchasers. One respondent commented that if a discretion were to be introduced, protection should be provided not only for third party purchasers, but for any innocent third party recipient of the property. Another argued that if protection were to be given in relation to third parties who acquire property rights, why not also to third parties who acquire contractual rights. Another respondent took an opposite approach. It was argued that it would give rise to too much uncertainty in such a crucial area as the passing of title if the courts were granted a discretion. It would therefore be better to provide that *no* title passes, but without prejudice to rights acquired by a bona fide purchaser for value without notice.

---

[21] CP 154, para 7.26.

[22] See paras 2.32 to 2.33 above.

THE WAY FORWARD NOW

5.24   There was less support from respondents in relation to the introduction of a discretionary approach to the recognition and protection of legal property rights in cases involving illegality than we found for a discretion in relation to the enforcement of contracts or claims for unjust enrichment. Given that we are no longer advocating the introduction of a statutory discretion in relation to contractual enforcement, we do not propose to recommend such a discretion in this area, where it would obviously prove to be more controversial.

5.25   As we explained in CP 154, we do not see any great problem with the outcomes created by the present law here. Sooner or later the courts may have to deal with the issues of uncertainty in this area of the law which we have highlighted. There are two main ones. First, in relation to goods that have not been delivered, where there is a danger that to allow the claim would amount to enforcing an otherwise unenforceable contract. Secondly, where a tenant under an illegal lease fails to pay rent. However we do not think these issues are pressing ones, nor that, using the more flexible approach advocated elsewhere in this paper, the courts would have any difficulty in reaching sensible results.

5.26   While we are disappointed that the reliance principle adopted by the case law does not allow the courts to focus on what we believe to be the true issues underlying the illegality defence, we appreciate the need for certainty in cases involving legal property rights. Therefore we do not propose any statutory reform here. There is, we suggest, scope for a small degree of flexibility where the property involved is such that it would be unlawful to be dealing in it at all.[23] But otherwise in relation to the creation, transfer or retention of legal property under a contract involving illegality, the illegality will be effectively ignored.

5.27   **We do not recommend any legislative reform to the illegality defence as it applies in relation to the recognition of contractually created, transferred or retained legal property rights.**

---

[23]   See para 5.12 above.

PART 6
ILLEGALITY AND TRUSTS

INTRODUCTION

6.1 In this Part we look at the effect that illegality may have on the recognition and enforcement of a beneficial interest under a trust. The trust arrangement is frequently found in the illegality case law as a vehicle for fraudulent behaviour. The division of the legal and equitable interests offers a unique opportunity to conceal the true beneficial ownership for illegitimate purposes – for example, in order to defraud creditors, tax authorities, or social security administrators.

6.2 The law in this area has reached a very unsatisfactory state. In many cases, it is simply not clear what rules are applicable or how they operate. What follows is an attempt to tease out some form of structure from the relevant case law and to fill in some of the gaps.

6.3 As we explained in the Introduction, it was a case about the effect of illegality on the enforcement of a resulting trust, *Tinsley v Milligan*,[1] that led to calls for the Law Commission to review the illegality doctrine. Because most of the case law has revolved around resulting trusts, we have found it easier to look at these first, before going on to consider how illegality may affect other trusts, such as express trusts and constructive trusts.

RESULTING TRUSTS: THE PRESENT LAW

1. The reliance principle

(1) Resulting trusts arising under arrangements set up for a fraudulent purpose

6.4 Where two or more parties purchase property together, it is not unusual for the legal title to that property to be held by only one of them. Alternatively one person may transfer property into the name of another, but intend to retain the beneficial ownership for him or herself. In both cases the law will generally presume that the legal owner of the property holds it on a resulting trust for the contributor or transferor.[2] These arrangements may be for perfectly legitimate reasons, such as the ease of any future sale. However, this structure also offers scope for fraudulent behaviour. The imposition of the resulting trust gives the contributor or transferor the opportunity of hiding the real ownership in the trust property from those who may have claims over it, without risking the loss of any interest in it.

---

[1]   [1994] 1 AC 340.

[2]   Different rules may apply where the property concerned is a home for the parties. We discuss this in greater detail in para 6.54 below.

6.5 In this section we look at how the illegality doctrine affects such arrangements. The position appears to be that, in general, illegality does not prevent a resulting trust arising under general trust principles, notwithstanding that the transaction was entered into in order to carry out some fraudulent purpose.[3] However, the beneficiary will only be able to enforce his or her interest under that resulting trust if, in order to prove the interest, the beneficiary does not need to plead or lead evidence of the illegality in which he or she is involved.[4] This is an application of the so-called "reliance principle" which we have already encountered in relation to the recognition and enforcement of legal interests.[5] In *Tinsley v Milligan* the House of Lords confirmed that the same rules should apply in relation to the recognition and enforcement of equitable interests. As Lord Browne-Wilkinson (giving the leading majority speech) explained:

> More than 100 years has elapsed since the administration of law and equity became fused. The reality of the matter is that ... English law has one single law of property made up of legal and equitable interests. Although for historical reasons legal estates and equitable estates have differing incidents, the person owning either type of estate has a right of property, a right in rem not merely a right in personam. If the law is that a party is entitled to enforce a property right acquired under an illegal transaction, in my judgment the same rule ought to apply to any property right so acquired, whether such right is legal or equitable.[6]

6.6 We saw that, in relation to legal interests, the reliance principle has little substantive effect. The result is that, in relation to the transfer or creation of legal interests, the illegality is effectively ignored. However, the consequences of applying the reliance principle are different in relation to equitable interests. Here it results in a sharp distinction being drawn between those cases where a presumption of resulting trust arises and those cases where there is the opposite presumption, one of gift. Illegality is ignored in the former cases, but prevents the enforcement of the trust in the latter cases.

6.7 Where a man transfers property to his wife or children, or purchases property in their name, then equity assumes that he has an intention to make a gift: there is a presumption of advancement. In order to displace this presumption, the husband or father will need to lead evidence that he intended to retain the beneficial interest and not make a gift. If this evidence discloses the fraudulent purpose of the trust, then he will not be able to rely on it. He will not be able to enforce the trust and his claim will fail.

---

[3] *Tinsley v Milligan* [1994] 1 AC 340.

[4] It does not matter which party raises the illegality in the pleadings, or indeed, whether it is raised by the court itself. The important question is whether the claimant has to plead or rely on it in order to prove his or her case: *Silverwood v Silverwood* (1997) 74 P & CR 453.

[5] See Part 5.

[6] *Tinsley v Milligan* [1994] 1 AC 340, 371.

6.8 However, if the parties are in any other relationship and the facts of the case give rise to a presumption of resulting trust, the beneficiary needs simply to rely on that presumption in order to prove his or her interest. There is no need for the beneficiary to lead any evidence in relation to the illegality, and, therefore, it can be ignored.

6.9 The presumptions of resulting trust and advancement which were developed by the courts of equity in order to guide them through the evidence are thus given a new and crucial significance. Prior to *Tinsley v Milligan* they were usually no more than initial starting points, which could be overturned by any relevant evidence of the parties' actual intent. After *Tinsley*, in a case involving an element of illegality, the presumption will determine the substantive outcome.

6.10 The application of the reliance principle to resulting trusts is perhaps best illustrated by looking at the facts of *Tinsley v Milligan*[7] and the cases which have followed it. In *Tinsley*, the parties purchased a home together, both contributing to its purchase price, and intending to share the beneficial ownership. However, the house was conveyed into the sole name of Miss Tinsley. This helped Miss Milligan to claim social security benefits on the fraudulent basis that she did not own her own home. The parties subsequently quarrelled, and Miss Tinsley moved out. She brought a claim for possession, based on her legal title. Miss Milligan counterclaimed for an order for the sale of the house and a declaration that it was held by Miss Tinsley in trust for both of them in equal shares. There was no dispute that, illegality apart, Miss Milligan's contribution to the purchase price would have led to a presumption of resulting trust in her favour. However, Miss Tinsley argued that because of the fraudulent scheme to defraud the Department of Social Security, Miss Milligan could not establish any interest in the house. Both parties had benefited from the fraudulent claims, and Miss Milligan had already admitted the fraud to the relevant Department.

---

[7] [1994] 1 AC 340. For comments on the case, see R Buckley, "Social Security Fraud as Illegality" (1994) 110 *Law Quarterly Review* 3; M Halliwell, "Equitable Proprietary Claims and Dishonest Claimants: A Resolution?" [1994] *The Conveyancer and Property Lawyer* 62; H Stowe, "The 'Unruly Horse' has Bolted: *Tinsley v Milligan*" (1994) 57 *Modern Law Review* 440; R Thornton, "Illegality, Implied Trusts and the Presumption of Advancement" [1993] *Cambridge Law Journal* 394.

6.11 A bare majority of the House of Lords upheld Miss Milligan's claim by applying the reliance principle.[8] Their Lordships reasoned that in order to establish her claim, Miss Milligan merely had to prove her contribution to the purchase price of the house. A presumption of resulting trust then arose in her favour. She had no need to rely on her illegality in any way. The House noted, however, that the outcome of the application of the reliance principle would have been very different if a presumption of advancement had arisen between the parties. The claimant would then have had to lead evidence sufficient to rebut the presumption of gift. In doing so, the claimant would normally have to plead, and give evidence of, the underlying illegal purpose of the arrangement.[9] This is not permitted, and the claim would fail.[10]

6.12 Lord Browne-Wilkinson was at pains to point out, however, that the effect of the illegality is not to prevent the proprietary interest from arising in equity or to produce a forfeiture of the right. Rather its effect is to render the equitable interest unenforceable in certain circumstances. Or, as he explained: "The effect of illegality is not substantive but procedural".[11] We look at this point further at paragraph 6.62 below, when we consider what the consequences of a trust being unenforceable by the beneficiary may be.

6.13 The principle laid down by *Tinsley v Milligan* has been frequently applied in subsequent cases.[12] For example, in *Silverwood v Silverwood*[13] an elderly grandmother was persuaded by one of her sons to transfer most of her savings into two accounts in the name of his children, the defendants. She subsequently applied to the Department of Social Security for income support without disclosing the two bank accounts. After her death, one of her other children, in his capacity as executor, claimed that the accounts were held for the estate on a resulting trust. Before the Court of Appeal, the grandchildren did not dispute that a resulting trust arose, but argued that the estate could not enforce it because it had led evidence of the benefits fraud in support of its case. Applying the reliance principle, the Court of Appeal found for the estate. In order to establish its equitable title, the estate had no need to prove why the money was transferred to the grandchildren. The illegality did not, therefore, form a necessary part of its case.

---

[8] The minority would have allowed Miss Tinsley's claim to possession of the home based on her legal title. Lord Goff (with whom Lord Keith agreed) was of the view that equity would not assist a person who transferred property to another for an illegal purpose. Lord Goff explained that this rule was founded on the "clean hands" maxim: the court will not assist a person seeking the aid of equity unless he or she comes to court with clean hands.

[9] [1994] 1 AC 340, 372.

[10] [1994] 1 AC 340, 375.

[11] [1994] 1 AC 340, 374.

[12] See, for example, *Anzal v Ellahi* 1999 WL 819140 (discussed at para 4.33 above); *MacDonald v Myerson* [2001] EWCA Civ 66, (2001) EGCS 15 (discussed at para 6.79 below); *Mortgage Express v McDonnell* [2001] EWCA Civ 887, (2001) 82 P & CR DG21 (discussed at para 6.17 below); *Candy v Murphy* [2002] WL 1039535; *Poojary v Kotecha* [2002] 2 P & CR DG15; *Slater v Simm* [2007] EWHC 951, [2007] WTLR 1043; *Knowlden v Tehrani* [2008] EWHC 54 (Ch) 2008 WL 168844; *Barrett v Barrett* [2008] EWHC 1061 (Ch) 2008 WL 2148139.

[13] (1997) 74 P & CR 453.

6.14   In *Lowson v Coombes*[14] the claimant and his mistress, the defendant, purchased a flat together. The flat was conveyed solely into the defendant's name in order to avoid any potential claim by the claimant's wife in future divorce proceedings. The flat was sold and a series of other homes bought and then sold in its place, each time legal title to the property being conveyed into the defendant's name only. After the relationship ended, the claimant applied for a declaration that the defendant held the property on trust for both of them and for an order for sale. His claim succeeded. Because the presumption of advancement did not apply between the parties, the claimant could establish a resulting trust in his favour simply by reason of his contribution to the purchase price. He had no need to rely on his illegal purpose to prove his interest.

6.15   In non-binding commentary in *SMQ v RFQ and MJQ*[15] Mrs Justice Black considered a case where the presumption of advancement did apply and the reliance principle would have prevented the beneficiary from enforcing the trust, although the case was in fact decided on the alternative claims based on proprietary estoppel and constructive trust. A father had transferred the legal title to his house into the joint names of his two sons. However the family intended that the sons should hold the property on trust for their father under a scheme designed to cheat the Inland Revenue of inheritance tax payable on the father's death. The intention was to conceal the true beneficial ownership so that it would appear to the Inland Revenue that the home had left his estate.

6.16   Mrs Justice Black said that there was a presumption that the father had given the property to his sons as an absolute gift. He could only rebut that presumption and prove a trust in his favour by leading evidence of their agreement to hold the property on trust for him. However, because this was an intrinsic part of their scheme for illegally evading tax, he was not allowed to rely on it.

---

[14]   [1999] Ch 373. For comments on the case see I Cotterill, "Property and Impropriety – The Tinsley v Milligan Problem Again" [1999] *Lloyd's Maritime and Commercial Law Quarterly* 465; and M P Thompson, "Illegal Transactions" [1999] *The Conveyancer and Property Lawyer* 242.

[15]   [2008] EWHC 1874 (Fam).

(2) Other circumstances in which the reliance principle might be applied to determine whether a beneficiary may enforce a resulting trust: illegally sourced trust property

6.17 The cases that we have so far considered in relation to the application of the reliance principle have all involved resulting trusts that had been created under arrangements intended to hide the real beneficial ownership of the trust property in order to commit some form of fraud. However, the reliance principle has been used in other cases where the illegality impinges on the resulting trust in some different way. One such example is *Mortgage Express v MacDonnell*.[16] The court had to consider whether a couple who had contributed to the purchase price of a house bought in the name of their brother-in-law could enforce the resulting trust which arose in their favour when the funds which they had used for the purchase resulted from a mortgage fraud. The Court of Appeal declared that the trust was enforceable. Although this case differed from *Tinsley v Milligan* - in that it involved an illegal source of funds rather than an illegal purpose – the reliance principle still applied. The couple had no need to lead evidence of the source of their funds in order to establish their claim.

2. The withdrawal exception

6.18 There is one general exception to the application of the reliance principle. This is the "withdrawal exception".[17] A claimant is allowed to rely on his or her illegality in order to establish an equitable interest arising under an illegal transaction, provided that the claimant is seeking to withdraw from the transaction before the illegal purpose has been wholly or partly accomplished. Its operation as a general exception was confirmed by the Court of Appeal in *Tribe v Tribe*.[18]

6.19 In *Tribe v Tribe* the claimant, the major shareholder in a retail company, was himself the tenant of the premises which the company occupied. As tenant, he anticipated that he would shortly be obliged to pay for significant repairs to the properties. He believed that he would have to sell his shares in order to meet the obligation. To avoid this consequence, the claimant transferred his shareholding to his son, the defendant, on the understanding that it would be held on trust for him pending the settlement of any dilapidations claim and that it would be returned to him once the claim was settled. The purpose of the arrangement was to deceive the claimant's creditors and protect his assets. In the event, the landlords made no demands for payment and the need to deceive creditors never arose. The father reclaimed the shares, but the son refused to return them. The father brought proceedings for a declaration that he was the beneficial owner of the shares and an order for delivery of them.

---

[16] [2001] EWCA Civ 887, (2001) 82 P & CR DG21.

[17] See paras 4.45 to 4.52 above.

[18] [1996] Ch 107. For criticism of the case see P Pettit, "Illegality and repentance" (1996) 10 *Trust Law International* 50; F D Rose, "Gratuitous Transfers and Illegal Purposes" (1996) 112 *Law Quarterly Review* 386; G Virgo, "Withdrawal from Illegal Transactions – A Matter for Consideration" [1996] *Cambridge Law Journal* 23. See also, *Painter v Hutchison* [2007] EWHC 758 (Ch), [2008] BPIR 170.

6.20 The Court of Appeal accepted the son's argument that a presumption of advancement arose between the parties. Under the reliance principle, the father would not be able to rebut that presumption where doing so would necessarily involve disclosing the illegality. However, the Court held that by way of an exception to this general rule, the claimant would be entitled to lead evidence of his illegality to rebut the presumption of advancement where the claimant was able to show that the illegal purpose had not been carried into effect. The father's claim therefore succeeded.

6.21 The precise limits of this "withdrawal exception" are not clear. It seems that genuine repentance of the illegality is not needed, but voluntary withdrawal is required. A claimant who is forced to withdraw because the illegal plan is discovered may not take advantage of the exception; but it is sufficient if the claimant voluntarily withdraws because the illegal transaction has ceased to be needed.[19]

6.22 How far a claimant who has participated in a transaction with an illegal purpose can go before he or she will be deprived of the opportunity to use the withdrawal exception was discussed in non-binding commentary in *SMQ v RFQ and MJQ*.[20] Mrs Justice Black considered whether the transferor would have been able to take advantage of the withdrawal exception in that case – an issue which would have been decisive had the court not allowed the claimant's alternative claims based on proprietary estoppel and constructive trust. As we have seen,[21] a father and his two sons entered into an arrangement whereby he transferred property to his sons on condition that he should retain control and ownership of it until he died. He signed documents to show to the Inland Revenue, if necessary, that the assets had been transferred to them. The intention of the arrangement was to cheat the Inland Revenue of inheritance tax on the father's death. The father continued to live in the property and the parties entered into a tenancy agreement in order to give the false impression that he was no longer the beneficial owner of it. The father paid rent into a building society account in the name of his sons and this rent was treated as theirs for tax purposes, although between themselves the parties regarded it as belonging to the father.

6.23 Because of the operation of the reliance principle, the father was unable to rely on the fraudulent scheme in order to rebut the legal presumption of advancement that arose in his sons' favour in respect of his transfer of the property. Instead the father argued that the withdrawal exception applied because the illegal purpose had not yet been carried into effect as inheritance tax would only have been due on his death. However, Mrs Justice Black said that the illegal purpose should be defined more broadly – "to deceive the Revenue" – and that it could be seen that constructive steps had already been taken towards this which had gone beyond the mere creation of authentic looking documents kept within the family and moved into the realms of actually presenting a false picture to the Inland Revenue. The father had therefore partly carried the illegal purpose into effect and would no longer be able to rely on the withdrawal exception.

---

[19] [1996] Ch 107, 135 by Millett LJ.

[20] [2008] EWHC 1874 (Fam).

[21] See para 6.15 above.

6.24   The combination of the reliance principle and the withdrawal exception means that, where a claimant transfers property into the name of the defendant for fraudulent purposes, intending to retain the true beneficial ownership, the claimant should be able to enforce a resulting trust in his or her favour before any third party has actually been deceived. This might be because the claimant can rely on a presumption of resulting trust in his or her favour and the defendant cannot rebut that presumption without relying on evidence of the fraudulent purpose of the transfer; or because, having withdrawn in time, the claimant is permitted to rely on evidence of the fraudulent purpose in order to rebut the presumption of advancement and so establish affirmatively the facts which give rise to the resulting trust. However, once a third party has been deceived, whether or not the claimant will be able to do so depends on the crucial relationship between the claimant and the defendant. If it is such as to give rise to a presumption of advancement, then it is likely that the claimant's claim will fail. The claimant is not permitted to lead evidence of the fraudulent purpose, and is therefore unable to rebut the presumption that a gift was intended. On the other hand, where no such relationship exists, the claimant will be able to rely on the presumption of a resulting trust and therefore should succeed.

3. Uncertainties relating to the application of the reliance principle to resulting trusts

6.25   As well as the uncertainties relating to the precise limits of the withdrawal exception, there are several other areas where the application of the reliance principle remains unclear. Because of its arbitrary nature, there is a strong temptation for courts to limit the application of the reliance principle by means of exceptions and fine distinctions. Apart from the withdrawal exception, there are indications in the case law of at least three other ways in which this might be achieved: first, by looking at the policy of any relevant legislation that has been infringed; secondly, by looking at any subsequent inconsistent conduct of the claimant; and thirdly, by looking at the nature of the trust property. The position is also complicated in the case of a voluntary conveyance of land, as opposed to personal property, where it is arguable that section 60(3) of the Law of Property Act 1925 has abolished the presumption of resulting trust that would usually apply. We look at all these points in detail below.

(1) The policy of the legislation that has been infringed

6.26   The first possible exception to the application of the reliance principle applies where the resulting trust is tainted with illegality because its formation or purpose has infringed legislation which provides, expressly or impliedly, what the response to such illegality should be. This is most clearly illustrated by the Australian case, *Nelson v Nelson*.[22] The High Court of Australia rejected the reliance principle in favour of an approach which looked at the policy of the relevant statutory provisions. A resulting trust would only be unenforceable if the statute, or its policy, clearly so required. A mother had purchased a house in the name of her two children. The arrangement was not intended to benefit the children, but instead to enable the mother to purchase another house with the benefit of a government subsidy which the relevant legislation declared was only available to those who did not already own homes. In order to obtain the subsidy the mother falsely declared that she did not own an interest in any other property. On the sale of the first house, the mother sought a declaration that she, rather than the children, had a beneficial interest in the proceeds of sale. The daughter counterclaimed that she beneficially owned a half share in the proceeds.

6.27   The High Court of Australia held that a presumption of advancement arose between the mother and daughter.[23] However a majority of the High Court rejected the application of the reliance principle which would have prevented the mother's claim.[24] Instead it was decided that the trust would only be unenforceable where the terms or policy of the legislation that had been infringed required this result. In this case, the Court noted that the relevant legislation provided that if the applicant had falsely claimed the subsidy, then that subsidy could be cancelled and any benefit recovered. There were also sanctions under the criminal law for fraudulent behaviour. The Court therefore held that, so long as the mother accounted for the benefit she received by fraudulently obtaining the State subsidy, the policy of the relevant legislation did not require such a drastic response as the mother's interest being unenforceable.[25]

---

[22]   (1995) 184 CLR 538. See P Creighton, "The Recovery of Property Transferred for Illegal Purposes" (1997) 60 *Modern Law Review* 102.

[23]   This is in contrast to the position in English law where it has been held that the presumption of advancement does not apply where a mother gives property to her children: *Sekhon v Alissa* [1989] 2 FLR 94. Nourse LJ, however, assumes that a presumption of advancement would apply from mother to son in *Silverwood v Silverwood* (1997) 74 P & CR 453, 458.

[24]   Dawson J used the reliance principle to decide the case. However he gave such a restrictive meaning to "reliance" that it is hard to see how it could ever prevent a transferor from enforcing a resulting trust in his or her favour. He said that a transferor could rely on evidence of the illegal purpose to show that he or she did not intend to make a gift to the transferee. In such cases what the transferor was relying on was his or her lack of donative intent, rather than any illegality. This approach would not seem to be consistent with that adopted by the House of Lords in *Tinsley v Milligan*: see the comments of Mance LJ in *Collier v Collier* [2002] EWCA 1095, [2002] BPIR 1057 at [103].

[25]   See also, *Damberg v Damberg* [2001] NSWCA 87.

6.28   Early English case law suggests that a similar approach might be adopted here, but since the cases predate the House of Lords' decision in *Tinsley v Milligan*, it is not clear to what extent they survive that decision. In *Curtis v Perry*[26] two ships were purchased with partnership funds, but registered in the sole name of one partner, Nantes. When the other partner, Chiswell, a Member of Parliament, discovered this, the ships were shown as partnership property in the partnership books. However, with Chiswell's agreement, the ships remained registered in the sole name of Nantes. This arrangement was maintained in order to hide Chiswell's interest and so evade a statutory prohibition against ships being used for government contracts if owned by a Member of Parliament. In a dispute between the partnership creditors and Nantes' separate creditors as to the ownership of the ships, Lord Eldon found in favour of the latter.

6.29   In a subsequent case, *ex parte Yallop*,[27] Lord Eldon explained that his decision in *Curtis v Perry* was based on two lines of reasoning. First, Chiswell would have to rely on his own fraud in order to prove his interest in the ships. Secondly, that it was contrary to the policy of the registration statute for him to assert ownership in the ships when he was not the registered owner. In *ex parte Yallop* itself, two partners purchased a ship using partnership funds, but registered it, for reasons that are not clear, only in the name of one. The registration was taken to be conclusive otherwise "the whole policy of these Acts may be defeated".[28]

(2) Subsequent actions of the transferor which are inconsistent with the resulting trust

6.30   In *Tribe v Tribe*[29] Lord Millett (then a judge of the Court of Appeal) raised a second possible refinement to the application of the reliance principle. He suggested that a transferor who could rely on a presumption of resulting trust would not invariably succeed. This is because the transferee might be able to rebut the presumption of resulting trust by leading evidence of the transferor's subsequent conduct to show that it was inconsistent with his or her retention of an equitable interest. If correct, such an approach would produce a sharp distinction between schemes where the illegal purpose had been acted on, and those where it had not. In the former case, the courts would not recognise the resulting trust (whichever presumption applies) because of the transferor's subsequent inconsistent behaviour. In the latter case, the courts would enforce the resulting trust (whichever presumption applies) under the withdrawal exception.

---

[26]   (1802) 6 Ves 739; 31 ER 1285.

[27]   (1808) 15 Ves 60, 33 ER 677.

[28]   (1808) 15 Ves 60, 66; 33 ER 677, 680.

[29]   [1996] Ch 107, 128-129.

6.31   The problem with this suggestion is that it is hard to see how it can be reconciled with the decision in *Tinsley v Milligan*[30] itself. There was no doubt that Miss Milligan had acted inconsistently with her retention of an equitable interest when she had fraudulently claimed benefits. Yet the resulting trust was enforced in her favour and there was no suggestion in their Lordships' speeches that Miss Tinsley could have led evidence of Miss Milligan's behaviour in order to rebut that presumption.

(3) Residual category dealing with cases where it would be unlawful for the claimant to possess the trust property or, possibly, where the illegality is very serious

6.32   Clearly no court will enforce a trust or make an order for the possession of property that it would be unlawful for the claimant to hold. We have already explained that this is an exception to the reliance principle when we considered its application in relation to the transfer of legal interests.[31]

6.33   There is also some suggestion in the case law that recovery would not be allowed under the reliance principle if the illegality is very serious.[32] However, the authority is very slight and the cases date back many years. Certainly in *Tinsley v Milligan*, Lord Goff seemed to be of the view that there was no exception to the reliance principle based on seriousness. He expressed concern about how the reliance principle would operate in cases where the illegality was serious. He gave the example of a case in which a group of terrorists or armed robbers secure a base for their criminal activities by buying a house in the name of a third party not directly implicated in those activities. He suggested that it would be difficult to distinguish between degrees of iniquity to prevent such claimants succeeding under the reliance principle.[33]

(4) Voluntary conveyances of land: section 60(3) of the Law of Property Act 1925

6.34   A further uncertainty arises in relation to voluntary conveyances of land. The claimant, instead of contributing to the purchase price of land, may transfer land directly into the name of the defendant, with the intention that it should be held in trust for him or herself. In the normal course of events, unless the claimant is the husband or father of the defendant, such a voluntary transfer would give rise to a resulting trust. Any issues of illegality would be effectively ignored under the reliance principle. However, section 60(3) of the Law of Property Act 1925 states that:

---

[30]   [1994] 1 AC 340.

[31]   See para 5.12 above.

[32]   See, for example, the suggestion in *Tappenden v Randall* (1801) 2 B&P 467, 471; 126 ER 1388, 1390 that the withdrawal exception does not apply if the transaction is "of a nature too grossly immoral for the Court to enter into any discussion of it". In *Bowmakers Ltd v Barnet Instruments Ltd* [1945] KB 65, 72 Du Parcq LJ said that there would be exceptions to the reliance principle, although he thought it unwise to speculate on what they might be.

[33]   [1994] 1 AC 340, 362.

In a voluntary conveyance a resulting trust for the grantor shall not be implied merely by reason that the property[34] is not expressed to be conveyed for the use or benefit of the grantee.

6.35   On a literal interpretation, this section would appear to abolish the presumption of resulting trust in relation to voluntary conveyances of land. A claimant who had conveyed land into the name of the defendant but intending to retain the beneficial interest for fraudulent purposes would therefore need to lead evidence of the trust. However, under the reliance principle the claimant could not do so if this were to involve relying on the illegal purpose. An alternative interpretation of the section, however, is that it was merely intended to overcome a previous technicality of the law. By virtue of the Statute of Uses, unless a voluntary conveyance of land provided that the gift was "unto and to the use of the grantee", a resulting trust automatically came into existence which the Statute of Uses executed so that the legal estate reverted to the grantor. However, the Statute of Uses was repealed by the Law of Property Act 1925. It has therefore been argued that the intention of section 60(3) was to make such a statement unnecessary, without doing anything to affect the presumption.

6.36   The literal interpretation was preferred by the High Court in its decision in *Lohia v Lohia*,[35] a case which did not involve any element of illegality. However, when the case reached the Court of Appeal,[36] Lord Justice Mummery and Sir Christopher Slade expressly preferred to leave the matter undecided since it was not necessary for them to reach a conclusion to decide the case. This issue therefore remains unresolved.

EXPRESS TRUSTS: THE PRESENT LAW

1. Introduction

6.37   So far, we have only considered how the doctrine of illegality applies to a resulting trust, since it is in this context that the majority of the case law has arisen. However, it is clear that illegality may also affect the operation of an express trust.

---

[34] In this section, "property" means land only: section 205(1)(ii) of the Law of Property Act 1925.

[35] [2001] WTLR 101. This case was cited with approval in *Ali v Khan* [2002] EWCA Civ 974, [2002] 30 EGCS 131.

[36] [2001] EWCA Civ 1691, 2001 WL 1890347.

6.38   Illegality may impinge on an express trust in a variety of ways. For example, a condition in an express trust may require or incite a beneficiary to do an unlawful act. Such a condition is void, and there is a fairly well established, although complex, set of rules which prescribe the effect, if any, this has on the beneficial interest.[37] Where several conditions are attached to one gift, the valid conditions may be severed from the invalid ones.[38] In practice, the strong tendency has been for the courts to strike out the illegal condition without upsetting the beneficial ownership, and there have been few cases where the interest has failed as a result. Similarly, a discretionary trust for a variety of objects, some legal and some illegal, is valid in respect of the legal objects, but the trustees cannot validly exercise their discretionary selection in favour of the illegal objects.[39]

6.39   In other cases the whole purpose of the trust is illegal and therefore held to be void. Most of the examples given in text books are not of trusts involving behaviour that is unlawful, but rather behaviour that is contrary to public policy. They include trusts which encourage the separation of spouses; or which purport to alter the ordinary rules for the devolution of property (for example, on bankruptcy). Where the express trust fails completely and the trust property is not otherwise disposed of, then under general trust rules, the trust property will usually[40] result back to the settlor.

6.40   However, it is now clear that in at least some cases an express trust established for an illegal purpose is *not* invalid. This is the position where the purpose of the trust is the fraudulent concealment of the beneficial ownership of the trust property. However, although valid, the enforcement of such a trust is governed by the reliance principle and the withdrawal exception. The beneficiary may therefore not be able to protect his or her interest. We look at these fraudulent concealment cases first, before going on to consider whether there are other express trusts to which the reliance principle might apply.

---

[37]   Broadly speaking, where the condition is a "condition subsequent", it may simply be struck out and the remainder of the trust enforced as normal. However, where the condition is a "condition precedent", the whole interest will fail in the case of a trust over land. Where the trust property consists of personal property, even in the case of a condition precedent, the interest will only fail if the condition is illegal because it involves *malum in se* (something wrong in itself). In any case, the interest will fail if performance of the condition was the sole motive for a bequest: *Re Wolffe* [1953] 1 WLR 1211. A determinable interest fails altogether if the determining event is illegal: *Re Moore* (1888) 39 Ch D 116.

[38]   *Re Hepplewhite Will Trusts, The Times* 21 January 1977.

[39]   *Re Piercy* [1898] 1 Ch 565.

[40]   Special rules apply where the trust that fails was a charitable trust.

2. Express trusts created for a fraudulent purpose – the reliance principle and withdrawal exception

6.41 So far we have only considered the operation of the reliance principle and withdrawal exception in the context of a resulting trust. However, following the Court of Appeal's decision in *Collier v Collier*,[41] it is clear that the same principles will be used to determine whether the claimant can establish an interest under an express trust[42] which has been created in order to conceal the beneficial ownership for fraudulent purposes. The facts of the case were complex and hard to discern, the judge concluding that both parties had lied to the court. However, the case provides a good example of the difficulties of applying the reliance principle. The claimant father, in financial difficulties, wanted to transfer two of his business properties to his daughter, the defendant, in an attempt to save them from his creditors and, in the event of his death, to hide them from the Inland Revenue in order to reduce his estate's inheritance tax liability. He granted his daughter a lease of the properties for a rent which was neither paid nor ever intended to be paid. The leases included an option for the daughter to purchase the freehold of the properties for a sum that was a considerable undervalue. The daughter registered the options. The father subsequently mortgaged the properties without informing the mortgagees of the options. The daughter exercised the options largely using money provided by the father, with the object of defrauding the mortgagees of their security. When her relationship with her father broke down, she sought to evict him from the premises.

6.42 Because of the ostensible requirement for the payment of rent and the consideration for the option, two members of the Court of Appeal[43] took the view that the grant of the leases had not been by way of gift. The presumptions of resulting trust and advancement were therefore not relevant. However, even if they had applied on the facts, the presumption of advancement arose between the parties, and, because of the illegal intention, could not have been rebutted by the father.

---

[41] [2002] EWCA Civ 1095, [2002] BPIR 1057.

[42] The judgments of the Court of Appeal refer to the trust alleged in this case as an "express trust": see Aldous LJ at [19] and Chadwick LJ at [65]. However, given that there was no writing evidencing the trust as required by section 53(1)(b) of the Law of Property Act 1925 the trust could only be enforceable under the equitable principle which prevents a statute being used as an instrument of fraud. There is some debate about whether such a trust should best be regarded as an express trust (the view preferred in *Rochefoucauld v Bousted* [1897] 1 Ch 196) or a constructive trust (the view preferred in *Paragon Finance plc v Thakerar* [1999] 1 All ER 400, 409). We have included the case in our section on express trusts since this was the terminology adopted by the Court of Appeal. For the purposes of examining the illegality doctrine, since the evidence required to establish the trust would be the same, it would not appear to make any difference whether it is treated as an express or constructive trust.

[43] Aldous and Chadwick LJJ. By contrast, Mance LJ was of the view that, since the leases were shams in the sense that neither party intended any rent to be payable under them, the presumption of advancement did apply. The father would not be able to rebut it because to do so would involve him leading evidence of his unlawful purpose.

6.43   Instead, therefore, the father argued that there was an express trust in his favour. He produced written documentation purporting to evidence this trust, but the Court of Appeal rejected it as either false or written on the daughter's behalf without her authority. In order to establish the express trust, therefore, the father needed to show that there was an agreement between himself and his daughter that she should hold the premises on trust for him. However, the reliance principle meant that he could not do this by relying on his illegality. The Court of Appeal unanimously rejected his claim, although each judge adopted a slightly different approach to the application of the reliance principle. All agreed that the withdrawal exception did not apply, because the fraudulent scheme had succeeded to the extent that the mortgagees had lost the protection of their security.[44]

6.44   Lord Justice Chadwick held that the father had not proved that there was any agreement that the interests should be held on trust; and even if there had been an agreement, its terms were impossible to identify with sufficient certainty to meet the requirements necessary for the creation of a trust. Lord Justice Aldous held that there had been an agreement to hold on trust, but it was a term of that trust that the leases should only be used to deceive creditors and the Inland Revenue. To recover the property, the father needed to rely on that agreement. Since the agreement included illegal terms, this would involve the father relying on illegality and he would not be permitted to do so. On the assumption that the presumption of advancement did not apply, Lord Mance (then a judge of the Court of Appeal) concurred that there was an agreement to hold on trust, but thought that dishonest behaviour was not necessarily a term of the trust. However, he also rejected the father's claim. The daughter's ostensible leasehold and freehold interests were "objective legal facts" which it was incumbent on the father challenging them to displace. To displace the legal position arising from these express interests, the father would have to rely on the proof of the purpose of their agreement. Under the reliance principle, this would not be allowed. Lord Mance said:

> To rebut the appearance of outright acquisition, the father had to explain the true transaction. This involved showing that it was agreed that the daughter was never to bear any burden under the leases and was to hold them and any freehold interest acquired on trust for her father. Either because it was necessary in order to know the full terms of the agreement, or simply because it was necessary evidently, the father could not do this, without disclosing the purpose, for which the trust was agreed.[45]

---

[44]   Aldous LJ also suggested that the illegal purpose of defrauding the Inland Revenue had been carried into effect. The father had had the benefit of the illegal purpose for a number of years, namely to defraud the Inland Revenue if he died: [2002] EWCA Civ 1095, [2002] BPIR 1057 at [46].

[45]   [2002] EWCA Civ 1095, [2002] BPIR 1057 at [98].

6.45   Lord Mance pointed out that if the father had been able to produce a simple express trust, duly recorded in writing, his claim would have succeeded. The properly recorded trust would have been an "objectively provable and apparently neutral fact"[46] on which he could rely (analogous to the contribution of money in a resulting trust case), and there would have been no need for him to rely on any illegality. This approach is consistent with comments made by Lord Millett in *Tribe v Tribe*[47] where he suggested that a transferor would be able to recover property transferred for an illegal purpose where there was an express declaration of trust in his or her favour.

6.46   Although neither father nor daughter was particularly meritorious in *Collier*, it is worth noting that the result of the decision seems to be, at least temporarily,[48] to reward the daughter's duplicitous behaviour by allowing her to keep the properties. Also, it is arguable that the decision would have been different if the claimant had been in almost any other relationship with the defendant (for example, mother, brother, grandparent or cohabitant). Then he might have argued that a resulting trust arose in his favour based on his contribution to the consideration payable under the options. The presumption of advancement would not have applied. This distinction is difficult to justify.

3. Other circumstances in which the reliance principle might be applied to determine whether a beneficiary may enforce an express trust?

(a) Express trusts created as part of a scheme to defraud the settlor

6.47   The reliance principle has been used to determine the enforceability of express trusts in a wider context than that outlined above. In *Halley v The Law Society*[49] the majority of the Court of Appeal used the reliance principle to deny the claimant an interest in an express trust that had been set up pursuant to a scheme to defraud the settlor. The claimant described himself as a "corporate funding broker", but was found by the judge to be basically a fraudster. He persuaded clients to enter into funding agreements which he knew to be worthless to them, but on the signing of which the clients paid a large arrangement fee. The arrangement fee was paid into the account of a solicitor (who had been struck off the Roll of Solicitors and was now represented by the Law Society). He held it in an escrow account on an express trust the terms of which were set out in an escrow agreement. Basically, once certain conditions relating to the documentation were satisfied, the fee should be paid to a corporate broker, who instructed that a portion of it should be paid to the claimant. Until then, it was held for the client. The conditions having been met, the solicitor released the arrangement fee to the corporate broker by transferring it into his client account. The next day, in accordance with the broker's instructions, the solicitor made entries in his client account which showed a transfer of the arrangement fee to the credit of the claimant. It was this sum that the claimant sought from the Law Society.

---

[46]   [2002] EWCA Civ 1095, [2002] BPIR 1057 at [105].

[47]   [1996] Ch 107, 134.

[48]   We discuss the outcome of this case in more detail at para 6.61 below.

[49]   [2003] EWCA Civ 97, [2003] WTLR 845.

6.48 The Court of Appeal refused his claim. Lord Justice Mummery, with whom Baroness Hale (then a judge of the Court of Appeal) agreed, based his decision on the illegality. He distinguished the facts of *Tinsley v Milligan*,[50] but nevertheless adopted a reliance based approach. The claim to the beneficial interest was founded on the claimant's implication in a fraud. He would have to plead and rely on the escrow agreement in order to establish his entitlement. The purported disposition of the beneficial interest was therefore unenforceable by him.

(b) Express trusts created for an illegal consideration

6.49 It seems likely that the enforceability of express trusts created for an illegal consideration would also now be decided by use of the reliance principle. Where the trust has already been constituted, such a trust is valid, and, would now seem to be enforceable by the beneficiary unless he or she needed to rely on evidence of the illegality to support the claim. This appears from the interpretation given by the majority in the House of Lords in *Tinsley v Milligan* to the early case, *Ayerst v Jenkins*.[51] In this case, the personal representatives of the settlor argued that a trust in favour of his deceased wife's sister was invalid because it had been created for an illegal consideration (an illegal marriage between the settlor and sister). The application failed, apparently on the ground that the trust was irrevocably constituted and was a valid trust. In *Tinsley v Milligan*, Lord Jauncey cited this case to support the proposition that: "A completely executed transfer of property or an interest in property made in pursuance of an unlawful agreement is valid and the court will assist the transferee in the protection of his interest provided that he does not require to found on the unlawful agreement".[52] Lord Browne-Wilkinson said that the "whole case proceeded on the footing that the defendant, even if a party to the illegality, was entitled to enforce against the trustees her equitable rights as beneficiary under the express trusts against the trustees".[53]

---

[50] [1994] 1 AC 340.

[51] (1873) LR 16 Eq 275. Although this case was not followed in *Phillips v Probyn* [1899] 1 Ch 811, a case on very similar facts, it is suggested that the grounds for distinction are not supportable.

[52] [1994] 1 AC 340, 366.

[53] [1994] 1 AC 340, 373.

4. Uncertainties relating to the application of the reliance principle to express trusts

6.50 Following these cases, it is clear that the enforcement of an express trust tainted by some form of illegality will, at least in some circumstances, be governed by the reliance principle. However, many uncertainties remain as to how that principle will operate in this context. It seems that a duly recorded express trust, even if set up for a fraudulent purpose, will be enforceable. This is because the beneficiary need not lead evidence of the illegality to establish his or her claim. What would the position be if the trust included a recital clearly setting out its unlawful purpose? Could the court shut its eyes to that part of the document? The decision in *Halley v The Law Society*[54] shows that in some cases the court may be willing even to look behind the face of the documentation in order establish whether there is some fraudulent scheme.

6.51 Further, what would be the position in a case such as *Collier* where no documentation exists, but the parties have had several conversations regarding the ownership of the trust property? Say, in the first conversation the daughter agreed to hold the property on trust for her father. It was only in the second conversation that the father explained the fraudulent purpose of the scheme. By separating out the discussion in this way, could the father have relied only on the first conversation and his claim have succeeded? It seems nonsensical that the courts might decide the outcome of the case by looking at selective pieces of the relevant evidence. Yet this seems to be the effect of the operation of the reliance principle in the case of express trusts.

CONSTRUCTIVE TRUSTS: THE PRESENT LAW

1. Introduction

6.52 Constructive trusts may be found in a large variety of situations. Broadly speaking, they are trusts which are imposed by law, when it would be unconscionable for the legal owner of the property to claim full beneficial ownership of it.[55] In this section we are primarily concerned with the "common intention constructive trust". As the name suggests, this is a trust which is imposed in order to give effect to the shared intention of the parties. It is within this category of constructive trust that issues of illegality have troubled the courts, and would appear to be more likely to do so in the future.

---

[54] [2003] EWCA Civ 97, [2003] WTLR 845.

[55] See the comments of Millett LJ in *Paragon Finance v DB Thakerar* [1999] 1 All ER 400, 409.

6.53 Following the House of Lords' recent decision in *Stack v Dowden*[56] it is clear that the common intention constructive trust will in future play a greater role in the determination of property disputes concerning interests in the domestic home. In this case, the House of Lords held, by majority, that the property rights of a cohabiting couple in the home that they occupied together and which was registered in their joint names should not be determined by reference to the presumptions of resulting trust and advancement. Rather, the starting point should be that equity follows the law: where the home is held by joint legal owners, it is presumed that there is joint beneficial ownership. The onus is on the person seeking to show that the beneficial ownership is different from the legal ownership, and in what way. This can be achieved by establishing a common intention constructive trust, discerned from "the parties' shared intentions, actual, inferred or imputed, with respect to the property in the light of their whole course of conduct in relation to it".[57] Only where the "facts are very unusual" is the presumption likely to be overcome.

6.54 It is not yet clear exactly when the rule laid down in *Stack v Dowden* will apply. The case concerned a home which was jointly owned at law, whereas in most of the cases involving a trust set up for an illegal purpose, legal title to the trust property is held by one party only. Several cases decided since *Stack* have applied its constructive trust analysis in a sole legal ownership situation,[58] although there has not been a decision stating that a resulting trust analysis can no longer be used in this situation. *Stack* has been followed not only where the dispute is between cohabiting couples, but also to other familial relationships. For example, it was applied in relation to a dispute between a parent and a child over their respective interests in the family home.[59] It has not been followed where the disputed property was held for investment rather than as a home.[60] What is clear is that where the court adopts a constructive trust analysis rather than holding that there is a resulting trust, the effect of any illegality in the transaction may be far greater.

[56] [2007] UKHL 17, [2007] 2 AC 432.

[57] [2007] UKHL 17, [2007] 2 AC 432 at [60].

[58] For example, *Abbott v Abbott* [2007] UKPC 53; *Williamson v Sheikh* [2008] EWCA Civ 990; and *Frost v Clarke* [2008] EWHC 742 (Ch). There has been much academic commentary on the possible ramifications of the decision. For example, see T Etherton, "Constructive trusts: a new model for equity and unjust enrichment" [2008] *Cambridge Law Journal* 265; S Gardner, "Family Property Today" [2008] *Law Quarterly Review* 422; N Piska, "Intention, Fairness and the Presumption of Resulting Trust after *Stack v Dowden*" [2008] *Modern Law Review* 120; M Pawlowski, "Beneficial Entitlement – no longer doing justice?" [2007] *Conveyancer and Property Lawyer* 354; and M Dixon, "The never-ending story – co-ownership after *Stack v Dowden*" [2007] *Conveyancer and Property Lawyer* 456.

[59] *Adekunle v Ritchie* [2007] BPIR 1177 and *Morris v Morris* [2008] EWCA Civ 257, 2008 WL 371068.

[60] *Laskar v Laskar* [2008] EWCA Civ 347, [2008] 2 P&CR 14.

2. Common intention constructive trusts – the reliance principle and withdrawal exception

6.55 There was no issue of illegality involved in *Stack v Dowden*[61] itself. What would be the outcome if there were an issue of illegality in such a case? Where the legal title is held jointly, a claimant might be able to establish that he or she was a joint beneficial owner simply by relying on the presumption that equity follows the law and without needing to plead any illegality. However, if the claimant wished to claim more than a half share of the beneficial interest, it is clear from *Stack* that he or she will succeed only in very unusual circumstances. In other words the claimant has an uphill struggle to displace the presumption of beneficial joint tenancy; and in doing so he or she must use the reasoning appropriate to a constructive trust. The court will look at the parties' whole course of conduct in relation to the property and not simply at financial contributions towards its purchase. The challenge would be for the claimant to produce the necessary "very unusual facts" without relying on an illegal purpose. Where the legal title is held by one party only, and if a resulting trust analysis can no longer be used (following *Stack*),[62] the claimant will have to rebut the presumption that equitable title follows the legal title without relying on any illegality.

6.56 However, the position is made more complicated by the suggestion in one Court of Appeal decision that a claimant who was the joint legal owner of a house might not be able to rely on any presumption of joint beneficial ownership where there was an issue of illegality involved. In *Gibson v Revenue & Customs Prosecution Office*[63] the claimant had acquired joint legal title to a home with her husband. Subsequently they agreed to use the proceeds of crime to pay the mortgage instalments. The defendant, seeking a confiscation order against the home, conceded that the claimant had acquired a joint beneficial interest on acquisition. Lady Justice Arden and Lord Justice Wall both queried what the position would have been had the husband and wife at the outset entered into an agreement to purchase the home jointly and use the proceeds of crime to pay off the mortgage, and no concession regarding ownership had been made. Lady Justice Arden pointed out that such an agreement would have been unenforceable and said that it was "an interesting question" whether the wife could have contended that a common intention to own the property should be inferred in accordance with *Stack* because of the joint legal ownership. Lord Justice Wall said that he preferred to reserve judgment on this point.[64]

6.57 If the comments made by Lady Justice Arden were subsequently followed, it is not clear what would be the claimant's position in such a case. Would she then be free to argue for a resulting trust? Would she be able to establish a constructive trust without the need to establish "very unusual facts" (as required following *Stack*) if she sought more than a half share? These are questions that we cannot at present resolve.

---

[61] [2007] UKHL 17, [2007] 2 AC 432

[62] See para 6.54 above.

[63] [2008] EWCA Civ 645.

[64] [2008] EWCA Civ 645 at [24] and [32] respectively.

6.58 There are some passages in Lord Browne-Wilkinson's opinion in *Tinsley v Milligan*[65] which suggest that the result in that case would have been the same had Miss Milligan based her claim on a common intention constructive trust, rather than a presumed resulting trust. That is, he suggested that Miss Milligan could have relied on her agreement with Miss Tinsley to share beneficial ownership without needing to rely on the illegal purpose of the arrangement. For example, he stated that Miss Milligan established the trust "by showing that she had contributed to the purchase price of the house and that there was a common understanding between her and Miss Tinsley that they owned the house equally".[66]

6.59 However, as we have seen, the Court of Appeal's decision in *Collier v Collier*[67] indicates that it would be difficult to rely on any agreement that was inextricably linked to an illegal intention. Lord Mance (then a judge of the Court of Appeal), in particular, stressed that Lord Browne-Wilkinson's remarks were not vital to the decision, and that later courts had regarded *Tinsley v Milligan* as turning on the recognition of a resulting trust. Lord Mance thought that to allow the parties to rely on a common but illegal intention would be inconsistent with the general tenor of the majority speeches.[68]

6.60 This latter interpretation of the application of the reliance principle has found favour in the recent High Court decision, *Barrett v Barrett*.[69] Thomas Barrett was the sole owner of a house which he lived in with his brother, John Barrett. Thomas went bankrupt and his trustee in bankruptcy accepted an offer from John to buy the house. John raised the purchase price largely by way of a mortgage. Thomas paid all the mortgage contributions, all other liabilities with regard to the house, carried out renovations and continued to live in it. When the house was sold, Thomas claimed the proceeds on the basis that he and John had entered into an agreement that John would hold the house on trust for him. The purpose of the arrangement was that Thomas could thereby conceal his interest from his trustee in bankruptcy. John was successful in striking out the application on the basis that Thomas would have to rely on his illegal purpose in order to prove his claim. The Court held that there was no express trust because of a lack of writing. Thomas' contributions to the mortgage instalments did not by themselves give rise to a resulting trust. In order to establish that the payments were intended to confer an interest in the property under a constructive trust, the contributions had to be referable to an agreement to this effect. Thomas could not rely on the agreement because it was not possible to separate the agreement from the illegal purpose. Without that purpose, the agreement had no rational explanation.

---

[65] [1994] 1 AC 340.

[66] [1994] 1 AC 340, 376.

[67] [2002] EWCA Civ 1095, [2002] BPIR 1057.

[68] [2002] EWCA Civ 1095, [2002] BPIR 1057 at [103].

[69] [2008] EWHC 1061 (Ch).

6.61 What, then, can a claimant seeking to prove a constructive trust rely on? According to Lord Mance in *Collier v Collier*, he needs an "objectively provable and apparently neutral fact, such as the payment of money"[70]. This would tend to suggest that, in deciding whether there is a constructive trust, and if so on what terms, the court will be able to consider some of the evidence, but only the part which is not intertwined with the illegal purpose. However, following Baroness Hale's opinion in *Stack v Dowden*[71] that: "The search is to ascertain the party's shared intentions, actual, inferred or imputed, with respect to the property *in light of their whole course of conduct in relation to it*", it may no longer be possible for the claimant to "cherry pick" the evidence on which he or she relies in this way. This suggests that the court will look at all the evidence relating to the parties' conduct. If this discloses that the shared intention had an unlawful purpose as its foundation, the claimant will not be able to rely on it. The position is simply unclear.

CONSEQUENCES THAT FOLLOW FROM A TRUST BEING UNENFORCEABLE FOR ILLEGALITY

6.62 As we have already noted,[72] under the reliance principle the disputed trust is not invalid. It notionally exists, but is unenforceable, at least by the beneficiary. This position is made clear by Lord Browne-Wilkinson's opinion in *Tinsley v Milligan*. He explained:

> The effect of illegality is not to prevent a proprietary interest in equity from arising or to produce a forfeiture of such right: the effect is to render the equitable interest unenforceable in certain circumstances. The effect of illegality is not substantive but procedural. The question therefore is, "In what circumstances will equity refuse to enforce equitable rights which undoubtedly exist".[73]

6.63 What appears to be the position, therefore, is that the beneficiary is under some sort of personal disentitlement. He or she is unable to enforce the existent trust. This leaves open two important questions. First, can any "innocent" third parties, such as creditors, legatees or dependants of the beneficiary, claim the equitable interest through the barred beneficiary? Secondly, if the beneficiary is unable to enforce the trust, can the trustee enjoy the benefit of the trust property? We consider these two questions in turn below.

[70] [2002] EWCA Civ 1095, [2002] BPIR 1057 at [105].

[71] [2007] UKHL 17, [2007] 2 AC 432 at [60].

[72] See para 6.12 above.

[73] [1994] 1 AC 340, 374.

1. The position of third parties?

6.64 In *Silverwood v Silverwood*[74] the Court of Appeal assumed that the executor of the settlor/beneficiary could be in no better position than the settlor herself. That is, if the grandmother had not been able to recover by way of a presumption of resulting trust, then neither would the executor. However, in *Collier v Collier*,[75] Lord Mance suggested that creditors may be in a different position. He raised the possibility that they may be able to enforce their security against an equitable interest held under an illegal trust by the beneficiary, even though the beneficiary himself could not enforce it. He said:

> Another possibility ... may arise because illegality is a procedural, rather than substantive bar capable only of affecting those party or privy to the illegality. ... It may perhaps be that innocent third parties in the mortgagees' position could thus rely upon the father's beneficial entitlement to, and enforce their claims against, the freehold of the Clapham property still held by the daughter ... despite the father's inability to do so.[76]

6.65 The position is simply not clear.

6.66 It has been held that a third party may receive good title to the trust property if conveyed to him or her by the trustee in accordance with the beneficiary's wishes, even if the beneficiary would not have been able to enforce the equitable interest against the trustee prior to that transfer. In *Hurndell v Hozier*[77] a director of a company that was to be listed on the Stock Exchange transferred five percent of the shares in that company to the claimant. This was to give the impression of complying with Stock Exchange rules that required a certain percentage of the shares to be owned by the public. However he fraudulently intended that the claimant should hold them merely as his nominee. In circumstances that are not clear from the evidence, the legal title to these shares was later transferred by the claimant to the defendant. On their subsequent sale, the claimant sought an account and payment of their highest value between the date of transfer and date of account or, alternatively, the net proceeds of sale. The defendant argued that the claimant had only ever held the shares as nominee of the director, and that the transfer to himself was in accordance with the wishes of the director.

6.67 The High Court carried out a thorough examination of the relevant evidence and concluded in favour of the defendant. In breach of the Stock Exchange rules, the director had intended the claimant to hold the shares merely as nominee for him and to retain the beneficial ownership himself. However, the claimant could not rely on this illegality in order to recover the value of shares of which he was not now the legal owner and of which he was never the beneficial owner.

---

[74] (1997) 74 P&CR 453.

[75] [2002] EWCA Civ 1095, [2002] BPIR 1057.

[76] [2002] EWCA Civ 1095, [2002] BPIR 1057 at [111].

[77] [2008] EWCH 538 (Ch).

2. What is the position of the trustee of a trust that is unenforceable?

6.68   If the trust is valid but unenforceable, the trustee still notionally holds the property on the illegal trust and so no default trust arises. However, the beneficiary cannot enforce the trustee's fiduciary obligations. In CP 154 we suggested that this left the trustee free in practice to treat the property as his or her own. If the trustee were to transfer the trust property to another, the trustee would incur no liability for breach of trust and would be able to pass title as if the full owner of the property.[78] In those cases where the reliance principle has prevented a transferor or contributor from enforcing a trust in his or her favour, it has been presumed that the legal owner then effectively holds the property beneficially for him or herself. There has been very little discussion of this point in the case law. However, this was assumed to be the position in judicial statements in both *Barrett v Barrett*[79] and *SMQ v RFQ and MJQ*.[80]

PROBLEMS WITH THE PRESENT LAW

6.69   There are three main criticisms that can be raised against the doctrine of illegality as it applies to determine the enforcement of equitable interests. These are: (1) that it operates in an arbitrary manner; (2) that it can result in unjust decisions; and (3) that in many respects its application is uncertain. We look at each of these problems in turn below.

1. Arbitrariness of the reliance principle

6.70   It was in the context of a resulting trust that the reliance principle was first used to determine whether a beneficiary could enforce an equitable interest that was tainted by illegality. Here, the reliance principle only rarely results in the non-recognition of the interest. This reflects the position at common law, from where the principle was adopted. The reliance principle was historically used to eliminate the adverse impact of illegality on transfers of legal property. However, in the resulting trusts context, the reliance principle does sometimes result in the non-recognition of the beneficial interest. Whether or not it does so depends on arbitrary considerations. These include the nature of the relationship between the beneficiary and the trustee. Unless the withdrawal exception applies, a father will not be able to bring a claim against his child or a husband against his wife. Subject to a few possible limited exceptions,[81] a claimant in any other relationship will succeed. There has been considerable judicial[82] and academic[83] criticism of this position.

---

[78]   CP 154, para 8.46.

[79]   [2008] EWHC 1061 (Ch) at [28].

[80]   [2008] EWHC 1874 (Fam) at [139].

[81]   See paras 6.25 to 6.36 above.

[82]   For example, see the comments by Nourse and Millett LJJ in *Tribe v Tribe* [1996] Ch 107, 118 and 134; the comments by Nourse LJ in *Silverwood v Silverwood* (1997) 74 P & CR 453, 458; and the comments of Robert Walker LJ in *Lowson v Coombes* [1999] Ch 373, 385.

6.71 Criticism of the reliance principle is neatly summarised by Justice McHugh in his judgment in the decision of the High Court of Australia, *Nelson v Nelson*. In rejecting its application, he said:

> [The reliance principle] has no regard to the legal and equitable rights of the parties, the merits of the case, the effect of the transaction in undermining the policy of the relevant legislation or the question whether the sanctions imposed by the legislation sufficiently protect the purpose of the legislation. Regard is had only to the procedural issue; and it is that issue and not the policy of the legislation or the merits of the parties which determines the outcome. Basing the grant of legal remedies on an essentially procedural criterion which has nothing to do with the equitable positions of the parties or the policy of the legislation is unsatisfactory, particularly when implementing a doctrine that is founded on public policy.[84]

6.72 The effect of applying the reliance principle to cases involving the presumptions of resulting trust and advancement has been to give the presumption of advancement a far more prominent role than was ever intended to be the case. Indeed for many years the presumption of advancement has been widely criticised as anachronistic and little notice has been paid to it. As long ago as 1970 Lord Diplock commented, in a case involving the division of a married couple's property following their divorce, that:

> It would, in my view, be an abuse of the legal technique for ascertaining or imputing intention to apply to transactions between the post-war generation of married couples "presumptions" which are based upon inferences of fact which an earlier generation of judges drew as to the most likely intentions of earlier generations of spouses belonging to the propertied classes of a different social era.[85]

[83] A G J Berg, "Illegality and Equitable Interests" [1993] *Journal of Business Law* 513, 517-518; N Cohen, "The Quiet Revolution in the Enforcement of Illegal Contracts" [1994] *Lloyd's Maritime and Commercial Law Quarterly* 163, 168; N Enonchong, "Illegality: The Fading Flame of Public Policy" (1994) 14 *Oxford Journal of Legal Studies* 295, 299; S H Goo, "Let the Estate Lie Where it Falls" (1994) 45 *Northern Ireland Law Quarterly* 378, 379; M Halliwell, "Equitable Proprietary Claims and Dishonest Claimants: A Resolution?" [1994] *Conveyancer* 62, 66; H Stowe, "The 'Unruly Horse' has Bolted: Tinsley v Milligan?" (1994) 57 *Modern Law Review* 441, 446; R A Buckley, "Law's Boundaries and the Challenge of Illegality" in R A Buckley (ed), *Legal Structures* (1996) p 229 at pp 231-234; D Davies, "Presumptions and Illegality" in A J Oakley (ed), *Trends in Contemporary Trust Law* (1996) ch 2.

[84] (1995) 184 CLR 538.

[85] *Pettitt v Pettitt* [1970] AC 777, 824.

6.73 The Government has accepted[86] that the presumption of advancement treats husbands and wives unequally and that this discriminatory operation means that legislation is needed to amend or abolish it before the Government can carry out its stated commitment to ratify Article 5 of Protocol 7 of the European Convention on Human Rights.[87] It is therefore particularly unsatisfactory that the use of the reliance principle has been to elevate the status of the presumption of advancement from a minor evidential role to one of determinative effect.

6.74 A different problem, but one which has an equally arbitrary effect, arises from the adoption of the reliance principle in the context of express and constructive trusts. Here, there is little relevant case law to guide us. In the case of an express trust we believe that the effect of applying the reliance principle will be that the claimant can use as evidence of his or her beneficial entitlement any "neutral" facts that go towards establishing the claim, but not any evidence that is tied up with the illegal purpose. Whether any particular piece of relevant evidence is tainted by the illegality, or can be separated from it, would seem to be essentially arbitrary and not a good reason on which to base the outcome of the decision.

2. Potential for injustice

6.75 The arbitrariness of the reliance principle in the trust context has the potential to result in injustice. We do not think that it permits the court to focus on the factors that should be relevant in deciding whether or not the claimant should succeed. In the vast majority of cases we believe that the involvement of illegality should not affect the beneficial entitlement of the claimant. Dealing with the element of illegality can be left to the criminal law. However in a small minority of cases we consider that the public policy principles that underlie the illegality doctrine mean that the civil law cannot simply ignore the illegal element and the claimant should be denied his or her usual rights. Whether or not the illegality has this effect should be determined by reference to such factors as the behaviour of the beneficiary, the seriousness of the illegality and the value of the interest at stake. Focusing purely on the state of the evidence and which party pleads the illegality could clearly lead to unsatisfactory outcomes.

3. Uncertainty as to how the reliance principle operates in some areas

6.76 As we have seen, we do not know for sure how the reliance principle will operate in many trust cases. We can speculate on when and how it might work in relation to express and constructive trusts, but the position is not clear. This uncertainty is particularly problematic in an area where not only the interests of the transferor and transferee may be in dispute, but also those of third parties, such as creditors or legatees. Nor is it clear to whom the equitable interest does belong where the reliance principle prevents the beneficiary from enforcing the trust.

---

[86] Written Answer, Hansard (HL) 21 April 1998, vol 588, col 197W.

[87] This Article states: "Spouses shall enjoy equality of rights and responsibilities of a private law character between them, and in their relations with their children, as to marriage, during marriage and in the event of its dissolution. This Article shall not prevent States taking such measures as are necessary in the interest of children".

6.77   Furthermore, even when we know that the reliance principle does apply, it is not always clear exactly what will amount to "reliance". To what extent may the court take any notice of any underlying illegal arrangement from which the beneficiary's interest arises? In particular, can the claimant lead evidence of an underlying illegal contract in order to establish his or her equitable interest, provided that he or she is not seeking to enforce the executory provisions of that contract?

6.78   The confusion surrounding this issue is apparent from Lord Browne-Wilkinson's judgment in *Tinsley v Milligan* when he explains how the reliance principle applies to determine legal title. At one point he takes a wide view of what amounts to reliance and is therefore impermissible. He states that property titles will only be enforced where the claimant can "establish such title without pleading or leading evidence of the illegality".[88] However, he later takes a narrower view of what is excluded by the reliance principle. He states that a claimant can enforce property rights provided that he or she does not rely on an illegal contract for any purpose "other than providing the basis of his claim to a property right".[89]

6.79   The result of such inconsistency is illustrated by contrasting the facts of *Macdonald v Myerson*[90] with *Halley v The Law Society*.[91] We do not intend to suggest that either case was wrongly decided, but they tend to show that a broad or narrow meaning can be attributed to what amounts to "reliance" in order to achieve the desired result. As Lord Justice Mummery commented in *Halley*, when considering who should be entitled to the funds held by the solicitor in the escrow account:

> This simple question admits of only one sensible answer, though it appears to be easier for a layman than for a lawyer to justify the answer.[92]

6.80   In *Macdonald v Myerson* the claimant had applied for a number of mortgages in different false names. He was found guilty of fraud charges and imprisoned. No confiscation order was made. This dispute related to the ownership of the proceeds of sale of two of the houses which the claimant had bought with the fraudulently obtained mortgages and which had been registered in false names. The claimant had instructed the defendant firm of solicitors to act for him on the sales, using forged powers of attorney from the non-existent title holders. The defendants carried out the conveyancing, and they now held the net proceeds of the sale (having discharged the mortgages) in their client account.

---

[88]   [1994] 1 AC 340, 369.

[89]   [1994] 1 AC 340, 370.

[90]   [2001] EWCA Civ 66, [2001] EGCS 15.

[91]   [2003] EWCA Civ 97, [2003] WTLR 845.

[92]   [2003] EWCA Civ 97, [2003] WTLR 845 at [93].

6.81 The claimant argued that since he had instructed the defendants they now held the proceeds of sale on trust for him. The Court of Appeal agreed that, despite his fraudulent scheme, the claimant was the owner of the money. The defendants raised an illegality defence, arguing that the claim was founded on a series of illegal transactions and no cause of action arose. This defence failed using the reliance test. All the claimant had to prove was that the defendants were retained by him and that they received the proceeds into their client account for the claimant's account. The background to the instructions was held not to be relevant for the purposes of proving his claim.

6.82 Yet in *Halley v The Law Society*[93] the Court of Appeal held that the claimant, the fraudster, *would* need to rely on the fraudulent investment scheme in order to make out his claim to the funds held by the defendant solicitor as escrow agent. The fraudulent scheme was not simply the background to his proprietary claim, but rather he was forced to rely on his own part in the fraud. This he was not allowed to do, and so the claim failed. It is not entirely clear why the background to the claim should be relevant here, when it was not relevant in *Macdonald v Myerson*.[94] The Court was quite clear that the claimant was not seeking to enforce any executory contractual claim, but rather to enforce an equitable interest arising under an express trust. It is arguable that simply leading evidence of the escrow agreement under which the interest arose would not amount to "reliance on the illegality" as contemplated by Lord Browne-Wilkinson in *Tinsley v Milligan*.[95] In any event, the argument based on illegality was unnecessary to determine the case, which would have been decided in the same way on the grounds that the whole transaction was so infected by fraud that it had no legal effect at all.[96]

6.83 There are also many problems in relation to the withdrawal exception. As we have seen, *Tribe v Tribe*[97] has extended its application to a point where it is difficult to see where its justification as an exception to the reliance principle lies. Whether or not the claimant can be said to have "withdrawn" from the illegal purpose depends largely on how narrowly or broadly that purpose is defined. On the one hand, if the illegal purpose was narrowly defined as hiding assets from his creditors, then the father in *Tribe v Tribe* could be said to have withdrawn before it was carried out because no creditors were deceived. On the other hand, if his illegal purpose was broadly defined as keeping his assets outside the reach of creditors until the danger had passed, then allowing him to reclaim those assets was more a completion of that purpose than a withdrawal from it.

[93] [2003] EWCA Civ 97, [2003] WTLR 845.

[94] [2001] EWCA Civ 66, [2001] EGCS 15.

[95] [1994] 1 AC 340.

[96] [2003] EWCA Civ 97, [2003] WTLR 845 at [42]-[56], by Carnwath LJ.

[97] [1996] Ch 107.

6.84   In conclusion, while, on the face of it, the reliance principle and withdrawal exception seem to provide strict rules by which parties can determine with certainty whether an equitable interest that is tainted by illegality will be enforced, this is not the true picture that emerges from the case law. Any certainty is more illusory than real. By adjusting between a broad and narrow definition of "reliance" and "purpose", the rules can be applied to the facts of a particular case in whatever way reaches the desired outcome.

OUR PROPOSALS ON CONSULTATION AND REACTION TO THEM

6.85   In CP 154 we provisionally proposed that the reliance principle should be abolished. We argued that it should be replaced with a statutory discretion to decide the effect of illegality which would apply to all "illegal trusts". This term was defined very broadly to include almost any way in which the creation or purpose of a trust could be tainted by some element of unlawfulness. The discretion was to be structured by a list of factors that should be considered in order to provide some guidance to the courts as to how they should reach their decisions.[98]

6.86   We received fewer responses to the provisional proposals in relation to trusts than we received in relation to contract. Only 25 consultees commented on the trusts options. Nearly all of these agreed that the reliance principle should be abandoned, and three-quarters agreed that a statutory discretion should be put in its place.

6.87   Although there was a large degree of support for our proposals to introduce a statutory discretion in relation to the enforcement of trusts involving illegality, we also received some forceful arguments against it. The responses showed that there was a widely held belief that it is less acceptable to have uncertainty in relation to property rights than in relation to contractual rights. It was suggested by several consultees that our reform proposals would introduce a large degree of uncertainty. In particular, there was concern over the scope of the proposed discretion. We had defined an "illegal trust" very broadly, in order to embrace virtually every way in which illegality might impinge upon a trust arrangement. Under our proposals more trusts would be affected by illegality than is presently the position. We had adopted this broad approach because we had found it hard to isolate those trusts to which the reliance principle applies from those to which it does not. Without any clear boundaries to work with, we had suggested that it would make sense to subject all types of illegal trusts to the proposed discretion. Even then, defining the scope of the discretion was not easy, and as one respondent commented:

---

[98] CP 154, Part VIII.

122

> I have the gravest doubts whether your recommendations in respect of trusts will work. The law of trusts in not in a parallel state [to the law of contract]. It is not a unit – some of its components are more amorphous than others; some are more techniques than concepts; some are economic wrongs. It is developing at an alarming rate into the commercial world where concealed illegal objectives are not unusual.[99]

6.88 In addition, a few respondents pointed to the uncertainty that our proposed discretion might bring to complex financial arrangements. We had focused largely on the one-off type of private trust arrangement that has given rise to litigation before the courts. However, trusts of one kind or another permeate business and particularly financial arrangements. In particular, the trust mechanism is quite legitimately used in the context of multiple shareholdings in order to ease the transfer in ownership of the shares. The legal title to the shares may be registered in the name of a nominee who holds on trust for the investor. The investor, who may be acting for himself or as an intermediary for the ultimate beneficial owner, can then buy and sell shares without the need to change the registered ownership. Such holdings may be very complex, multi-tiered and cross international boundaries. A breach of a statutory criminal regulation, quite possibly inadvertent, at some stage by one of the holding bodies seems not unlikely, and yet it would be enormously disruptive for the financial community if this were to put in doubt the ownership of the holdings. We do not think that the present law on illegality would affect such an arrangement, and we do not intend that our reforms should do so either.

OPTIONS FOR REFORM

6.89 We remain of the view that the position reached by the present law is indefensible and needs reform. Since the rules which we seek to reform have been laid down by the House of Lords, judicial reform seems unlikely. We therefore provisionally recommend that some legislative reform is appropriate.

6.90 We have considered a range of possible reform options.

1. A statutory discretion to apply to all trusts tainted with illegality as outlined in CP 154

6.91 Bearing in mind the responses that we received on consultation, we are reluctant to recommend any scheme that might increase significantly the number of trusts affected by the illegality doctrine. Our provisional proposals were deliberately widely drafted, and would have brought within the discretion many trusts that are in some way tainted by illegality but which would not be void or unenforceable under the present law. We no longer advocate such broad reform.

---

[99] Mr Derek Davies.

2. The abolition of the presumption of advancement

6.92   At one stage we considered simply proposing that legislation should be introduced to abolish the presumption of advancement. It is the interaction of the reliance principle with the presumption of advancement which prevents the courts from looking at the true intention of the parties and results in the most criticism of the present law. Although not a perfect solution, we considered that the abolition of the presumption of advancement would resolve most problems and, at least in resulting trust cases, bring about a position in equity that is the same as that which applies at law – the illegality would simply be ignored. As we have explained, the Government is already committed to the abolition of the presumption of advancement, and this approach therefore seemed likely to gain Parliamentary approval.

6.93   With this end in mind, we published a short paper in December 2006, asking lawyers and administrators whether they had any practical experience of the presumption of advancement. We are very grateful for the comments that we received. No one who responded to us was aware of any case in which the presumption of advancement had made a difference to the outcome. However, before we had finalised our recommendations, the House of Lords gave its judgment in *Stack v Dowden*.[100] As we have seen, that case determined that where a family home is jointly owned at law, the courts will presume that it is jointly owned in equity too. Only in exceptional circumstances will one of the parties be able to claim a greater than half share under a constructive trust. A resulting trust analysis is not to be used. Subsequent decisions have applied the same analysis in the sole legal owner cases too, which make up the majority of the illegality case law. If a resulting trust analysis is no longer to be used in this situation,[101] it is clear that abolishing the presumption of advancement would not have any impact in these cases. We considered that the position is sufficiently unclear that we needed to reconsider our recommendations.

---

[100] [2007] UKHL 17, [2007] 2 AC 432.

[101] See para 6.54 above.

3. Abolition of the illegality defence in relation to the enforcement of equitable interests

6.94 We have considered at length the possibility of simply abolishing the illegality defence in relation to the recognition of equitable interests. As we have seen this is generally the effect of applying the reliance principle to cases dealing with the transfer of legal interests. There are forceful arguments for aligning the position between law and equity. Yet we remain of the view which we expressed in CP 154 that the illegality defence should be retained in at least some form. This is largely based on two reasons. First, we do not believe that the illegality should be ignored in every trust situation. There may be cases where the claimant's conduct or purpose is so heinous that the policies that underlie the illegality defence justify the loss of protection which the court would usually provide for his or her equitable interest. We do not consider that it is sufficient to point to the various legislative provisions which provide for the forfeiture or recovery of assets to the State (see paragraphs 2.32 to 2.33 above) because the case in question may not fall within their remit or it might be highly unlikely that these provisions would in practice be used.

6.95 For example, we have explained that one of the policies that underlies the illegality doctrine is the need to support the rule that the claimant has infringed. There could be cases where enforcing the trust would further the illegal purpose of the claimant, but refusing to enforce the trust would defeat it. One example of such a case is provided by the facts of *Chettiar v Chettiar*.[102] A father had purchased a rubber estate in the name of his son in order to avoid a legislative provision restricting the maximum area of rubber land that any individual could own. Allowing the father to rebut the presumption of advancement and enforce the resulting trust would have assisted his illegal purpose, whereas denying his claim defeated it.

6.96 A second example might be where the claimant transfers the legal title of assets to the defendant intending to retain the beneficial ownership but attempting to give the false impression that the defendant has greater assets than is really the case. The purpose of the fraud is to encourage third parties to invest in or otherwise deal with the defendant. Should creditors then find themselves in dispute with the defendant, their claim may have more chance of success if the assets remain with the defendant rather than be returned to the claimant. This is the type of example found in *Re Great Berlin Steamboat Company*.[103] The directors of a company were attempting to persuade investors to buy shares in the company. In order to make it appear more solvent than was really the case, the claimant transferred some of his own money into the bank account of the company for the purpose of deceiving potential investors. When the company went into liquidation, the claimant sought to recover this sum. His claim failed.

---

[102] [1962] 1 All ER 494.

[103] (1884) 26 Ch D 616.

6.97 A second reason for believing that the illegality defence should be retained in the trusts context is that we need to consider the interaction with our proposals elsewhere in cases which involve illegality. In some instances claims under the different areas actually overlap. For example, a claim for proprietary restitution and an equitable claim under a resulting trust could be tantamount to the enforcement of the same interest, and so should be treated the same way under our proposals. As we have seen, the illegality defence does have a role to play in these other areas of the law, and nothing we propose should contradict that position.

4. A statutory discretion to apply to a limited range of trusts affected by illegality

6.98 Having decided that simple abolition is not an option, we considered whether it was possible to devise a set of statutory rules that might regulate how the illegality defence applies to all trusts. However, this has not proved to be a workable solution. There are so many competing factors at play – not only between the parties (which may include settlor, trustee, beneficiaries and other third parties) but also involving issues of wider public policy – that a set of rigid rules is simply unworkable here. Only a discretion would enable a court to balance all of the policy factors that are involved. We have already explained that in contract and unjust enrichment cases the courts have, and should develop further, an element of flexibility in reaching their decisions. Although not formally called a discretion, in effect the courts do already take into account such factors as the seriousness of the claimant's conduct and the purpose of the invalidating rule, when deciding the outcome of disputes.

6.99 We therefore remain of the view that some form of discretionary approach is required. However, in order to avoid the uncertainty referred to above, we considered the possibility of narrowing the scope of its application to a limited category of trusts. Our review of the case law shows that there is one type of arrangement that has caused most of the recent litigation – that is, where the trust institution is being used in order to conceal the true arrangement between the parties for an unlawful purpose. We believe that this narrow ambit for the recommended discretion should catch most, if not all, of those cases that have caused concern, but should not create unnecessary uncertainty over a wider area.

6.100 **Accordingly, we provisionally recommend that the courts should be given a statutory discretion to decide the effect of illegality on trusts in at least some cases.**

6.101 The final version of this report will explain in detail what we recommend the exact parameters of that discretion should be, how the discretion should operate, and what the effects of its exercise might be. In particular, we will explain that we recommend that the statutory discretion should only apply to cases where the trust arrangement has been created or exploited in order to conceal the beneficiary's equitable interest in the trust property in connection with the commission of an offence. The final report will include a draft Bill.

PART 7
ILLEGALITY IN TORT

INTRODUCTION

7.1 In this Part we consider when the doctrine of illegality prevents a claimant from enforcing the usual right to a remedy arising from a tortious act committed against him or her. So, for example, can a claimant who is injured in a car accident as a result of the defendant's negligence claim damages for any injuries suffered even if the claimant was speeding when the accident occurred? Or can a burglar sue his or her intended victim if during the course of breaking into a house he or she sustains injuries caused by the householder's negligence or even deliberate assault?

THE PRESENT LAW

1. Introduction

7.2 Some early cases raised doubts as to whether the illegality defence applied in tort at all.[1] It is now clear that it does,[2] and that it may apply as a defence to all torts, not simply those based on negligence. It may also apply to defeat just one particular head of damages without affecting the rest of the claim.[3] However, the policies that justify its use, and how it should be applied to the facts of any particular case, remain uncertain. This has resulted in a body of case law that is complex and hard to reconcile. As one commentator has noted: "as things stand … the law here seems to offer not so much a principle as a safety valve".[4]

7.3 We consider first what different considerations apply when examining the policies which lie behind the illegality defence in tort as opposed to contract or trusts. We then go on to look at how the defence has been used in the case law.

---

[1] For example, in *National Coal Board v England* [1954] AC 403, 419 Lord Porter said: "The adage itself is generally applied to a question of contract and I am by no means prepared to concede where concession is not required that it applies also to the case of tort".

[2] *Clunis v Camden and Islington Health Authority* [1998] QB 978, 987.

[3] For example, in *Hewison v Meridian Shipping* [2002] EWCA Civ 1821 (Unreported) the claim for loss of future earnings was denied as the claimant had obtained his job by making false representations to his employer, but his claim for damages for personal injury succeeded.

[4] A Burrows (ed) *English Private Law* (2nd ed 2008) p 1268.

2. The policies underpinning the illegality defence in tort

7.4 In Part 2 we have already discussed the general policies that underlie the justification of the illegality defence across all areas of law. However, two of these policies, those based on not profiting from a wrong and deterrence, would seem to bear less relevance in a tort context. This means that greater weight must be borne by the policies based on the furtherance of the underlying rule that the claimant has infringed, consistency and the integrity of the legal system. Indeed in Canada, consistency is now seen as the only justification for the application of the defence in tort law and as a result its application has been severely curtailed.[5] It can never be used to deny a claim for personal injury caused to the claimant by the defendant's tort while the claimant was engaged in some illegal activity. We look at all these issues below.

7.5 In addition, negligence claims, based on the finding of a duty of care, raise some further issues not relevant to other areas.

(1) In a claim in tort, the claimant is generally seeking compensation rather than profit

7.6 In Part 2 we have suggested that one of the principles underlying the illegality defence is that the court should not assist a claimant in profiting from his or her criminal act.[6] However, this policy is often not applicable in tort cases, where the claimant is seeking compensation for a physical injury or loss which he or she has suffered, rather than a financial profit. In *Revill v Newbery*[7] Lord Justice Evans drew the distinction in the following terms:

> It is one thing to deny a plaintiff any fruits from his illegal conduct, but different and more far-reaching to deprive him even of compensation for injury which he suffers and which otherwise he is entitled to recover.[8]

7.7 It would seem, therefore, that the "no profit from a wrong" policy cannot be used to bar a claim for personal injury sustained during an illegal activity. Another alternative policy ground must be found to justify adopting the illegality defence in such cases.

---

[5] See para 7.10 below.

[6] See paras 2.16 to 2.18 above.

[7] [1996] QB 567.

[8] [1996] QB 567, 579.

7.8 However, in a minority of tort cases where the claimant is seeking to obtain a profit or an indemnity for his own liability, this policy has been used to justify the application of the illegality defence. In *Askey v Golden Wine Co Ltd*,[9] the claimant had been purchasing for resale large quantities of cocktails manufactured by the defendants' company. Despite knowing that the defendants already had criminal convictions arising from supplying adulterated drinks, the claimant failed to make any checks of his own to determine that the cocktails were safe. He merely relied on the defendants' assurances. It subsequently transpired that the cocktails had also been contaminated during manufacture, resulting in the claimant being convicted of offences under the Food and Drugs Act 1938 for failing to take proper steps to ensure the drink was fit for sale. He was duly fined, ordered to pay costs and had to give refunds to his customers. He sought to recover these amounts in a fraud claim against the defendants. The court accepted that his claim was defeated by the illegality defence . It held that the criminal punishment was personal to the offender, and, relying on the "no profit from a wrong" principle, that public policy required that no right of indemnity or contribution or damages should be enforced in respect of expenses which the claimant had incurred by reason of being compelled to make reparation for his crime.

(2) Deterrence

7.9 Another policy that we have suggested underlies the illegality defence is that of deterrence. However, it could be argued that this bears less relevance in many of the tort cases than it may do in, for example, the contract or trusts area. In the latter cases, the parties are generally entering into some sort of financial arrangement from which they hope to reap a profit. The risk of losing this profit, or even their initial stake, because of the involvement of illegality, might deter them from entering into the arrangement. In many such cases the chance of detection and level of potential criminal sanction is low. The position is different in tort law. In several of the reported tort cases, the illegality committed by the claimant consists of a serious criminal offence against life[10] or safety.[11] It is difficult to suggest that a person who is not deterred from these activities by the threat of criminal sanction will be deterred by the possibility that he or she may not receive compensation for any loss suffered in the course of, or as a result of, committing the offence.

---

[9]   [1948] 2 All ER 35.

[10] For example, *Clunis v Camden and Islington Health Authority* [1998] QB 978.

[11] For example, *Pitts v Hunt* [1991] 1 QB 24.

(3) Consistency - the Canadian approach

7.10   The Supreme Court of Canada has adopted the concept of "consistency" as the only justification for the illegality defence in tort law.[12] This concept has been narrowly interpreted so that the defence is only relevant where the tort claim would allow a person to profit from illegal conduct or to evade a penalty prescribed by the criminal law. It can never successfully defeat a claim for a personal injury award since permitting such a claim would not produce any "inconsistency" with the criminal law.

7.11   In CP 160 we said that we were not inclined to go as far as the Supreme Court of Canada and assert that consistency was the only valid rationale for the doctrine of illegality in tort. We asked consultees whether other rationales could be adopted to allow the illegality defence to defeat a claim for personal injury.[13] The large majority of those who responded thought that the illegality defence should be available to deny a personal injury claim. Various policy arguments were put forward for this view, generally based on those we had already identified, such as the integrity of the legal system, furthering the purpose of the rule infringed by the claimant, preserving the dignity of the court and punishment.

(4) No duty of care, or a defence to an otherwise valid claim?

7.12   There has been discussion in the case law as to how the rules on illegality operate to prevent a claim succeeding. Some judges have been influenced by the approach taken by the High Court of Australia in *Jackson v Harrison*[14] where it was held that, because of the illegality, the court might be unable to determine the correct standard of care. This may lead to the conclusion that because of the illegality there is no duty of care owed at all:

> A more secure foundation for denying relief, though more limited in its application – and for that reason fairer in its operation – is to say that the [claimant] must fail when the character of the enterprise in which the parties are engaged is such that it is impossible for the court to determine the standard of care which is appropriate to be observed.[15]

---

[12]   See *Hall v Hebert* [1992] SCR 226 (referred to in para 2.14 above) and *British Columbia v Zastowny* 2008 SCC 4.

[13]   CP 160, para 4.98.

[14]   (1977-1978) 138 CLR 438. See also *Gala v Preston* (1991) 172 CLR 243.

[15]   *Jackson v Harrison* (1977-1978) 138 CLR 438, 455 by Chief Justice Mason.

7.13   Several English judges have adopted this approach, including Mr Justice Ewbank in *Ashton v Turner*[16] and Lord Justice Balcombe in *Pitts v Hunt*.[17] More recently, the Court of Appeal in *Vellino v Chief Constable of Greater Manchester*[18] has suggested that the practical effect is the same, irrespective of the analysis. Sir Murray Stuart-Smith said:

> It is common ground that if the facts are such that the maxim ex turpi causa non oritur actio is applicable, it does not matter whether the correct legal analysis is that the Defendants owed no duty of care, ... or that the maxim affords a free standing reason for holding that the cause of action does not arise or cannot be pursued.[19]

7.14   However, we do not find this to be a useful approach. Not all actions in tort are founded on a duty of care. It therefore seems conceptually inconsistent to suggest that the rules on illegality prevent a duty of care arising in the case of negligence (thus denying a cause of action), yet operate as a defence to an otherwise valid cause of action in the case of an intentional tort.[20]

7.15   Moreover, it is possible to imagine situations where this approach would cause difficulties even within the law of negligence. This might occur, for example, where an erratically driven getaway car containing two criminals crashes into an innocent third party motorist. The court would be obliged to determine the relevant standard of care owed to the third party, and so it seems artificial to say that it was unable to consider the same act in relation to the driver's passenger. Indeed, it is not at all clear when the courts would find it "impossible" to determine the standard of care.

7.16   Such an approach also fails to explain how an illegal act can prevent recovery of only certain heads of damages within a claim for negligence. For example, in *Hewison v Meridian*,[21] the claimant was unable to recover for his loss of earnings, but recovered damages under other heads.

3. The practical application of the illegality defence in tort

7.17   The manner in which the illegality defence operates in tort is difficult to predict with certainty. The number of factors to take into account, and the varying significance placed on the conceptual justifications for the defence, mean that the cases have not always followed the same reasoning. This has made it difficult to predict the outcome of a case, and has resulted in more litigation. However, it is possible to identify a number of criteria which the courts will consider. We look at these below.

---

[16]   [1981] QB 137, 146.

[17]   [1991] 1 QB 24, 51. Compare the comments of Beldam LJ in the same case who was "not convinced" by this approach (at p 47) and instead held that the claimant was "precluded" from recovering (at p 46). For the facts of this case, see para 7.47 below.

[18]   [2001] EWCA Civ 1249, [2002] 1 WLR 218.

[19]   [2001] EWCA Civ 1249, [2002] 1 WLR 218 at [62].

[20]   For example, *Murphy v Culhane* [1977] QB 94.

[21]   [2002] EWCA Civ 1821 (Unreported).

(1) The reliance principle

7.18 In some tort cases, particularly those where there is an underlying transaction involving illegality, the court has refused to permit a claim to succeed where the claimant would have to rely on his or her illegal conduct to found the claim. This is the same "reliance principle" laid down by the House of Lords in *Tinsley v Milligan* which we have already seen as having the central role to play in relation to the transfer of legal and equitable property rights. Indeed it has been suggested that this is the only relevant test to be applied in the tort cases. For example, in *Standard Chartered Bank v Pakistan National Shipping Corporation* Lord Justice Aldous said:

> There is in my view but one principle that is applicable to actions based upon contract, tort or recovery of property. It is, that public policy requires that the courts will not lend their aid to a man who founds his action upon an immoral or illegal act. The action will not be founded upon an immoral or illegal act, if it can be pleaded and proved without reliance upon such an act.[22]

7.19 The reliance principle was applied to a claim for conversion in *Webb v Chief Constable of Merseyside Police*.[23] The claimant was seeking to recover money which the police had lawfully seized in the belief that it was the proceeds of drug trafficking. The Chief Constable sought to retain the money on the basis that, although the police's statutory power to retain it had been exhausted,[24] it was against public policy to allow the claimant to recover it because it represented the proceeds of drug trafficking. The Court of Appeal unanimously held that the claimant did not have to rely on any illegal act to establish an entitlement to possession, and could therefore recover the money.[25] It was irrelevant that the illegality surrounding his acquisition of the money was pleaded in defence or emerged in evidence.

---

[22] [2000] 1 Lloyd's Rep 218, 232.

[23] [2000] QB 427.

[24] The claimant had not been convicted of a criminal offence and so the statutory provisions then in force relating to criminal confiscation did not apply.

[25] The position would have been different if the claimant had been asking for the return of property which it would be unlawful to deal in at all, for example controlled drugs: [2000] QB 427, 444.

7.20 The reliance principle has been most recently used as the decisive test for the application of the illegality defence by the Court of Appeal in *Moore Stephens v Stone & Rolls Ltd*.[26] An individual used the claimant company, which he owned and directed, to commit various frauds on a Czech bank. The bank successfully sued the company and was awarded substantial damages. The company went into liquidation. It brought a claim in negligence against its auditors, the defendants, alleging that the defendants had negligently failed to detect the fraud in its books. The defendants sought to strike out the claim on the basis of illegality. They were successful in the Court of Appeal. Lord Justice Rimer said that the relevant question was whether, to advance the claim, it is necessary for the claimant to rely on the illegality. If so, then "the axe falls indiscriminately and the claim is barred, however good it might otherwise be. There is no discretion to permit it to succeed".[27]

7.21 Although more frequently used in cases where there has been an underlying illegal transaction, the reliance principle has been used as the relevant test in a wider range of cases. One example is *Clunis v Camden and Islington Health Authority*.[28] The claimant had been discharged from hospital following his detention under the Mental Health Act 1983. Less than two months later, he stabbed a man to death in an unprovoked attack. He pleaded guilty to manslaughter on the grounds of diminished responsibility, and was detained in a secure hospital. The claimant then brought an action against the health authority for damages for his second detention, alleging that the authority had failed to treat him with reasonable professional care and skill after his original release. One of the grounds[29] on which the claimant's claim failed was that it arose out of, and depended upon proof of, his commission of a criminal offence.[30]

7.22 However, the reliance principle is not the only test that has been used for the application of the illegality defence, and the fact that a claimant does not need to rely on his or her illegal act in order to prove the claim will not guarantee that the illegality defence does not succeed. Even where illegality is not pleaded, or where the claimant does not 'rely' on the illegal act to found the claim, the court may raise the issue of illegality of its own initiative:

---

[26] [2008] EWCA Civ 644, [2008] 3 WLR 1146.

[27] [2008] EWCA Civ 644 at [16].

[28] [1998] QB 978. The decision was followed in *Worrall v British Railways Board* (Unreported) 29 April 1999 where the claimant sought damages in respect of imprisonment and lost earnings. He had been convicted for serious sexual offences which he alleged that he had committed after suffering a personality disorder caused by the defendant's negligence.

[29] The Court of Appeal also held that the defendant's obligations arose out of the Mental Health Act 1983 and did not give rise to a common law duty of care.

[30] [1998] QB 978, 989. The Court of Appeal suggested that the defence would not have succeeded if the claimant could show that he did not know the nature and quality of his act or that what he was doing was wrong.

> I do not believe that there is any general principle that the claimant must either plead, give evidence of or rely on his own illegality for the principle to apply. Such a technical approach is entirely absent from Lord Mansfield's exposition of the principle.[31]

7.23 In the paragraphs that follow we look at other factors that the courts have used in order to determine the applicability of the illegality defence.

(2) The proximity of the illegality to the claimant's loss or injury

7.24 This proximity based test, increasingly used by the courts, looks at the closeness of the connection between the claimant's loss or injury and the illegal conduct. It seems to involve a loosening of the rigid boundaries of the reliance test, in some cases increasing and in others decreasing the scope of the defence. It thus allows a certain amount of flexibility that is not permitted by the reliance test.

7.25 The requirement for some form of proximity between the illegal conduct and the claim is apparent from the early case law. In *National Coal Board v England*,[32] Lord Asquith said that if the loss or injury suffered by the claimant is unrelated to his or her unlawful act, then illegality will not be available as a defence. He suggested that if two burglars, A and B, agree to open a safe using explosives and A so negligently handles the explosive charge as to injure B, B might find some difficulty in maintaining an action for negligence against A. On the other hand, if A and B are proceeding to the premises which they intend to burgle, and before they enter B picks A's pocket and steals his watch, A would be able to sue in tort. The theft was totally unconnected with the burglary.[33]

7.26 In looking for a connection between the illegality and the tort, the courts have tended to adopt a pragmatic approach. This is illustrated by the case of *Saunders v Edwards*.[34] Here the claimants had agreed to purchase the leasehold to a flat, including a roof terrace, from the defendant. The claimants suggested that some of the accompanying chattels should be over-valued in order to reduce the amount of stamp duty payable. Soon after completion, the claimants discovered that the defendant had installed the roof terrace without the landlord's permission and consequently that they had no right to use it.

7.27 The claimants sought damages for fraudulent misrepresentation, but the defendant raised the defence of illegality based on the fraudulent over-valuation. The Court of Appeal held that the apportionment of the price was wholly unconnected with the claim. Lord Bingham (then a Court of Appeal judge) remarked:

---

[31] *Cross v Kirkby*, The Times, 5 April 2000, by Beldam LJ.

[32] [1954] AC 403.

[33] [1954] AC 403, 428-429.

[34] [1987] 1 WLR 1116.

On the whole the courts have tended to adopt a pragmatic approach to these problems, seeking where possible to see that genuine wrongs are righted so long as the court does not thereby promote or countenance a nefarious object or bargain which it is bound to condemn. Where the [claimant's] action in truth arises directly *ex turpi causa*, he is likely to fail... Where the [claimant] has suffered a genuine wrong, to which allegedly unlawful conduct is incidental, he is likely to succeed.[35]

7.28 Lord Justice Kerr agreed that the claimants' fraud on the Inland Revenue was independent of, and unconnected with, the fraud done to them. The claimants' loss caused by the defendant's fraudulent misrepresentation would have been the same, even if the contract had not contained the illegal element. The claimants' action was allowed to proceed.[36]

7.29 The Court of Appeal endorsed this need for close proximity between the illegality and the claim in *Cross v Kirkby*.[37] The claimant had attacked the defendant with a baseball bat whilst attempting to disrupt a hunt. The defendant had wrestled the bat from the claimant and hit him with considerable force causing a fractured skull. The claimant's claim for compensation failed on the basis, *inter alia*,[38] that it was "inextricably linked"[39] with his criminal conduct. Lord Justice Beldam (with whom Lord Justice Otton agreed) said that the reliance test was not the right test to use to decide whether the illegality defence applies. Rather the defence applies when:

the claimant's claim is so closely connected or inextricably bound up with his own criminal or illegal conduct that the court could not permit him to recover without appearing to condone that conduct.

7.30 This requirement for an "inextricable link" has been used in several subsequent cases. For example, in *Hall v Woolston Hall Leisure Limited*[40] the claimant had brought an action against her employer for sexual discrimination. During her period of employment, her payslips had shown a lower net income than was actually the case. She had queried this with her employer, but was told that it was the way they operated. Her employer argued that, because the employment contract had been tainted by this illegality, the employee's claim could not succeed. Lord Mance (then a Court of Appeal judge) said:

---

[35] [1987] 1 WLR 1116, 1134.

[36] [1987] 1 WLR 1116, 1127. Nicholls LJ reached the same conclusion as Kerr and Bingham LJJ although he took a slightly different approach, applying the public policy test derived from *Thackwell v Barclays Bank Ltd* [1986] 1 All ER 676.

[37] *The Times*, 5 April 2000.

[38] The Court of Appeal held that, in any event, the action failed because the defendant had acted in self-defence.

[39] See the judgment of Judge LJ.

[40] [2001] 1 WLR 225.

While the underlying test therefore remains one of public policy, the test evolved in this court for its application in a tortious context thus requires an inextricable link between the facts giving rise to the claim and the illegality, before any question arises of the court refusing relief on the grounds of illegality. In practice... it requires quite extreme circumstances before the test will exclude a tort claim.[41]

7.31 Most recently it has been used by the Court of Appeal in the well publicised case, *Gray v Thames Trains Limited and Network Rail Infrastructure Limited*.[42] The claimant had been injured as a result of the defendant rail companies' negligence in the Ladbroke Grove rail crash. Although his physical injuries were slight, as a result of the accident the claimant suffered a severe form of post traumatic stress disorder. He underwent a significant personality change. Having previously sought to avoid confrontation whenever possible, two years after the crash, following a minor altercation with a stranger in the street he fetched a knife and stabbed the stranger to death. He pleaded guilty to manslaughter on the grounds of diminished responsibility and was detained in hospital. Following *Clunis v Camden and Islington Health Authority*,[43] he conceded that he could not claim damages from the defendants for the consequences of the detention itself, but he claimed for his loss of earnings since the date of the accident.

7.32 The defendants admitted liability for the loss of earnings up until the date of the manslaughter, but denied liability for any losses thereafter on the basis of the illegality defence. Sir Anthony Clarke MR (giving the judgment of the Court) held that the reliance principle was not the correct test to apply in a case such as this where it is not suggested that the cause of action arose out of an illegal act. In this context the reliance principle was too narrow. The correct test was that set out in *Cross v Kirkby* - whether the relevant loss is inextricably linked with the claimant's illegal act or, so closely connected or inextricably bound up with the criminal conduct that the court could not permit him to recover without appearing to condone that conduct.

7.33 Applying that test here, the Court of Appeal held that the illegality defence did not apply. Assuming that the manslaughter did not break the chain of causation between the defendants' negligence and the loss of earnings, then it could not be fairly said that the loss of earnings was inextricably linked with the claimant's illegal act or so bound up with it that allowing him to recover would appear to condone the conduct.[44] The case would have to be remitted to a judge for the issues of foreseeability, causation and contributory fault to be decided.

[41] [2001] WLR 225, 248.

[42] [2008] EWCA Civ 713.

[43] [1998] QB 978. The case is considered at para 7.21 above.

[44] *Worrall v British Railways Board* (Unreported) 29 April 1999 (see para 7.21 fn 28 above) was distinguished on the basis that in that case the claimant had claimed for loss of earnings pursuant to his detention in prison. His attempts to raise a new argument in the Court of Appeal – that the loss of earnings were caused by the accident (and thus the defendant's negligence) and not by the commission of the criminal offences or period of imprisonment – was not permitted.

(3) The seriousness of the claimant's illegality

7.34 Another factor that the courts will consider is the seriousness of the alleged illegal conduct on the part of the claimant. Some judicial comments suggest that even where the claim is inextricably linked to the illegality, criminal conduct of a serious nature is required for the defence to apply. In *Clunis v Camden and Islington Health Authority*, Lord Justice Beldam accepted a submission by counsel that there are many summary criminal offences which are not sufficiently serious to warrant the invocation of the defence.[45]

7.35 Sir Murray Stuart-Smith in *Vellino v Chief Constable of Greater Manchester*[46] said:

> In the case of criminal conduct this has to be sufficiently serious to merit the application of the principle. Generally speaking a crime punishable with imprisonment could be expected to qualify. If the offence is criminal, but relatively trivial, it is in any event difficult to see how it could be integral to the claim.[47]

7.36 Similarly, in *Hewison v Meridian Shipping*[48] Lord Justice Ward said:

> There is no doubt in my mind that the claimant's conduct must be shown to be so clearly reprehensible as to justify the condemnation of the court... Where to draw the line between what is serious and what is trivial is not always easy.[49]

7.37 However, there are other judicial statements to the effect that the illegality defence is not confined to criminal conduct.[50] In *Standard Chartered Bank v Pakistan National Shipping Corporation*, the Court of Appeal were clearly of the view that tortious behaviour (in this case deceit without any element of criminal dishonesty) could be sufficient to bring the defence into play.[51]

---

[45] [1998] QB 978, 988.

[46] [2001] EWCA Civ 1249, [2001] 1 WLR 218.

[47] [2001] EWCA Civ 1249, [2001] 1 WLR 218 at [72].

[48] [2002] EWCA Civ 1821 (Unreported).

[49] [2002] EWCA Civ 1821 (Unreported) at [71].

[50] For example, *Kirkham v Chief Constable of Greater Manchester Police* [1990] 2 QB 283, 291.

[51] [2000] 1 Lloyd's Rep 218.

(4) Proportionality of denying relief to the illegality

7.38   It is important to be specific when defining the concept of "proportionality" in the context of the illegality defence. Cases employing the public conscience test have balanced the actions of the claimant against those of the defendant. This is the approach that has been criticised by the House of Lords in *Tinsley v Milligan*,[52] and is no longer to be used in tort cases. Here we are comparing the seriousness of the claimant's conduct to the loss that he or she will suffer if relief is denied. As Lord Justice Ward explained in *Hewison v Meridian Shipping*:

> The disproportion is between the claimant's conduct and the seriousness of the loss he will incur if his claim is not allowed. This test of proportionality is not quite the same as judging whether the claimant's wrongdoing is disproportionate to the defendant's wrongdoing. Judging their respective actions in that way may be reintroducing through the back door the public conscience test which we are not allowed to apply.[53]

(5) Participation

7.39   Another factor that the courts have taken into consideration is whether the claimant participated in the illegal act. In *Hall v Woolston Hall Leisure Ltd*,[54] the claimant's participation in the PAYE fraud, put at its most serious, could only be described as acquiescence. This was not sufficient involvement for her claim to be defeated by the illegality defence. In *Clunis v Camden and Islington Health Authority*,[55] Lord Justice Beldam said that public policy only requires the court to deny assistance to a claimant if he or she was implicated in the illegality.[56]

---

[52]   [1994] 1 AC 350. See, also, the judgment of Sir Murray Stuart-Smith in *Vellino v Chief Constable of Greater Manchester* [2001] EWCA Civ 1249, [2001] 1 WLR 218 where he said: "The defendant's conduct is irrelevant. There is no question of proportionality between the conduct of the claimant and defendant". Although note that section 329 of the Criminal Justice Act 2003 requires a comparison to be made between the claimant and defendant's conduct in cases where an offender brings civil proceedings for trespass to the person. Where the claimant has been convicted of an imprisonable offence, committed on the same occasion as the alleged act, proceedings can only be brought with the permission of the court. Permission will only be granted where there is evidence that the defendant's act was grossly disproportionate, or, broadly, that the defendant was not acting to prevent injury to himself, others or property. The defendant will have a defence if it can be proven that both of the above conditions are not met.

[53]   [2002] EWCA Civ 1821 (Unreported) at [72].

[54]   [2001] 1 WLR 225, the facts of which are set out at para 7.30 above.

[55]   [1998] QB 978.

[56]   [1998] QB 978, 987.

(6) The statutory context

7.40   When determining whether the illegality defence applies, the courts have also examined any relevant legislation to see whether its policy sheds any light on the availability of the defence. In *National Coal Board v England*[57] a collier claimed damages for personal injuries suffered when an explosive charge fired unexpectedly whilst he was connecting the detonator wires. Although the claimant's act of connecting the wires had constituted a breach of regulations under the Coal Mines Act 1911 designed to prevent this very occurrence, the House of Lords found that the policy behind the legislation did not preclude recovery in tort.[58]

7.41   In *Revill v Newbery*[59] Lord Justice Neill examined the Occupier's Liability Act 1984 to show that Parliament was of the view that an occupier did owe a duty of care to a burglar, albeit that in this case the defendant's duty was one at common law. The claimant had trespassed onto the defendant's allotment with the intention of committing a burglary. The defendant, who had been sleeping in his shed in order to protect his property, was woken by the attempted break-in and, without looking, fired a shot through a hole in the door thereby injuring the claimant. The claimant was found guilty of various offences, whilst the defendant was acquitted of wounding. In an action for damages for personal injury, the defendant raised the illegality defence. The Court of Appeal unanimously rejected the application of the defence.[60] The 1984 Act showed that it was not Parliament's policy that a trespasser should be treated as an outlaw.

7.42   Similarly, in *Pitts v Hunt*[61] Lord Justice Beldam said that the primary source of public policy in the use of motor vehicles must be the relevant Acts of Parliament themselves.

---

[57]   [1954] AC 403.

[58]   [1954] AC 403, 428.

[59]   [1996] QB 567.

[60]   Damages were, however, reduced to one third to take into account the claimant's contributory negligence.

[61]   [1991] 1 QB 24. For the facts of this case see para 7.47 below.

(7) Non-condonation

7.43 A number of cases also refer to the question of whether allowing a claim to succeed would appear to condone the claimant's illegal conduct, or whether it would encourage others to engage in similar behaviour. In *Thackwell v Barclays Bank Ltd*,[62] Mr Justice Hutchison accepted the argument advanced by counsel for the defendants that the defence would succeed when a finding for the claimant would have the effect of indirectly assisting or encouraging the claimant in his illegal act.[63] Lord Justice Nicholls in *Saunders v Edwards*[64] held that this test was a "useful and valuable one", supplementing it with the words "or encouraging others in similar criminal acts".[65]

7.44 Although, at the time, non-condonation appeared to form part of the public conscience test, it seems to have survived the rejection of that test in *Tinsley v Milligan*. As Lord Justice Ward pointed out in his comprehensive summary of the relevant case law in *Hewison v Meridan Shipping*, it has been referred to in several recent Court of Appeal judgments.[66] He explained that "it retains its place because it is an inherent aspect of the public policy which informs the doctrine as a whole".

4. Rejection of the public conscience test

7.45 In Part 2 we have described the "public conscience test". Many of the cases in which this test was developed were tort cases. In *Thackwell v Barclays Bank Ltd*,[67] Mr Justice Hutchison said that the court should look at the quality of the illegality relied on by the defendant and answer two questions:

> First, whether there had been illegality of which the court should take notice, and, second, whether in all the circumstances it would be an affront to the public conscience if by affording him the relief sought the court was seen to be indirectly assisting or encouraging the plaintiff in his conduct.[68]

7.46 Subsequent cases gave support to this approach. In *Saunders v Edwards*[69] Lord Justice Nicholls said:

---

[62] [1986] 1 All ER 676.

[63] [1986] 1 All ER 676, 689.

[64] [1987] 1 WLR 1116.

[65] [1987] 1 WLR 1116, 1132.

[66] For example, *Cross v Kirkby, The Times*, 5 April 2000, *Hall v Woolston Hall Leisure* [2001] WLR 225, 237 and *Reeves v Commissioner of Police for the Metropolis* [1999] QB 169, 185.

[67] [1986] 1 All ER 676.

[68] [1986] 1 All ER 676, 687.

[69] [1987] 1 WLR 1116.

> I think that the [public conscience] test is a useful and valuable one, summarising neatly and explicitly the essence of the task on which, in broad terms, the court is engaged when seeking to give effect to the requirements of public policy in this field. I would add, however, at the end of the formulation the words 'or encouraging others in criminal acts'.[70]

7.47 So, for example, in *Pitts v Hunt*[71] Lord Justice Beldam asked whether compensating the claimant would shock the public conscience. The claimant was the pillion passenger on a motorcycle driven by a rider whom the claimant had encouraged to drink heavily and drive dangerously prior to an accident in which the claimant was badly injured and the rider was killed. The claimant sought damages against the rider's estate. Given the serious nature of the claimant's conduct, Lord Justice Beldam decided that it would be contrary to public policy to allow the claim and accordingly held that the illegality defence applied to defeat the claim for personal injuries.

7.48 However, as we have seen, in *Tinsley v Milligan*[72] both the majority and the minority of the House of Lords rejected the public conscience test. Yet there remained some confusion over whether the public conscience test could still be used in tort claims. Several subsequent Court of Appeal decisions have held that the public conscience test no longer applies to tort claims either.[73]

7.49 Yet other cases still made use of the public conscience test. For example, it was referred to by all members of the Court of Appeal in *Reeves v Commissioner of Police of the Metropolis*.[74] The deceased had managed to commit suicide while in police custody despite the fact that the police were aware that he was a suicide risk. His estate sued for damages for negligence. The police argued that, although no longer unlawful, suicide remained contrary to public policy and the illegality defence applied to defeat the deceased's claim. The Court of Appeal rejected this argument on the basis that the public conscience would not be shocked by allowing such a claim.

---

[70] [1987] 1 WLR 1116, 1132.

[71] [1991] QB 24.

[72] [1994] 1 AC 340.

[73] See, for example, *Webb v Chief Constable of Merseyside Police* [2000] QB 427, 445; *Vellino v Chief Constable of Greater Manchester* [2001] EWCA 1249, [2002] 1 WLR 218 at [68]; and *Hewison v Meridian* [2002] EWCA Civ 1821 (Unreported) at [49].

[74] [1999] QB 169. The pragmatic approach adopted by Evans LJ in *Standard Chartered Bank v Pakistan National Shipping Corporation* [2000] 1 Lloyd's Rep 218 under which he compared the relative merits of the claimant and defendant's conduct is similar. See, also, the decision in *Daido Asia Japan Co Ltd v Rohen* [2002] BCC 589 (Ch D) where the court declared that affording the claimant relief for the tort of deceit when it had also practised a deceit on a third party would not affront the public conscience.

7.50   Similarly, Mr Justice Langley used the public conscience test in *Moore Stephens v Stone & Rolls Limited*[75] (referred to in paragraph 7.20 above) to dismiss the application to strike out the claim. He said that the public would find nothing repugnant in allowing the claim to succeed. However, when the case reached the Court of Appeal, the judges were unanimous in rejecting such an approach. They declared that the public conscience test had been abolished by *Tinsley v Milligan* for all purposes.[76] The Court of Appeal had been wrong to use the test in *Reeves*.

7.51   This emphatic rejection of the public conscience test in *Moore Stephens v Stone & Rolls Limited* would appear to bring to an end any confusion over its continued relevance. Certainly for tort claims, as well as property claims, the public conscience test is no longer to be used.

PROBLEMS WITH THE PRESENT LAW

7.52   As with other areas of the law relating to the application of the illegality defence, we do not criticise the outcome of the tort decisions. Whatever language is used in the judgments, the courts have, by and large, adopted a fairly pragmatic approach and by using the relevant rules flexibly, they have reached appropriate decisions.[77] However, the conceptual basis on which the judges make their decisions is uncertain. Different judges have analysed the defence in different ways. A whole range of tests has been suggested as appropriate, in some cases to the exclusion of any other. As a result, it is difficult to predict an outcome or to explain the outcome in terms of the apparent rationales behind the illegality defence.

7.53   Of the various tests that have been adopted by the courts, we consider the application of the reliance principle to be particularly difficult in the context of a negligence claim. Exactly which parts of the factual background are essential and necessary for the claimant to rely on in making out his or her case will often be unclear. The reliance principle may be either under-inclusive or over-inclusive, depending on the facts of the particular case. However, the inherent vagueness of what amounts to "reliance" means that unjust decisions can be avoided. Indeed although this test has been described as "an axe which falls indiscriminately",[78] the real position seems to be that there is such flexibility in deciding whether the claimant "relies" on the unlawful conduct that the preferred outcome can be reached.

---

[75]   [2007] EWHC 1826 (Comm), (2008) PNLR 4.

[76]   [2008] EWCA Civ 644, [2008] 3 WLR 1146.

[77]   Perhaps the one decision that stands out as difficult, and which has been subsequently criticised, is *Meah v McCreamer* [1985] 1 All ER 367.

[78]   *Moore Stephens v Stone & Rolls Limited* [2008] EWCA Civ 644, [2008] 3 WLR 1146 at [16].

REFORM

1. Consultation Paper recommendations

7.54 When we published CP 154, we were not aware of any significant difficulties arising from the application of the illegality defence to tort law, and felt that to include tort would have made the project unwieldy. As one author commented, "the overall approach of the courts tends ultimately to be pragmatic and very much dependant on the facts of the particular case".[79]

7.55 However, a number of respondents to CP 154 felt that there was a need to review the illegality defence in tort. The most common justification was a desire to have a consistent test, founded upon the same principles, applying to all branches of the law. In light of this, we produced CP 160 in 2001. In the Introduction to that Paper, we said:

> We appreciate the comments made by some consultees about the inconsistency that would arise as between our provisional proposals for legislative reform in contracts and trusts and the common law of tort. We think there is particular force in this point where there are concurrent or parallel claims in contract and tort... If our provisional proposals for contracts and trusts were to be implemented, but the defence in tort left untouched, a court might be required to apply both the statutory discretion and a series of common law rules in relation to the same illegal conduct in the same case, depending on which cause of action it was considering. We do not think this outcome would fulfil our statutory duty to work towards "systematic development and reform" of the law.[80]

7.56 As a consequence, in CP 160 we provisionally suggested adopting a statutory discretion similar to that proposed in CP 154. We proposed an over-arching test, under which the court would make its decision based on a number of factors, such as the seriousness of the illegality, and proportionality of denying relief.[81]

7.57 In CP 160 we also considered the alternative case for judicial reform. We identified that most cases on illegality in tort had been at Court of Appeal level or lower, and so it was possible for the House of Lords, presented with a suitable opportunity, to reform the law. However, we concluded that the chance of such an opportunity arising was limited because most cases involving illegality were also determined on additional grounds which would render an appeal on the illegality point ineffective.

7.58 More significantly, we were influenced by the responses to CP 154, which appeared to support the development of a consistent rule on illegality that would apply to all branches of the law. We felt it important to avoid two different mechanisms for overlapping areas of law. As a consequence, at the time we felt that judicial reform was not the best option to be proposing.

---

[79] *Clerk & Lindsell on Torts* (19th ed 2006) para 3-24.

[80] CP 160, para 1.4.

[81] See CP 160, paras 6.21 to 6.43.

7.59 We also considered the possibility of abolishing the illegality defence to tort claims altogether. Indeed, it could be argued that our provisional proposals would have severely limited its application in the case of claims for personal injuries. By suggesting that "consistency" in the law should be the over-arching principle by which the discretion should be exercised, we would have ruled out the defence applying to such claims except in very exceptional circumstances. However, we concluded that it should be retained for two reasons. First, a claimant might otherwise avoid the consequences of the operation of the doctrine in contract or other areas simply by framing his or her claim in tort. Secondly, the claimant might sue in tort for damages in respect of imprisonment or the recovery of a fine imposed on him or her, or for the recovery of property which it would be illegal to possess. To allow such claims would, we suggested, undermine other parts of the law.

2. The response to CP 160

7.60 We received 43 responses to CP 160. All but one of the respondents agreed with our provisional proposal that the illegality defence should be retained in some form. Three quarters also agreed that general reform of the illegality defence in tort is desirable. As well as these formal responses we received numerous letters from the general public who had read media reports on CP 160 and were very concerned that our proposals would enhance the rights of those who are injured during the course of committing an offence.

7.61 We also asked whether consultees agreed that there would be a real risk of confusion and inconsistency if the law in relation to contracts and trusts were to be reformed by legislation, but tort law was left unreformed. A majority agreed that this reason was sufficient to include the illegality in tort rules in our proposed statutory discretion.

7.62 We questioned whether reform would be best achieved by legislation, rather than judicial reform. A majority agreed that legislation would be the best method. However, a significant minority favoured judicial reform. A typical concern was that a statutory discretion would not allow sufficient flexibility to take account of the very wide range of factual situations arising in tort law. Additionally, it was pointed out that a statutory definition would still retain an element of uncertainty.

3. The way forward now

7.63 As we have explained in Part 3, we are no longer provisionally recommending statutory reform in relation to contracts affected by illegality. We received a number of responses to both CP 154 and CP 160 which set out strong arguments for not adopting a statutory discretion. In addition, we encountered difficulty when attempting to draft such a discretion.[82] The scope of the discretion that we had proposed in CP 160 – "to bar a claim when the claim arises from, or is in any way connected to, an illegal act on the part of the claimant" – was very wide. Many negligence cases, particularly those involving road accidents, would have fallen within the scope of the discretion when there is no possibility that they would be defeated by the illegality defence under the present law. We would therefore be potentially adding to the uncertainty of the present law rather than removing from it. We found it difficult to narrow down the scope of the proposed statutory discretion by any sensible criteria that were universally applicable.

7.64 We have already explained in Part 3 that our new preferred approach in relation to the rules on illegality in contract is for incremental reform by case law development. In part, this was prompted by several recent decisions in tort law,[83] which had suggested that the courts are beginning to find their own way in striking an appropriate balance with the use of the illegality defence.

7.65 As we have outlined at paragraph 7.56 above, one of the main reasons for proposing legislative reform of the law of illegality in tort in CP 160 was to achieve consistency with the rules in contract law. We continue to think that there is a need for consistency in how the defence applies in contract and tort. As we are no longer provisionally proposing legislative reform in contract law, we believe that it is now inappropriate to proceed with a similar provision for tort law.

7.66 However, we were initially concerned that development through the case law was no longer possible in the tort area following the decision of the Court of Appeal in *Moore Stephens v Stone & Rolls Limited.*[84] Here Lord Justice Rimer was emphatic in his view that the illegality defence depended on the application of the reliance principle and that no discretionary element was allowed. However, on reflection we do not think that lower courts should regard this decision as the final word on the application of the illegality defence in tort. There was little argument before the Court of Appeal as to the correct approach to apply. Both sides conceded, rightly, that the public conscience test had been abolished. As Lord Justice Rimer noted, it was unnecessary for the court to consider the precise limits of the circumstances in which the illegality defence applied. There was no dispute that, whatever language was used, in the present case, the company's claim relied upon, was based substantially upon, arose out of and was inextricably linked with the claimant's illegal conduct.

---

[82] We set out our reasons in more detail in Part 3.

[83] Particularly *Cross v Kirkby, The Times,* 5 April 2000 and *Hall v Woolston Hall Leisure* [2001] 1 WLR 225.

[84] [2008] EWCA Civ 644, [2008] 3 WLR 1146.

7.67 We seemed to be justified in this view when, a few days later, a differently constituted Court of Appeal gave its judgment in *Gray v Thames Trains.*[85] Here the Court adopted the broader proximity based approach set out in *Cross v Kirkby.*[86] While we do not necessarily find the search for one single test that determines the application of the illegality defence productive, this approach clearly allows the court to take into account many of the factors that we have explained underlie the application of the defence. We think that it would be helpful if in future the courts were able to focus directly on those relevant factors. This would ensure that they fully enunciate their reasoning in order to promote greater transparency and consistency.

7.68 The House of Lords has given leave to appeal in both the *Moore Stephens* and *Gray* cases, with the hearings due in February 2009 and March 2009 respectively. We hope that these cases will provide their Lordships with an opportunity to consider the application of the illegality defence in tort for the first time in many years.

7.69 **We provisionally recommend that the courts should consider in each individual case whether the application of the illegality defence to a claim in tort can be justified on the basis of the policies that underlie that defence. These include: (a) furthering the purpose of the rule which the illegal conduct has infringed; (b) consistency; (c) that the claimant should not profit from his or her own wrong; (d) deterrence; and (e) maintaining the integrity of the legal system. In reaching its decision the court will need to balance the strength of these policies against the objective of achieving a just result, taking into account the relative merits of the parties and the proportionality of denying the claim. Whenever the illegality defence is successful, the court should make clear the justification for its application.**

---

[85] [2008] EWCA Civ 713.

[86] *The Times* 5 April 2000.

PART 8
LIST OF PROVISIONAL RECOMMENDATIONS

PART 2 – WHY DO WE NEED ANY DOCTRINE OF ILLEGALITY?

8.1 The illegality defence should be allowed where its application can be firmly justified by the policies that underlie its existence. These include: (a) furthering the purpose of the rule which the illegal conduct has infringed; (b) consistency; (c) that the claimant should not profit from his or her own wrong; (d) deterrence; and (e) maintaining the integrity of the legal system. (Para 2.35)

PART 3 – ILLEGALITY AND CONTRACTUAL ENFORCEMENT

8.2 We no longer recommend that the law on illegality and contract should be reformed by way of the introduction of a statutory discretion. (Para 3.122)

8.3 The courts should consider in each case whether the application of the illegality defence can be justified on the basis of the policies that underlie that defence. These include: (a) furthering the purpose of the rule which the illegal conduct has infringed; (b) consistency; (c) that the claimant should not profit from his or her own wrong; (d) deterrence; and (e) maintaining the integrity of the legal system. Against those policies must be weighed the legitimate expectation of the claimant that his or her legal rights will be protected. Ultimately a balancing exercise is called for which weighs up the application of the various policies at stake. Only when depriving the claimant of his or her rights is a proportionate response based on the relevant illegality policies, should the defence succeed. The judgment should explain the basis on which it has done so. (Para 3.142)

8.4 The courts should consider whether illegality is a defence to the particular claim brought by the particular claimant, rather than whether the contract is "illegal" as a whole. (Para 3.144)

8.5 The courts should not use the reliance principle to determine whether the claimant can succeed in a case involving the enforcement of an executory contract. (Para 3.148)

PART 4 – ILLEGALITY AND THE REVERSAL OF UNJUST ENRICHMENT

8.6 The courts should consider in each case whether the application of the illegality defence to the unjust enrichment claim can be justified on the basis of the policies that underlie that defence. In reaching its decision the court will need to balance the importance of these policies against the objective of achieving a just result, taking into account the relative merits of the parties and the proportionality of denying the claim. Whenever the illegality defence is successful, the court should make clear the justification for its application. (Para 4.44)

8.7 We do not recommend any legislative reform to the use of illegality as a ground for a claim for the reversal of unjust enrichment. (Para 4.59)

8.8 The courts should disallow the defence of change of position because the defendant has been involved in some unlawful conduct only where the disapplication of that defence can be firmly justified by the policies that underlie the existence of the doctrine of illegality. (Para 4.62)

PART 5 – ILLEGALITY AND THE RECOGNITION OF CONTRACTUALLY TRANSFERRED, CREATED OR RETAINED LEGAL PROPERTY RIGHTS

8.9 We do not recommend any legislative reform to the illegality defence as it applies in relation to the recognition of contractually created, transferred or retained legal property rights. (Para 5.27)

PART 6 – ILLEGALITY AND TRUSTS

8.10 The courts should be given a statutory discretion to decide the effect of illegality on trusts in at least some cases. (Para 6.100)

PART 7 – ILLEGALITY IN TORT

8.11 The courts should consider in each individual case whether the application of the illegality defence to a claim in tort can be justified on the basis of the policies that underlie that defence. These include: (a) furthering the purpose of the rule which the illegal conduct has infringed; (b) consistency; (c) that the claimant should not profit from his or her own wrong; (d) deterrence; and (e) maintaining the integrity of the legal system. In reaching its decision the court will need to balance the strength of these policies against the objective of achieving a just result, taking into account the relative merits of the parties and the proportionality of denying the claim. Whenever the illegality defence is successful, the court should make clear the justification for its application. (Para 7.69)

APPENDIX A
THE PROCEEDS OF CRIME ACT 2002

THE STATUTORY REGIMES FOR CRIMINAL CONFISCATION AND CIVIL RECOVERY

A.1   We explained in Part 2 that an important principle underlying the illegality defence is that a person should not be able to benefit from his or her own wrong. Parliament has enshrined this principle into legislation by providing that in defined circumstances benefits obtained as a result of criminal conduct may be confiscated or recovered by the State. Special provisions apply in relation to certain crimes, for example terrorism, but the two main schemes are found in the Proceeds of Crime Act 2002.

1. Criminal confiscation orders[1]

(1) The legislation

A.2   Where a defendant is convicted of an offence, the Crown Court may make a confiscation order, designed to deprive the criminal of the benefits of his or her crime. The first step in the making of such an order is for the court to determine whether the defendant has a "criminal lifestyle".[2] This will be the case if one of three conditions is satisfied in relation to the offence committed: (a) it is one specified in Schedule 2 to the Act (including drug trafficking; money laundering; arms trafficking and directing terrorism); or (b) it forms part of a course of criminal activity; or (c) it was committed over a period of at least six months.[3] If the defendant is found to have a criminal lifestyle, then the second step is for the court to determine whether he has benefited from "his general criminal conduct".[4] However, in making that determination and assessing the level of benefit, the court makes certain assumptions. These include that any property transferred to him in the previous six years was obtained by him as a result of his general criminal conduct; that any expenditure incurred by him in the previous six years was met by him from property so obtained; and that any property held at the date of conviction was obtained by him as a result of his general criminal conduct.[5] These assumptions do not apply if they are shown to be incorrect or would result in a serious risk of injustice.[6]

---

[1]   Proceeds of Crime Act 2002, Part 2.

[2]   Proceeds of Crime Act 2002, section 6(4)(a). For a definition, see section 75.

[3]   In the case of conditions (b) and (c) the benefit obtained must have been not less than £5000: Proceeds of Crime Act 2002, section 75(4).

[4]   Proceeds of Crime Act 2002, section 6(4)(b).

[5]   Proceeds of Crime Act 2002, section 10.

[6]   Proceeds of Crime Act 2002, section 10(6).

A.3 Alternatively, if the court decides that the defendant does not have a "criminal lifestyle", then it may find that he has benefited from "his particular criminal conduct" – that is, the offences for which he is to be sentenced.[7] In this case, the court must determine the level of benefit from the conduct concerned, but without the use of any of the assumptions. A wide definition is given to benefit – a person benefits from criminal conduct "if he obtains property as a result of or in connection with the conduct".[8]

A.4 In either case, the court must then make a confiscation order for the value of the benefit the defendant has obtained ("the recoverable amount")[9] or, if less, the amount that the defendant is worth ("the available amount").[10] In assessing the available amount, the court must include the total value of all property held by the defendant and all "tainted gifts" made by the defendant.[11] Where it has been decided that the defendant has a criminal lifestyle a gift is tainted if (i) it was made in the six year period ending with the commencement of the proceedings; or (ii) regardless of when it was made, it consists of, or represents, property obtained by the defendant as a result of or in connection with his general criminal conduct. Where it has been decided that the defendant does not have a criminal lifestyle any gift is tainted if made after the relevant offence was committed.

(2) Application to cases that fall within our legislative reform proposals

A.5 These provisions for criminal confiscation are clearly very broad, and we have had to consider whether their potential application displaces the need for any illegality defence at all. For example, if the State can simply confiscate the trust property at the end of the day, why go through the hurdles of determining whether the beneficiary can enforce his or her interest?

A.6 Provided that there has been a successful criminal prosecution, the criminal confiscation provisions apply to the type of case that falls within our proposals for legislative reform. Our proposals affect cases where a person has deliberately concealed his or her assets in order to obtain benefits fraudulently. The value of those benefits would be included in the "recoverable amount" for the purposes of any confiscation order. In other cases, no property as such will have been obtained, but rather a payment due avoided – for example to tax authorities or creditors. The Act provides that where the defendant's benefit is a pecuniary advantage, he is taken to have obtained a sum equal to the value of that advantage.[12] In some cases, the defendant may be assessed as having a criminal lifestyle – for example where a social security fraud has continued for more than six months.

---

[7] Proceeds of Crime Act 2002, section 6(4)(c).

[8] Proceeds of Crime Act 2002, section 76(4).

[9] Proceeds of Crime Act 2002, section 7.

[10] Proceeds of Crime Act 2002, section 9.

[11] Proceeds of Crime Act 2002, sections 77-78.

[12] Proceeds of Crime Act 2002, section 76(5).

A.7 However, the provisions of the Act would not generally appear to bite against the trust property itself. This is not "recoverable property" because it was not obtained "as a result of or in connection with" the criminal conduct – it is property that the defendant already owned, and attempted to conceal, prior to any crime being committed.[13] If the defendant has been found to have a criminal lifestyle there is a prima facie assumption that any property held at the time of trial is recoverable property. However, where the defendant can show that the assumption is incorrect, it will not be applied.[14]

A.8 It is possible that the person holding the legal title to the trust property might be convicted of an offence in connection with the fraudulent scheme. For example, his or her involvement in the deliberate concealment for criminal purposes may have amounted to a conspiracy. In such a case, it would be arguable that his or her title was obtained "in connection with the crime". What is not clear from the authorities is whether, for the purposes of any confiscation order, he or she is to be treated as having obtained a benefit equal to the full value of the property or merely the nominal value of the bare title. In one case, the Court of Appeal has stated that where the legal title to real property has been transferred as a result of or in connection with a fraudulent scheme, it will generally be appropriate to regard the transferee as having obtained the full value of that property within the meaning of the relevant provisions of the Criminal Justice Act 1988 (the forerunner of the Proceeds of Crime Act 2002), especially where the transferee was himself or herself a party to the fraud.[15] However, in a subsequent case, decided under the provisions of the 2002 Act, the Court of Appeal held that the beneficial interest in the property had not passed to the transferee in such a case. The value of the benefit to the transferee was therefore only the nominal value of the bare title and the confiscation order that had been made against him was quashed.[16]

A.9 In any event, in the vast majority of illegality cases that have come before the civil court, there has been no criminal conviction[17] and therefore no confiscation order. Where the trust property is not itself the proceeds of crime, the application of the provisions of the Proceeds of Crime Act to the trust property has therefore not been tested. We therefore believe that there remains a role for the doctrine of illegality in these cases.

---

[13] An exception would be a case such as *R v David Edward Dale* [2006] EWCA Crim 1889 (see para A.10 below) where the trust property itself has been acquired as part of the fraudulent scheme.

[14] Proceeds of Crime Act 2002, section 10.

[15] *Ilyas v Aylesbury Vale District Council* [2008] EWCA Crim 1303.

[16] *R v Michael Anthony Richards* [2008] EWCA Crim 1841.

[17] Exceptions to this include *MacDonald v Myerson* [2001] EWCA Civ 66 and *Mortgage Express v McDonnell* (2001) 82 P & CR DG21. In neither case was a confiscation order made.

A.10　What is clear is that the criminal courts will not allow the illegality defence to be used in order to prevent their powers to make criminal confiscation orders from having full effect. This is illustrated by *R v David Edward Dale*.[18] The defendant had been convicted of large-scale mortgage fraud. As part of his fraudulent scheme he had transferred title to some of the properties purchased to friends and relatives, to be held as nominee for him. He tried to argue that since his interest under these trusts would not be enforceable by him under the doctrine of illegality, the confiscation order could not include their value. The Criminal Division of the Court of Appeal rejected such arguments summarily. It stated:

> The purpose of this legislation is to deprive criminals of the proceeds of their crime. It cannot have been the intention of Parliament to allow a sound principle of civil law to prevent the enforcement by the state of the very provisions by which it is seeking to deprive criminals of the benefits of their crimes.

2.　Civil recovery of the proceeds of unlawful conduct[19]

(1) The legislation

A.11　The Proceeds of Crime Act 2002 introduced a new civil recovery scheme. It provides very broad powers for the recovery of property which is, or which represents, "property obtained through unlawful conduct".[20] The proceedings are directed against the property, and not at the criminality of any particular individual. Indeed, these powers may be exercised whether or not any criminal proceedings have been brought.[21] The Act provides that "a person obtains property through unlawful conduct (whether his own conduct or another's) if he obtains property by or in return for the conduct".[22] All such property is deemed to be "recoverable property".[23]

---

[18]　[2006] EWCA Crim 1889.

[19]　Proceeds of Crime Act 2002, Part 5.

[20]　Proceeds of Crime Act 2002, section 240.

[21]　Proceeds of Crime Act 2002, section 240(2).

[22]　Proceeds of Crime Act 2002, section 242.

[23]　Proceeds of Crime Act 2002, section 304.

A.12 Since the respondent to the proceedings is the holder of the recoverable property and not necessarily the alleged criminal, the property may be followed into the hands of any transferee.[24] However, property ceases to be recoverable property if it reaches a bona fide purchaser for value without notice[25] or it if is obtained in civil proceedings by a claimant whose claim is based on the unlawful conduct.[26] Alternatively, where the alleged criminal has disposed of the recoverable property, the Act also allows the court to recover property which he or she has obtained in its place.[27]

A.13 From 1 April 2008, the responsibility for undertaking civil recovery has been passed to the Serious Organised Crime Agency (SOCA) following the abolition of the Assets Recovery Agency.[28] SOCA states that it will consider a case for adoption if a number of criteria are met.[29] These include, first, that a criminal investigation and prosecution must have been considered and either failed or been impossible. Secondly, there must be, on a balance of probabilities, evidence of criminal conduct. Thirdly, recoverable property must have been identified to a value of at least £10,000 and must include property other than cash or negotiable instruments.

(2) Application to cases that fall within our legislative reform proposals

A.14 Do these provisions for civil recovery displace the need for any illegality doctrine? They clearly may be relevant to the type of case that falls within our proposals for legislative reform. Where a person has deliberately concealed his or her assets in order to obtain a benefit to which he or she would not otherwise be entitled, the amount of those benefits would be recoverable property. This applies whether or not that person is convicted of any offence. Similarly, where a person avoids the payment of an amount owing by the same means, then he or she is treated as having obtained a sum of money equal to that pecuniary advantage, and this sum of money is recoverable property.

A.15 It is less clear whether the civil recovery provisions could be used to attack the trust property itself. At least where the transferee is in collusion with the transferor in relation to the criminal purpose to the extent that there is a criminal conspiracy between them, it could be argued that the transferee obtains the trust property "by" the unlawful conduct – the conspiracy. As such, then it too would become recoverable property, even though the transferee holds only a bare title.

---

[24] Proceeds of Crime Act 2002, section 305(3).

[25] Proceeds of Crime Act 2002, section 308(1).

[26] Proceeds of Crime Act 2002, section 308(3).

[27] Proceeds of Crime Act 2002, section 305(1) and (2).

[28] Serious Crime Act 2007, section 74.

[29] Serious Organised Crime Agency, http://www.soca.gov.uk (last visited 16 Jan 2009).

A.16   In any event, it is quite clear that even where the civil recovery provisions are applicable, the Serious Organised Crime Agency does not have sufficient resources to institute proceedings in every case in which property has been obtained through unlawful conduct. It will also not do so unless another law enforcement agency refers the case to it, having considered, but failed to obtain, a criminal prosecution. The vast majority of cases are therefore simply not within its attention.

3. Conclusion

A.17   Our recommendations for legislative reform of the illegality doctrine must be viewed against this background of provision for State confiscation and recovery. In some cases, at least, where the parties are disputing the ownership of property following a transaction tainted by illegality, the State may step in and confiscate the property. However, in many cases the legislative provisions will not bite against the trust property itself, or for a variety of reasons will not have been used. They do not, therefore, displace the need for an illegality defence.

APPENDIX B
LIST OF RESPONDENTS

RESPONDENTS TO CONSULTATION PAPER 154

Judiciary

Committee of Council of HM Circuit Judges

The Right Honourable The Lord Goff of Chieveley

Queen's Bench judges

The Right Honourable Lord Justice Thomas

Barristers

Mr Peter Birkett QC

Chancery Bar Association

Commercial Bar Association

General Council of the Bar

Mr Michael Lerego QC

New Zealand Law Commission

North Eastern Circuit

Mr Alan Tunkel

Western Circuit

Solicitors

Mr Trevor Aldridge QC

Commercial Law Committee of the City of London Law Society

Law Society

Litigation Sub-Committee of the City of London Law Society

London Solicitors' Litigation Association

Academics

Professor Jack Beatson QC

Centre for Research into Law Reform

Professor Nili Cohen

Professor Brian Coote

Professor Stephen Cretney QC

Dr Gerhard Dannemann

Mr Derek Davies

Mr John Davies

Professor Nelson Enonchong

Professor Harold Ford

Professor Daniel Friedmann

Professor David Hayton

Mr Hugo van Kooten

Professor Hector MacQueen

Professor Jill Martin

Mr Philip Pettit

Dr Lionel Smith

Mr Peter Sparkes

SPTL Contract and Commercial Law Group

Professor Richard Sutton

Professor Andrew Tettenborn

Professor Sir Guenter Treitel

Ms Janet Ulph

Professor Stephen Waddams

Professor Graham Virgo

Government

Lord Chancellor's Department

Treasury Solicitor's Department

Organisations

Financial Law Panel

Law Reform Committee for Northern Ireland

Legislative and Policy Committee of the Employment Lawyers Association

Phonographic Performance Limited

RESPONDENTS TO CONSULTATION PAPER 160

Judiciary

Association of District Judges

The Right Honourable Lord Justice Buxton

Civil Sub-committee of the Council of Circuit Judges

The Right Honourable Sir Anthony Evans

His Honour Judge Peter Heppel QC

Barristers

Mr Stuart Brown QC and Mr Richard Copnall

General Council of the Bar

Mr Michael Lerego QC

Personal Injuries Bar Association

Wales and Chester Circuit

Mr Robert Weir

Solicitors

City of London Solicitors' Company Litigation Sub-committee

City of Westminster and Holborn Law Society

Forum of Insurance Lawyers

Law Society

Academics

Professor Patrick Atiyah

Mr Roderick Bagshaw

Professor Dr Christian v. Bar

Professor Richard Buckley

Professor Andrew Burrows

Mr Peter Cane

Mr Brian Childs

Mr Derek Davies

Professor James Davis

Professor Nelson Enonchong

Professor Margaret Fordham

Dr Paula Giliker

Professor Rick Glofcheski

Ms Laura Hoyano

Professor Michael Jones

Mr Mark Lunney

Mr Nicholas McBride

Professor David Miers

Mr Ken Oliphant

Mr Horton Rogers

Mr Marc Stauch

Professor Andrew Tettenborn

Ms Janet Ulph

Professor Stephen Waddams

Dr Kevin Williams

Government

Lord Chancellor's Department

Organisations

Metropolitan Police Service

Motor Insurers' Bureau

Printed in the UK for The Stationery Office Limited
on behalf of the Controller of Her Majesty's Stationery Office
ID 6035955 01/09

Printed on Paper containing 75% recycled fibre content minimum.